This is a facsimile reprint of the 1950 edition first published by Harper & Brothers, New York.

Library of Congress Catalog Card Number 71-109181

The Story of Our Names

by

ELSDON C. SMITH

DETROIT • 1970
Gale Research Company • Book Tower

To My Wife:

CLARE

Contents

Foreword

FOR more than a quarter of a century, much of my spare time has been spent in the study of the names people bear, and their origin and meaning. I have attempted to read everything in the English language on the subject. In doing this, I have compiled a bibliography of more than three thousand items.

For books on surnames and Christian names I have explored second-hand bookstores until I have made myself a nuisance even to that most patient group—the booksellers. I have pored over booksellers' catalogues until I have collected what is, I believe, by far the largest collection of books in existence on personal names.

For articles in old periodicals and various references in books I have spent innumerable hours in all the largest libraries in this country and in England, and have spent my vacations, not in staggering from one tavern to another, but in proceeding from one library to another, followed, at times, by a protesting family.

In all my research I have not found in any one work a full, readable story of the names people bear. Many of the best books on the subject are dry (and therefore learned?) expositions with which the ordinary, busy person has little patience. For easier reading I have not cluttered up the pages with numerous footnotes, valuable as they are to the scholar. There are, however, respectable authorities for most statements. The idea for this type of book has been in my mind for many years, and notes I have made about the subject provided enough material for half a dozen books of this size.

Authorities mentioned in the body of the work by surnames only may be identified in the bibliography at the end. Both the terms *Anglo-Saxon* and *Old English* have been used and the author means them as synonymous.

For much of my data I am indebted to the tendency of newspaper editors to include notices and articles about odd names, or the coincidence of name-meaning and action. Knowing of my interest, many friends and acquaintances have sent me clippings about names and have told me of the unusual names they have observed.

Everyone is interested in the origin and meaning of his own name, and in the odd names of others. All are quick to note an appropriate name. When Noel Coward cast aspersions on the valor of Brooklyn's fighting men, their defenders were quick to make use of his surname in expressing their contempt for him.

This book is not meant as a dictionary or guide by which one may find out all about his own name. Books for this purpose are listed in the bibliography. The author hopes that the reader may learn about the origin, history and means of deriving names of persons, and thus understand how his own names arose even though he may not know the exact, detailed derivation. But from the facts and examples given most readers will be able to work out the origin and meaning of their own names.

There are many casual writers on names who have rhapsodized on their own ideas of the subject without even a feeble effort toward accuracy. While I have spared no pains in making sure that the statements I have made were authoritative, I cannot pretend to be infallible. The odd names have been carefully collected over a period of twenty years. Since then, it is possible that some of the persons bearing them have moved or passed away.

It is curious that of the many persons who have applied to me for help in naming babies in late years, the man, rather than his wife, is the one who writes, even though he be a soldier in the South Pacific. Do appropriate names mean more to men than to women?

To my friends who have called my attention to material, and to odd and unusual names, I express my sincere thanks. To the many who have discussed problems with me and given their opinions on the subject I must express my appreciation. To those who have helped directly with this book I express my sincere gratitude.

Some have spent many long hours in helping check the manuscript. To Clyde B. Clason, Charles Walker, Merle Morrison and Naomi Bowles especially I must here say, "Thank you." Their help and suggestions have been invaluable.

But the most help has come from my wife, Clare. Her steady aid and encouragement have been responsible for any real merit this work may possess.

Suggestions for improvements, or additional items of personal name interest, will be welcomed whether or not the publishers can be persuaded to importune the author to revise and correct the book for a second edition.

322 Sherman Avenue,   ELSDON C. SMITH
Evanston, Illinois

THE STORY OF
OUR NAMES

CHAPTER I

Our Christian Names

*A good name is rather to be chosen
than great riches.*
—Proverbs xxii, 1

WHEN the early converts to Christianity took a new name to symbolize their new life at the baptismal ceremony, the new name came to be designated as the "Christened" or "baptismal" name, and this term was continued after surnames were adopted to distinguish the first name from the family name. "Christian name" is probably a corruption of the now almost obsolete "Christened name." Perhaps when Saul altered his name to Paul, he took the first *Christian* name. The name given at baptism is the true name of an individual, the surname merely being a description added to assist in identification of the family. Now the term "Christian name" is so common, particularly in England, that we often designate the forenames given to Jews as Christian names, and dictionaries define it simply as a *given* name or *first* name.

As the Church thus came to take such an important part in naming babies, it very early took the stand, grounding its practice on *James* ii, 7, compared with *I Peter* iv, 15, that only the names of saints and martyrs could be given at the time of baptism. The Council of Nicaea, in A.D. 325, forbade the use of names of heathen gods. Even the Church of England, in the sixteenth century, prohibited all names of heathen origin. St. Chrysostom suggested to the Christians of his day that their names ought to refer to holy persons. The Council of Trent in the sixteenth century advised the use of a saint's name in baptism. Canon 761 of the Catholic Church now provides that if the parents are perversely determined to give the child an unworthy name the pastor shall "add to the name given by the parents the name of some Saint and enter both in the Baptismal Register." The Church soon concluded that this baptismal name could not be changed except at confirmation. As the Church had its priest present at the rites of baptism and confirmation, it was able to make sure that its rules on this subject were universally obeyed. Even in our time both the baptismal and marriage services know only one name—the Christian name.

While names today are not given with any particular consciousness of meaning, that was not true in early times and among more primitive peoples. Then names were chosen because of some unusual circumstance which attended the birth of the baby, or because of some hope or desire upon the part of the parents on behalf of the infant. If we investigated, we would find that most names used today have a pleasant meaning. This is true simply because most of those with offensive connotations have disappeared from our nomenclature. A very few names with meanings which are not agreeable have survived, such as *Claude* or *Claudia*, meaning "lame," and *Ursula*, "little she-bear"; *Cecil* means "blind" and *Calvin*, "bald."

The earliest personal names among all peoples had definite meanings, and primitive peoples even today sometimes give names to their children with acute consciousness of their meanings. Instances of this among the American Indians and with the early Hebrews are given in Chapters VI and VIII.

Practically all of our common Christian names are derived from five languages, i.e., the Hebrew, Greek, Latin, Celtic and Teutonic tongues. The Hebrew names often relate to deity, both Christian and pagan; the Teutonic names tend to emphasize warlike terms and qualities, while the Greek, Latin and Celtic names are apt to refer to abstract qualities and personal characteristics. Many Celtic names may also chronicle a worship of God.

Most of the Teutonic names are dithematic, which means simply that they consist of two elements linked together with nothing to show any grammatical relation between them. *Roger*, for example, literally means "fame, spear"; *William*, "helmet, resolution"; *Wulfstan*, "wolf, stone." Hebrew names, on the contrary, are based upon one idea, such as *James*, "supplanter," and *Elizabeth*, "oath of God." Many Greek and Latin names consist of only one word.

Before the Norman Conquest, in 1066, English names were chiefly from the Anglo-Saxon. Most of the common given names that we know so well today were practically unknown in England until after the Normans came. The true, early English type of names were names like those compounded with *æthel* (noble), such as *Æthelred, Æthelstan* and *Æthelwulf,* or with *ead* (rich), such as *Eadward, Eadmund* and *Eadric,* or with *ælf* (elf), such as *Ælfred, Ælfric* and *Ælwine.* We have some of these in modern form: *Edward, Edmund, Alfred. Ethel* is now a recognized girl's name. Originally names beginning with *Ethel* could be borne only by the younger sons of the hereditary kings or earls.

With the Conquest there came the Norman names, mostly of Teutonic origin, like *William, Robert, Hugh, Raoul* (Ralph), *Richard, Roger, Geoffrey, Walter* and *Fulk.* Biblical names like *Samson* and *John* also appeared in greater number. First the Anglo-Saxon nobles and more important people adopted the new Norman style of names; and then the peasantry followed suit until the old Anglo-Saxon names, at least for a long time, became exceedingly rare. Most of those now in use are reintroductions.

Even before the Conquest there was some tendency to adopt saints' names; afterward, the Normans caused this custom to flourish. To our medieval ancestors, whose life was a constant effort to wrest a poor living from the soil, the protection of the canonized was real; and the saint on whose day the child was born was looked upon with a practical reverence. There is little wonder, then, that up to the time of the Reformation, there was a steadily increasing use of the names of the more popular Catholic saints.

The Name Day, so often celebrated by Catholics, is the date of the feast of the saint after which one is named. The Feast Day is not the birthday of the saint, but is generally, though not always, the anniversary of the saint's death. In 1945, President Manuel Avila Camacho of Mexico, in celebration of his Name Day, released 179 German prisoners from internment.

Due to the recrudescence of classical learning in the fifteenth and sixteenth centuries there was some importation of Greek and Roman, so-called pagan names such as *Diana, Venus, Ulysses* and *Pompey.* Greek abstract nouns also came into use, and we come across names like *Alethea* (truth), *Sophia* (wisdom) and *Irene* (peace). When one calls to mind the difficulties of traveling from one country to another, one does not wonder at the slow infiltration of foreign names.

The publication of the Genevan Bible in 1560, the first Bible used by the common people, gave a powerful impetus to the adoption of Scriptural names. An edition of the Book for use by all naturally gave the people a knowledge of all the Biblical characters, formerly the exclusive preserves of the clergy, and in view of their pious inclinations, made them think of Holy Writ when they began to consider a name to be given the new arrival. Baptismal registers became a record of Bible names.

Some odd situations arose because of the layman's imperfect knowledge of the Scriptures. Near Manchester a workman with the surname of *Lees* applied to his employer for a Biblical name. *Tellno* was suggested, facetiously, no doubt, since in Lancashire a lie is a *lee*. The father had not seen that particular name in the Bible, but, liking it all the better for its unfamiliarity, he chose it for his son. Too late, he realized the hoax. A clergyman in Hampshire, England, was requested to christen a child *Sirs*. When he hesitated he was told, with some asperity, that it was a Scriptural name to which he had no right to object, and *Acts* xvi, 30, was quoted to him, "Sirs, what must I do to be saved?"

Bardsley tells the story of a clergyman who requested the chosen name from a group of women clustered around the baptismal font. "Ax her," said one. "What name?" he asked the woman who appeared to be designated. "Ax her," she replied. The next woman on being queried gave the same reply. At last he discovered the name they were trying to say was the scriptural *Achsah*, Caleb's daughter.

Before the Protestant Reformation about the only Old Testament names used with any frequency were *Adam, Elias, Samson, David, Solomon, Daniel, Joseph* and *Benjamin*. The popularity of Old Testament names largely depended on the extent to which they were used by the religious drama of the Middle Ages. The Protestant Reformation brought about a complete change.

Although the Puritans hated the devil, they hated the Papists more, and everything connected with the Catholic religion was tainted in their eyes. They consequently avoided the saints' names and resolutely turned to the more unusual of the Bible names. English names not in the Bible they rejected as "pagan." Names like *Elijah, Nathaniel, Moses, Sarah, Aaron, Joshua, Priscilla* and *Gideon* became common. Even *Maher-shalal-hash-baz*, the longest name in the Bible, was freely used. They had no scruples against using New Testament names of evil repute like *Ananias* and *Sapphira*. After exhausting the Old and New Testaments, the Puritans turned to abstract nouns such as *Patience, Grace, Truth, Experience, Deliverance, Tribulation, Peace, Rejoice, Silence, Mercy, Faith, Hope* and *Charity*. Names like *Ac-*

cepted, Redeemed, Renewed, Comfort, Humility, Repentance, Lament and *Freewill* were encountered everywhere.

Where the devout Puritans found these names is not hard to discover. The following, being the first five verses of the fifth chapter of *Romans*, produces eight names:

Therefore being justified by *faith*, we have *peace* with God through our Lord Jesus Christ: by whom also we have access by faith into this *grace* wherein we stand, and *rejoice* in *hope* of the glory of God. And not only so, but we glory in tribulations also: knowing that *tribulation* worketh *patience; and patience, experience;* and experience, hope: and hope maketh not ashamed; because the love of God is shed abroad in our hearts by the Holy Ghost which is given unto us.

Besides the names italicized above the Puritans also used *Love.* The well-known Increase Mather of early American history probably owes his Christian name to the fourteenth verse of the One hundred fifteenth *Psalm* where it is promised:

The LORD shall increase you more and more, you and your children.

In general, names of sad import were preferred by the Puritan fathers. Thus *Benoni* (son of my sorrow) was six times as popular as *Benjamin* (son of the right hand).

Not being satisfied with the difficult old Hebrew names, and having whetted their appetite on the abstract nouns, the most extreme Puritans turned to exhortatory sentences, pious ejaculations, brief professions of Godly sorrow for sin, or exclamations of praise for blessings received, and so stamped their offspring. *Learn-wisdom* and *Hate-evil* tried to live up to their names. *Faint-not* and *Fear-not* became quite common for a while. *Help-on-high, Sorry-for-sin* and *Search-the-Scriptures* each named more than one luckless babe. Longer names have been turned up, such as *Fight-the-good-fight-of-faith, Job-rakt-out-of-the-ashes* and *Hew-agag-in-pieces-before-the-Lord.* In the eighteenth century there resided in Rhode Island a man whose parents had conferred upon him the gentle appellation, *Through-much-tribulation-we-enter-into-the-kingdom-of-heaven.* His surname was *Clapp.* According to Hume's *History of England* (Volume VII, page 230, edition of 1787) the brother of Praise-God Barebone, the fanatical Puritan leather dealer of Fleet Street, London, was named, *If-Christ-had-not-died-for-thee-thou-would-have-been-damned Barebone.* This name was effectively shortened to "Damned" Barebone.

In the baptismal register of Waldron, England, is the following entry:

Flie-fornication, the bace sonne of Catren Andrewes, bapt. ye 17th Desemb., 1609.

This name is matched, however, by that given an English foundling girl, in 1644, at Baltonsborough, Somerset—*Misericordia-adulterina*. The early Puritans considered the names *Lament* and *Trial* appropriate for girls born out of wedlock. For boys the name of the reputed father was usually given, a practice that is often followed today.

Eccentric Puritan names arose quickly in England but the flood subsided almost as quickly, and it never spread as far north as Scotland. The period from 1580 to 1640 marks the cycle of peculiar Puritan names in England. Some have said that the Puritans bequeathed permanent names to the English group, such as *Faith, Hope, Charity* and *Grace,* but these are all found before the Puritan Age.

Many Puritans migrated to America and brought their ideas in respect to nomenclature with them, so that, with the Catholics on the other side, most of our early names in this country were Biblical in origin. *Adam, Isaac, David, Samuel, Elijah, Ephraim, Obadiah, Moses, Ebenezer, Josiah, Ichabod, Abraham, Jeremiah,* and *Benjamin,* together with *James, John, Thomas, Peter* and *Andrew,* fill our early directories. Moreover the custom died out much more slowly in America. This was probably due to the fact that in the backwoods of the new country there were not so many to poke fun at eccentric nomenclature.

In England the constantly growing list of Christian names was further augmented by importations from the Scotch, Irish and Welsh. Through Scotland and Ireland, and also directly, names came in from the Scandinavian countries. English children bore such names as *Torquil* (Thurkil), *Brenda* and *Desmond.*

The accession of the Georges to the throne brought in new Teutonic names: *Carl, Frederick, Ernest* and *Adolphus,* as well as feminine names like *Caroline, Charlotte* and *Wilhelmina.* In the last hundred or more years feminine flower names like *Daffodil, Dahlia* and *Orchid* were selected to go with the earlier similar names like *Rose* and *Violet.* Other vegetable products have produced names such as *Hazel, Ivy, Lavender* and *Myrtle.* Precious stones have given us the girls' names of *Beryl, Ruby, Opal* and *Coral,* and the boys' names of *Jasper* and *Garnet.*

Names from the months of the year are not uncommon. In the

latter part of the last century names associated with places, and, indeed, with almost everything, have appeared. Finally, parents, just to be different, have not hesitated to invent their own, and have adopted sounds, phonetically spelled, as names.

Since the time of the Puritans the history of Christian names has not been so much different in England and the United States, although Yonge says that English name habits are exaggerated in America, which is probably true. Americans, however, have had more of a tendency to go to extremes. Also, in this country the past hundred years, streams of immigration from the Scandinavian countries, Russia and South European states have enriched our supply of names by the foreign forms current in the countries from which the great immigrations have come.

From time to time we turn to foreign forms: *Ivan, Olga* and *Sonia* have come to us from the Russian; *Dolores* and *Alphonso* are, of course, Spanish. German, French and Italian names are easily recognized. After Danish Crown Princess Ingrid visited the United States in 1939, the name *Ingrid* became popular, particularly in the Northwest. In the past *Jonathan* has been referred to as our peculiarly national prenomen, but now it appears to have lost that position although probably no particular name can be said to have taken its place.

The list of Christian names in this country is much larger than in England, due not only to the many diverse, unassimilated groups here, but also to the change of names in order to be different, and the more daring desire of Americans to differ from the norm. In the early years of our country grotesque Christian names were very common. *The American Cyclopædia*, compiled about 1861, observes that there are only about fifty-three male Christian names that can be used without appearance of singularity, of which thirty-two are from the Bible.

In the Middle Ages the people relied almost entirely on about twenty name for each sex. About four-fifths of the men were called either *John, William, Thomas, Richard, Robert* or *Henry*. Most of the rest were named *Roger, Walter, Hugh, Rolf, Edmund, Nicholas* and *Philip*. Ample proof of the popularity of these names is found in the recurrence of the surnames today derived from these names. For example, *John* is represented by Jones, Johnson, Johnston, Jenkins, Jenks and Jackson; *William* produces Williams, Williamson, Wilson, Willis, Wills, Wilkins and Gill; *Thomas* gives us as surnames besides Thomas, Thompson, Thoms and Tomkins. The women were called: *Agnes, Alice, Cicely, Joan, Matilda, Margaret, Elizabeth, Isabel, Helen, Elaine,*

Emma, Katharine, Mabel, Sibyl, Beatrice. Some may be surprised to find *Edward* and *Alfred* not on the list of men's names, but the truth is that the Anglo-Saxon names had about died out by the fourteenth century. *Charles* did not become popular in England until the time of Charles I (1625-1649).

Some names have been particular favorites of royalty. *Louis,* for example, was the name of eighteen kings of France. *Henry, Edward* and *George* are favorites of English rulers; *Frederick* of the monarchs of Prussia and Germany; and *Charles* of Swedish sovereigns. In Denmark, *Frederick* and *Christian* have alternated as the name of the ruling monarch for more than four hundred years. The ruling houses of almost every Western country have had a few names preferred for the reigning king.

For four centuries after the Conquest the paucity of personal names in general use stimulated the rise of nickname, or pet, forms and diminutives. Thus for Richard we have *Rick, Hick, Dick, Rich, Hitch, Digg* and *Higg;* for John, *Jack, Jenk* and *Jock;* for Robert, *Rob, Hob, Dob* and *Bob;* Henry, *Harry* and *Hal;* and there are a hundred other well-known ones. Some of these pet forms are, at present, obsolete; others are modern. For example, today we call Robert, *Rob,* or more often *Bob,* but we do not call him *Hob* or *Dob.* Yet the number and prevalence of surnames formed from *Hob* and *Dob* testify eloquently to their early popularity. Richard has kept only *Dick* and, to a minor extent, *Rick.*

Some of these pet forms have become so popular that they have become Christian names in their own right. We have, among many others, *Jack* from John and *Harry* from Henry. For girls there is *May* from Mary and *Maud* from Matilda. Indeed, it will be found, upon close examination, that quite a few of our Christian names are pet forms of other Christian names.

The Catholic Church disapproves of pet names at baptism. The story is told of a friend meeting a new father in the congested Italian Quarter of New York. "Whata you call da bambino, eh?"

"What I name heem? I say to the priest, 'Please, you baptize my baby Tom'; and he say, 'No, no, not Tom, there ees no Santo Tom,—Thom*ass.*'"

A few months later they met again, and Thomas' father congratulated the other on the birth of a fine baby boy. "And whata you theenk to nam the babee?"

"Oh, I theenk hees nam shall be Jack."

"Santa Maria!" bellowed the other, "Not Jack! Not Jack! For da priest he weel say, 'There ees no Santo Jack,—Jack*ass*.' "

Nowadays the custom of using diminutives is much lessened. We do use *Willie* and *Johnnie* and some other *-ie* suffixes to denote small children, but we are not always, even then, acutely conscious of the diminutive ending. In the Middle Ages every English name of some popularity had attached to it (and to its pet forms) in daily conversation one or more of the more popular diminutives, *-kin, -cock, -in, -on,* and *-et,* to produce variants. Thus Tom was easily distinguished from Tomkin; John from Jockin or Jenkin; William from Willin, Wilcock, Wilkin or Willet; Richard from Diccon, Hitchin or Hitchcock; and Robert from Robin, Dobbin or Hobkin. The use of a diminutive ending may make a name look entirely different. *Alison* is a common girls' name and means "little Alice," but it appears like the "son of Ali."

The use of diminutives came slightly later than the shortening of the name into a pet form. *Thomas* and *Nicholas* had to be reduced to *Tom* and *Col* or *Cole* before *Tomkin* and *Collin* could make their appearance. The proof of the enormous popularity of these pet and diminutive forms is frozen for our inspection in the popular list of English surnames.

For almost nine hundred years *William* and *John* have vied for the post of most popular boys' name. After the Conquest, *William* was the leader, but from time to time since then we have had more *Johns* than *Williams*; and, taking the English and American people as a whole, there have been distinctly more *Johns* than *Williams.*

Among girls' names, for many centuries, *Mary* has been the undisputed leader, due chiefly to the church's veneration of the Mother of Jesus. Indeed, the Hebrew names, *John* and *Mary*, have been popular in all countries of the Western world, and each nation has its favorite form of these names, as follows:

Country	John	Mary
Arabia	Yahya	Maryam
Belgium	Jehan	Marie
Czechoslovakia	Jan	Marie
Denmark	Johan	Maria
England	John	Mary
Esthonia	Johan	Marri
Finland	Jussi	Maria
France	Jean	Marie
Germany	Johann(es) (Hans)	Maria

Country	John	Mary
Greece	Ioannes	Mariam
Hawaii	Ioane	Mele
Holland	Jan	Maria
Hungary	Janos	Maria
Ireland	Sean	Maire
Isle of Man	Juan	Moirrey
Italy	Giovanni	Maria
Lapland	Jofan	Marja
Lithuania	Jõnas	Marijà
Mexico	Juan	María
Norway	Johannes	Maria
Poland	Jan	Marja
Portugal	João	Maria
Russia	Ivan	Marya
Scotland	Ian	Môr
Spain	Juan	María
Sweden	Johan	Maria
Switzerland	Johann(es)	Marie
Turkey	Iahaja	Meriem
United States	John	Mary
Wales	Evan	Mair

The choice of Christian names is influenced markedly by the names of the reigning monarchs or rulers of a country. Particularly when a king is crowned or a president is nominated or elected, the publicity then given is likely to stimulate the use of their forenames by numerous parents. The popularity enjoyed by many of our leading Christian names was occasioned by royalty, and in England and America we thus have *Albert, Anne, Charles, George, Victoria* and *William.* Famous heroes have energized names: the Duke of Wellington has produced many *Arthurs*; Washington, more as a popular hero than as our first president, has given rise to the many *Georges* in America; Abraham Lincoln has stimulated the vogue of *Lincolns*; Florence Nightingale has popularized *Florence*; St. Thomas of Canterbury, *Thomas*; Lindbergh, *Charles*; and Churchill has now made *Winston* a popular name in England, while General Douglas MacArthur's exploits have caused many little boys to be christened *Douglas*. Of course, it is impossible to calculate the strength given to names by popular heroes now living. Some of them give only a temporary impetus to the use of their names. Others give a momentum which continues a thousand years, rolling up renewed vigor. Popular Hollywood actors and actresses now give a temporary vogue to their names or to the professional ones they adopt.

Names selected by prominent poets and novelists for their characters are likely to cause hundreds of persons to start life with those appellations. For example, *Edna* owes its popularity to Edna Lyall, the novelist, who probably made it up, as her real name was Ada Ellen Bayly; *Vanessa*, once popular, is indebted to Swift; and *Pamela* to Sidney in his *Arcadia* and later to Richardson; Charlotte Brontë first gave vogue to *Shirley*; and Scott revived the Anglo-Saxon *Edgar*. Marie Corelli gave impetus to *Thelma* by her novel of that name. Dickens, Scott, Richardson, Thackeray, Yeats and Spenser are among those writers who have been responsible for the adoption of many Christian names. Even modern novels like *Gone With the Wind* have produced *Scarlett,* and some have named their daughters after the principal character in *Forever Amber*. Indeed, Christian names, in any given period, give an idea of what the people are thinking about—books, popular figures, religion, poetry.

Girls' names are subject to ever fluctuating fashion. Boys' names remain more stable, yet even they change over the years, as examination of the names of our Revolutionary soldiers will plainly show. Girls' names that were once rare are now among the most popular. Early numbers of *Notes and Queries* listed *Eunice* and *Alma* as curious and worthy of note. Bardsley, writing in 1880, said, "Joyce fought hard, but it was useless," and "Barbara is now of rarest use." Yet *Joyce* and *Barbara* became exceedingly common though they are now waning again. *Dorothy* was in demand in England from about 1450 to 1570 and again from 1750 to 1820, and Bardsley predicted that it might turn up again about 1990. In this country it has already been in common use in recent years.

Each generation, by adding new elements of nomenclature, reveals its characteristics. People living today know the generation which called its Elizabeths *Betty*, as well as the one which preferred *Eliza* or *Lizzie*; going further back, we recognize them as *Betsy*. Margaret used to be *Peggy* or *Maggie*, but *Marge* is now more usual. Many years ago *Molly* and *Polly* were common for Mary, but nowadays Mary has a tendency to stand alone without pet forms. Now certain middle names go with certain first names, as *Carol Ann, Nancy Jean* and *Barbara Jean*.

Names are an index to the habits and moods of the parents. Romantic people reflect the names of popular novel heroes and heroines;

enthusiastic ones mark famous incidents and commemorate great men; fashionable people select the new names currently popular at the moment; pious persons are careful to adopt the names approved by their church; nonconformists choose unusual names. Some parents leave the selection of names for their children to Providence by opening the Bible at random and taking the first name that agrees with the sex of the child, meeting their eye. Today some turn on the radio and adopt the first name they hear.

One family, after failing to agree on the baby's name, put the letters of the alphabet into a hat from which each of the five members drew in turn until they had enough vowels and consonants to form a name. A boy thus received *Dwish*, and another son, in the same manner, was named *Koyit*. It has been said that parents should not create names but should endeavor to discover them. A name should have a reason for its bestowal.

In many parts of Scotland and the North of England it was an unwritten law that the paternal grandfather and grandmother have namesakes in the eldest son and daughter. Even today in this country young couples often give their newborn baby the name of one of the four grandparents instead of attempting to pick an appropriate name for the baby. Honoring a rich uncle or aunt, with an eye cocked to his or her will, is by no means unknown. Other parents pat their own backs by giving their own names to their children. Continuance of this practice produces hereditary Christian names in the family, and this occasionally aids the genealogist. Baring-Gould tells of the Reuss family, which, he claims, have given every son, since 1162, the name of *Henry*.

Some name their children after men they admire. Charles Dickens named each of his seven sons after a literary personage. The eldest son, born in 1837, he named Charles Culliford Boz, the first name being after himself. The next son, born four years later, was named Walter Landor, after the writer who was then sixty-six years of age. In 1843 he bestowed the name of Francis Jeffrey (then seventy years of age) on his third son. Next, in 1845, Alfred Tennyson Dickens commemorated the poet who was then only thirty-eight years old. Although Sidney Smith left this world in 1845, Dickens named the son born in 1847 Sydney Smith Haldimand Dickens. William Haldimand, a former member of Parliament, was an intimate friend of Dickens. The sixth son was named Henry Fielding Dickens, in 1849, after the novelist who had died almost a century before. Finally, in

1852, the last son was named Edward Bulwer Lytton Dickens, after the novelist, who was then forty-nine years old. On each, Charles Dickens bestowed a nickname.

Some parents have given their children middle initials with the idea that they would fill them out when they wanted to. Other parents have given only initials for Christian names, and they have been used for that purpose throughout the lifetimes of their progeny. Some of these initial combinations can be spelled out as when AB, FE, KC, LB, LN an OP are lengthened into *Abie, Effie, Casey, Elbe, Ellen* and *Opie.*

In England there is a tendency to call men by the initials of their forenames plus the surname, as *H. G. Wells* and *A. A. Milne.* This custom is also found over here, particularly among business associates, but the tendency is not quite so strong as among the English. In America it is more usual to use the first name and middle initial plus the surname, as *John D. Rockefeller* and *John Q. Public.*

There are many more feminine than masculine names. One reason for this is that practically all boys' names can be used for girls by adding feminine endings such as *-a, -abel, -abella, -een, -ella, -elle, -ena, -ene, -eta, -etta, -ette, -ia, -ibel, -ie, -ila, -ina, -inda, -ine, -o, -otta,* and *-otte.* Almost no girls' names have masculine forms, probably because boys regard anything adapted for their use from the possession of members of the feminine sex as "sissy." Probably Mary is about the only feminine name that has produced masculine forms, as *Mario* and sometimes *Marion* and *Maria.* Another reason for the greater number of feminine forms is that the above suffixes may also be added to girls' names to make variants. There are more than a score of different ways of calling a girl Mary, Elizabeth, Anna or Rose.

As many of the odd and unusual names have no sex, it is not surprising that there are many established Christian names used by both sexes. Some, like *Jesse-Jessie* and *Francis-Frances,* are pronounced the same but spelled differently. In these examples the first spelling is masculine and the second feminine. There is a slight tendency to distinguish female from male names, otherwise similarly spelled, by the addition of *-e* as in *Carol, Carole* and *Lynn, Lynne;* but this is not by any means a universal rule and many boys' names have the *-e* ending. *Florence, Vivian* and *Evelyn* are often found as names of men, the latter two particularly in England. President Truman's younger brother is known as Vivian, although that is his middle name.

In 1940, in Indiana, a newspaper announcement, concerning Ora Jones marrying Ora Jones, exemplified the fact that some Christian names are in common use for both sexes. Manuel Prenner, in an article in the April, 1942, issue of *American Speech*, listed 122 names, which he had recently found, designating both men and women. Bearers of names which do not indicate the sex are continually running into amusing or embarrassing situations arising from mistakes as to the gender of the person. When Mr. Clare McCullough toured Europe, during the war, with other radio executives, Army officials, thinking Clare was a lady, assigned him to a room by himself. Representative Clare Hoffman, from Michigan, has undoubtedly had similar experiences. Emily Post thinks that there is nothing else for men whose given names are often used by women to do except to put "Mr." in parentheses with their signatures.

Particularly are many girls given pet or nursery names generally reserved for boys. For instance, it is not uncommon to find girls christened *Billie, Bobbie, Frankie, Terry* and *Tommy*. Others carry these names as nicknames. A woman married at Hammersmith, in England, had the Christian name of Mailliw (William spelled backwards).

It is probable that several names have changed sex. For example, *Alice* undoubtedly was originally a man's name and so was *Emma*, and *Maud* may have been. Some authorities have contended that *Anne* and *Lucy* were also ancient men's names. Anna was king of East Anglia in the seventh century. Many men in both England and France have had *Maria* or *Anne* for their given name. Girls in France have been given the name of *Joseph*. General de Gaullé's full name is Charles André Joseph Marie de Gaullé; that of the Marquis de Lafayette was Marie Joseph Yves Gilbert Du Motier Lafayette. In recent times *George* has been a rather common girls' name. In 1932 the Supreme Court of Czechoslovakia ruled that the given name, *Maria*, would not be permitted any longer for males in such combinations as *Erich Maria* and *Ludwig Maria*. The tribunal decided that a given name must clearly indicate an individual's sex.

The giving of girls' names to boys and boys' names to girls sometimes comes about from disappointment as to the sex of the baby after the parents had decided to use a name of the sex they desire the infant to be. The most frequent cause, however, is sheer ignorance on the part of the parents as to Christian names and their spelling. A desire to be "different" or to achieve distinctiveness in spelling is sometimes the cause. In some cases the influence of languages other than English brings about the incongruous name. We usually think of the *-a* ending, for instance, as designating the feminine sex; yet in Anglo-Saxon names it indicates the masculine sex, as *Adda* and *Odda*.

Lord Coke, in his *First Institute* (Coke upon Littleton), says that a man cannot have two baptismal names. Camden, in the early part of the seventeenth century, stated that two Christian names were rare in England and that outside of royalty he could remember only two men with two Christian names. As Camden probably knew more of the families and pedigrees of the English aristocracy than any other man of his day (he was Clarenceux King of Arms), he spoke with authority. Perhaps the earliest recorded instance of a middle name in England was John Philip Capel of Fineham, in 1363; then there was John Severelle Love, a surgeon mentioned in 5 Henry V, A.D. 1417, Journal 1, fol. 19.

The custom of two Christian names came to England from France, through Scotland, in the first instance. Across the channel the practice is found to have existed as early as the twelfth century. In Spain double Christian names were frequent before the year 1000. In the time of the Georges the custom in England became intensified due to the influence from Germany, where the double baptismal name had been in aristocratic use since the fifteenth century. In the Roman Catholic countries of Italy and Spain the custom of giving to boys a female saint's name, usually that of the Blessed Virgin, as a middle name, arose as early as the sixteenth century. In a similar way Joseph was sometimes given to girls in France.

For a long time, in the seventeenth century, the few English persons baptized with more than one Christian name either did it to commemorate royalty and thus used names patronized by the royal house, or used *Posthuma* or *Maria* as the middle name. *Posthuma*, or *Posthumus*, of course, commemorated the earlier death of the father. *Maria* was used by both sexes and designated a child specially committed to the protection of the Virgin. Many of these double font-names were combined in one, as *Maryanne*, in the feeling of something akin to illegality in their use. The higher nobility in England slowly copied the practice within the above limits, but the common people did not adopt double Christian names in great numbers until the early part of the nineteenth century.

In the United States more than one Christian name was rare before the Revolutionary War, except with the Pennsylvania Dutch. Of our presidents, John Quincy Adams was the first to have two baptismal names, and most of the men we read about in the early years of our country had only one given name. Many of the early middle names in this country were surnames, as witness Henry Wadsworth Longfellow and William Hickling Prescott. President Adams' middle name is from the surname of his mother's grandfather, John Quincy. An English writer has observed that middle names may be either Christian names or surnames.

The adoption of three or four Christian names was almost unheard of before the nineteenth century, and even today only about two per cent of the people have more than two forenames, and this is brought about chiefly by the German influence. Weekly tells of *Thomas Hill Joseph Napoleon Horatio Bonaparte Swindlehurst Nelson* living in Lancashire in 1876. In 1944, the Preble County draft board of Eaton, Ohio, drafted *Noah Harvey Herman Daniel Boone Buster Brown David Longworth*. When William Cary of Seattle, Washington, came on the scene, his father was so excited that he christened him with the surnames of all the officers of his Civil War regiment, his full name being *Oscar William Free Omlis Fitz Allen John Don Pedro All Fonlas Mell Tare Gustofson Tittle Tuttle Step Carl Cary*. He died in 1946 at the ripe old age of eighty-two. Perhaps the extreme record is *Ann Bertha Cecilia Diana Emily Fanny Gertrude Hypatia Inez Jane Kate Louisa Maud Nora Ophelia Paula Quince Rebecca Starkey Teresa Ulysis Venus Winifred Xenophon Yeni Zeus*, daughter of Arthur and Sarah Pepper, born at Liverpool, England, December 19, 1882. Listed on a stone in the churchyard of Whitchurch Canonicorum, Dorset, England, is a lady who died July 9, 1871, at the age of sixty, a concatenation of Christian names: *Arabella Jenecenna Racatenna Abacel Grinter*.

Nowadays, in both England and America, about eighty per cent or more of the people have middle names. Where the surname is a common one, the middle name is extremely useful as a means of identification. Today everyone is expected to have a middle name, and all kinds of forms to be filled out provide a space for it. During the early part of World War II, if a man had no middle initial, the Army gave him three—N.M.I.—meaning "no middle initial." One should have a middle name if only to have an answer to the question, What is your middle name? On its Social Security forms the Government requires married women to give their maiden *first* name, their maiden *last* name (in place of the middle name), and their husband's last name.

The reasons that have guided parents in the selection of middle names are infinite. Salmon Portland Chase, formerly Chief Justice of the United States, received his first name from his Uncle Salmon. But he was named Portland because that important uncle died in Portland, Maine. The Chief Justice was in the habit of asserting, rather mournfully, that he was his uncle's monument.

The surname of the mother is often given to a baby as a middle name, and the practice tends to manufacture new Christian names out of surnames. In England and America surnames are often given as the first Christian name. In 1605 Camden mentions the growing practice, and observes that it does not happen elsewhere in Christendom. That most famous name in world fiction, Robinson Crusoe, tells us that he was christened Robinson from his mother's maiden name. The Catholic clergy, of course, oppose this practice because of their rule that the name given should be that of a saint. Some surnames, such as *Dudley, Sydney,* and *Howard,* have become so common that they are now recognized Christian names. The early practice was, for the most part, limited to the English aristocracy. Surnames as given names for babies are augmented by the custom of naming after the doctors who deliver them.

Surnames have been freely used as Christian names in America. After the Revolution the surnames of the founding fathers became quite common, as *Washington Irving, Washington Alston, Hamilton Fish, Franklin Delano Roosevelt* and *Jefferson Davis.* When Washington Irving visited Rome he was the recipient of attentions more flattering than he could account for, until, just as he was going away, he was asked if he was a relative of General Washington. Most of our presidents have so lent their surnames, and a name like *Lincoln* has become an acknowledged Christian name, and there are *Lincoln Steffens, Lincoln Schuster* and a host of other Lincolns. On the Continent surnames and unusual Christian names are impossible of adoption as both church and state unite in refusing to register what is not recognized as in use.

A curious practice, sometimes found, is that of duplicating the family name. Thus Sir Creswell Creswell was a famous English judge. Ford Madox Ford is a prominent British writer; Holling C. Holling is an author of various children's books. During the late depression Fish Fish was listed on the London dole. There was recently in Chicago a high school boy named Christ Christ. A bank cashier in Chicago was originally Moussa Moussa Moussa, but he inserted a medial *K* in place of the middle Moussa. England has a man named James Ashburner James Ashburner, and another named William Prior Johnson

William Prior Johnson. In Wales combinations like Edward Edwards and Owen Owens are common. In this country appellations like John Johnson and Robert Robertson can be found in any directory. The Dutch family of Lefferts, in America, had an old custom of calling one of the sons Leffert Lefferts.

An ancient practice, now practically obsolete, is that of giving the same Christian name to each boy in the family. An example is that of the famous Sir John Pasto (1442-1479), who had a younger brother John. In 1612 one John Willes made bequests to his brother John Willes "the elder" and to John Willes "the younger." Salverte tells of a Scotchman, an enthusiastic admirer of the Stuarts, who named each of his fourteen sons Charles Edward, in honor of the Pretender. Twins have been furnished with identical names transposed, as James Reginald and Reginald James. Brothers have also received identical names transposed; James Caesar Petrillo, the music czar, has an orchestra leader brother, Caesar James Petrillo.

In early times there was a comparatively small stock of Christian names, but that would be little excuse for giving several in the same family the same name. Duplicate Christian names were sometimes due to the practice of naming after the grandparents. When the two grandparents had the same forename, the only way of bestowing the honor was to name two sons or daughters alike. Oftentimes the same Christian name was given to several children to make sure that the name would not die out through the early demise of the elder children. Now some superstitious people believe that to give a child the name previously given to a deceased brother or sister will cause it, also, to die at an early age.

There is a small group of boys' names, mostly Anglo-Saxon in origin, which, in England, and particularly in America, are contemptuously referred to as "sissy" names. The reason for this is not easy to discover, as many of them have been borne by men who were rough, fearless pioneers, vikings and seafaring men, who could not by any stretch of the imagination be termed other than the most virile of men. Some of them have been included in this list because of reputations acquired through characters so designated in newspaper comic strips. These names are *Marmaduke, Algernon, Percy, Egbert, Cuthbert, Cedric, Cadwallader* and *Montague*. Perhaps they are too fancy. Other names which are regarded by some as sissy names, but are not so known by others, are *Clarence, Claude, Harold, Horace, Howard* and *Cecil*.

The *New York Times* on June 15, 1945, carried an editorial entitled, "Calling All Clarences," commemorating Pfc. Clarence B. Craft of California for killing thirty Japanese on Okinawa. It pointed out that well-meaning mothers who had pinned the name of Clarence on their defenseless darlings were now justified before all men, and observed that there must be great rejoicing among all the Clarences in the world. Back in 1922, Clarence Massey of Cleveland, Ohio, formed the Clarence-Anti-Defamation League to stop vaudeville actors from making fun of the name. P. E. Foxworth, the New York area head of the Federal Bureau of Investigation, defiantly stated, "The *P* in my name stands for Sam—but it's really Percy. Do you blame me?"

Among girls, names like *Amarilla, Ermentrude, Hypatia, Mehitable, Euphemia, Dulcibella* and *Cleopatra* are just generally unpleasant, at least at the present time. Also in this category, for both men and women, are the more unusual of the Biblical names. Some names have a humorous social distinction, as *Bridget* for a cook.

Among us, the names of *Jehovah* and *Jesus* are considered to be too sacred for human beings. Yet in Spain, Portugal and South America the people have no compunctions against using *Jesus* as a Christian name, and we find it in this country among the Spanish- and Portuguese-speaking peoples. The Greeks, and some Scandinavians, have no hesitancy about using *Christ* as a Christian name.

New Christian names may be easily manufactured simply by taking a few letters and shaking them around until they drop into a pronounceable pattern. A name-father can also obtain new names by taking a place-name or word which is then prominent in the news, and at the same time get a few lines of newspaper publicity. A few children born on December 7, 1941, received the appellation of *Pearl Harbor*. Some girls born on the day of the invasion of France were named *Invasia*. Those who were born on the day of victory, to become *Victor* or *Victoria*, fared better. A well-known example is Kenesaw Mountain Landis who was christened after Sherman's forces fought the battle of Kenesaw Mountain. But when you meet these people in the future you will know exactly how old they are. Liberty Bond Dvorak, the Chicago lady lawyer, cheerfully admits that her acquaintances know how old she is, but contends that she has not reached the critical age, and, with her disposition, she probably never will. But after dropping *Bond* she was forced to smile at the quotations, "Give me Liberty or give me death" and "Give me Liberty or the Saturday Evening Post."

To summarize, almost all given names selected by parents, either civilized or barbarian, may be placed in at least one of the following classes:

I. To honor another person:

    a) From given name of grandparent or more distant ancestor.
    b) From given name of parent.
    c) From maiden surname of mother.
    d) From name of uncle or aunt or other relative.
    e) From given name or surname of friend.
    f) Beginning with a certain initial to honor parents, grandparents or others, as *Charles*, when the two grandfathers are named Clifford and Cyrus.

II. In admiration of a famous personage:

    a) From given name or surname of a political character.
    b) From name of sovereign.
    c) From name of military personage.
    d) From name of religious character, particularly from the Bible.
    e) From name of poet, writer or musical celebrity.
    f) From name of star of stage, screen, radio or television.
    g) From name of fictitious character.

III. Because it is "pretty" or seems to be harmonious with the surname:

    a) From a surname, as *Farley, Sydney, Sumner* or *Stanley*.
    b) A pleasant nickname, as *Jack* or *Betty*.

IV. From some event or circumstance of birth:

    a) Place of birth, as *Lydia, Kent, Oceanus, Portland*.
    b) Time of birth, as *Easter, Noel, June, Monday*.
    c) With reference to number, as *Enough, Finis, Omega, Wenonah* (first), *Octavius* (eighth), *Tertius* (third).
    d) Twins, as *Thomas*; or *Avery* and *Ivory*; or triplets, as *Faith, Hope* and *Charity*.
    e) Event happening on or near day of birth, as *Pearl Harbor, Invasia*.
    f) Event happening to parents on or near day of birth, as soldier father receiving *Furlough* and so naming son.

V. From some hope or aspiration on the part of the parents:

    a) Of a religious nature, as *John* (gracious gift of God), *Grace, Hope, Elizabeth* (oath of God), *Fight-the-Good-Fight*.

b) Of a warlike nature, as *Gertrude* (spear, maiden), *Lorraine* (famous, war), *Luther* (famous, warrior).

VI. Descriptive of the child:

a) From complexion, as *Blanche* (white), *Douglas* (dark gray), *Maureen* (dark).
b) From color of hair, as *Flavia* (yellow), *Rufus* (red-haired), *Xanthe* (yellow-haired).
c) From a bodily imperfection, as *Cecil* (blind), *Claude* and *Gladys* (lame), *Calvin* (bald).
d) From size, as *Vaughn* and *Paul* (small).
e) From action of the child, as *Balbus* (stammerer).
f) From disposition of the child, as *Dirty* or *Gentle*.
g) From real or fancied resemblance to something, as *Ursula* (little she-bear).

VII. From an object:

a) A flower or plant, as *Daisy, Pansy* or *Violet*.
b) A jewel or gem, as *Margaret, Pearl, Opal, Ruby*.
c) An animal or insect, as *Columbine* (dove), *Caleb* (dog), *Deborah* (bee), *Dorcas* (gazelle).
d) A weapon, as *Ledyard* (people's spear).
e) A clan emblem, as *Ajax* (eagle), *Leo* (lion).
f) A modern term, as *Dynamo*.

VIII. Because of association or relation with the surname:

a) Of a humorous nature, as *Lily White, Happy Sadd*.
b) Same or similar to the family name, as *James James, John Johnson*.
c) For the sake of alliteration, as *Charley Chadwick*.
d) From sound or rhyme of name, as *Peter Streeter*.

IX. From error or ignorance:

a) Medical words, as *Vagina, Appendix*.
b) Misspelled names.
c) Odd pronunciations, as *Libertine* for Liberty.

X. Oddities (which are often less so when rightly understood):

a) Of a different sex, as boy named *Mary*.
b) Queer pet name, as *Skeezix*.
c) Composed of single letters, as *LB* or *OP*.
d) Short or long name, as *Ex* or *Jafkeranaegzia*.

XI. As a result of chance:

   a) From drawing after various names are written on paper, sticks or other things.
   b) From first name seen after opening the Bible, or other religious book, at random.
   c) From name of first person met at a certain time.
   d) From first words uttered by a person present at the birth or on other occasion.
   e) From first name heard after turning on the radio.

XII. From invention:

   a) Changing spelling of an ordinary name, as *Ethyle* for Ethel.
   b) Spelling a sound without meaning, as *Cona, Tala*.

The examples given, it must be recognized, may also be found in other classes. Since the above table refers only to names selected by parents, it does not include those primitive peoples who paid an oracle or priest to name their children, when the oracle or priest selected the name in addition to bestowing it.

Everyone feels that Christian names should harmonize with the surname, but few know any tests other than saying the names over and over. There should be harmony in sound, pronunciation, nationality and rhythm. Since the entire name is only a few syllables, rhythm is difficult for some to identify. A name should be a poem, not a prose cacophony. Alliteration is conducive to euphony, but rhyming tends to produce a comic effect. In early times a name was given because of its significance, but now the reason is, "It sounds nice and goes well with ——— [the surname]." Everyone can name a baby, but few can do it well. Giving a child an absurd or insignificant name is tying a stone around his neck.

About the easiest way for the normal person to attain harmony is to refrain from having all the names contain the same number of syllables. Specifically, three names each composed of a single, short syllable are too staccato, as *John Paul Jones*; when each has three or more syllables, it is too long and cumbersome. If the surname has only one syllable, the two given names should each contain two syllables, as *Edgar Allan Poe* and *William Howard Taft*, or one of them should have two syllables and the other three syllables, as *William Robertson Smith* and *Oliver Wendell Holmes*. Common surnames with only one syllable, like *Brown, Jones* and *Smith*, are the most difficult with which to fit harmonizing given names. If the surname contains two syllables, the two names added should be of one and three syllables in either order, as *Margaret Lee Runbeck* and *Charles Augustus Lindbergh* or be composed of one and two syllables in that order, as *John Jacob Astor*. If the surname is of three syllables, the names selected should be of one or two syllables in either order, as *Ralph Waldo Emerson* and *William Gibbs McAdoo*. Particular attention should be given to accent. Two accented syllables should not come together except, perhaps, when the first name is one of a single syllable. Especial care should be given to avoid adoption of a middle name with rising accents, unless the surname is of the same character.

In the future some names will be popular which are rare or unknown today, and many of our common names will become unusual. It is impossible to forecast the trend of names as instanced by the dismal predictions made by the nomenclatural scholars in the past. Also many of the statements made in this chapter will seem untrue to some who have been familiar with certain names in their own locality. The author has attempted to avoid purely local situations in respect to certain names and has tried to outline their influence in the country as a whole. Simple names, once popular in England, like *Fulk, Odo* and *Hamo,* as shown by the surnames derived from them, have become quite rare now, but may return in the future.

For those who are interested in seeing how popular their given names are, the following lists, carefully compiled by the author, of the hundred most common girls' names and the hundred most common boys' names with estimated numbers of each in the United States are here set out:

GIRLS

Rank	Name	Estimated Number	Rank	Name	Estimated Number
1.	Mary	3,720,000	11.	Nancy	1,020,000
2.	Elizabeth	1,788,000	12.	Patricia	947,000
3.	Barbara	1,785,000	13.	Jane	945,000
4.	Dorothy	1,770,000	14.	Alice	900,000
5.	Helen	1,725,000	15.	Joan	840,000
6.	Margaret	1,485,000	16.	Betty	830,000
7.	Ruth	1,395,000	17.	Dolores	825,000
8.	Virginia	1,365,000	18.	Eleanor	810,000
9.	Jean	1,170,000	19.	Anne	795,000
10.	Frances	1,155,000	20.	Florence	750,000

Rank	Name	Estimated Number	Rank	Name	Estimated Number
21.	Ann	690,000	61.	Sally	247,000
22.	Rose	660,000	62.	Edna	246,000
23.	Lillian	655,000	63.	Pauline	244,000
24.	Marie	645,000	64.	Julia	243,000
25.	Shirley	640,000	65.	Joyce	240,000
26.	Lorraine	585,000	66.	Susan	235,000
27.	Irene	570,000	67.	Jacqueline	230,000
28.	Grace	540,000	68.	Esther	227,000
29.	Marjorie	525,000	69.	Marian	226,000
30.	Anna	510,000	70.	Theresa	224,000
31.	Josephine	500,000	71.	Kathryn	216,000
32.	Louise	495,000	72.	Caroline	210,000
33.	Mildred	465,000	73.	Rita	208,000
34.	Janet	460,000	74.	Judith	204,000
35.	Evelyn	450,000	75.	Priscilla	200,000
36.	Marion	440,000	76.	Violet	195,000
37.	Katherine	420,000	77.	Beatrice	190,000
38.	Doris	405,000	78.	Geraldine	185,000
39.	Lucille	390,000	79.	Hazel	184,000
40.	Ellen	375,000	80.	Beverly	180,000
41.	Lois	370,000	81.	Norma	179,000
42.	Marilyn	365,000	82.	Emma	178,000
43.	Martha	362,000	83.	Gladys	174,000
44.	Harriet	360,000	84.	Adeline	170,000
45.	June	345,000	85.	Stella	168,000
46.	Bernice	344,000	86.	Carolyn	166,000
47.	Jeanne	343,000	87.	Agnes	165,000
48.	Charlotte	330,000	88.	Catherine	164,000
49.	Phyllis	328,000	89.	Elsie	161,000
50.	Loretta	315,000	90.	Laura	160,000
51.	Katharine	305,000	91.	Constance	155,000
52.	Elaine	300,000	92.	Eileen	154,000
53.	Carol	287,000	93.	Genevieve	150,000
54.	Clara	285,000	94.	Rosalie	148,000
55.	Edith	284,000	95.	Emily	147,000
56.	Sarah	270,000	96.	Cecelia	146,000
57.	Gertrude	255,000	97.	Joanne	143,000
58.	Sylvia	252,000	98.	Carmella	140,000
59.	Gloria	250,000	99.	Vivian	137,000
60.	Rosemary	249,000	100.	Lucy	135,000

BOYS

Rank	Name	Estimated Number	Rank	Name	Estimated Number
1.	John	5,837,000	42.	Lewis	221,000
2.	William	5,365,000	43.	Eugene	220,000
3.	Charles	3,023,000	44.	Hugh	200,000
4.	James	2,998,000	45.	Howard	197,000
5.	George	2,940,000	46.	Isaac	186,000
6.	Robert	2,404,000	47.	Nathaniel	180,000
7.	Thomas	1,910,000	48.	Roy	178,000
8.	Henry	1,668,000	49.	Raymond	172,000
9.	Joseph	1,597,000	50.	Edmund	166,000
10.	Edward	1,407,000	51.	Donald	165,000
11.	Samuel	1,147,000	52.	Lawrence	154,000
12.	Frank	1,120,000	53.	Earl	149,000
13.	Richard	783,000	54.	Horace	148,000
14.	Harry	724,000	55.	Martin	146,000
15.	Francis	707,000	56.	Jesse	145,000
16.	Frederick	705,000	57.	Oliver	144,000
17.	Walter	684,000	58.	Oscar	143,000
18.	David	682,000	59.	Augustus	139,000
19.	Arthur	637,000	60.	Edgar	134,000
20.	Albert	607,000	61.	Anthony	127,000
21.	Benjamin	587,000	62.	Patrick	124,000
22.	Alexander	527,000	63.	Jonathan	123,000
23.	Daniel	486,000	64.	Elmer	122,000
24.	Louis	463,000	65.	Stanley	117,000
25.	Harold	374,000	66.	Herman	114,000
26.	Paul	361,000	67.	Franklin	113,500
27.	Fred	359,000	68.	Abraham	111,000
28.	Edwin	352,000	69.	Leonard	109,000
29.	Andrew	342,000	70.	Nathan	108,000
30.	Alfred	339,000	71.	Norman	107,000
31.	Peter	334,000	72.	Russell	106,000
32.	Ralph	300,000	73.	Matthew	105,000
33.	Philip	298,000	74.	Julius	99,000
34.	Herbert	283,000	75.	Nicholas	98,500
35.	Stephen	273,000	76.	Allen	97,000
36.	Jacob	264,000	77.	Chester	96,000
37.	Carl	258,000	78.	Leo	92,000
38.	Theodore	244,000	79.	Guy	91,500
39.	Clarence	243,000	80.	Kenneth	91,000
40.	Ernest	242,000	81.	Otto	90,500
41.	Michael	235,000	82.	Josiah	89,000

Rank	Name	Estimated Number	Rank	Name	Estimated Number
83.	Bernard	88,000	92.	Archibald	78,500
84.	Claude	87,500	93.	Jeremiah	78,000
85.	Christopher	87,000	94.	Rufus	77,000
86.	Sidney	86,500	95.	Leon	76,500
87.	Harvey	86,000	96.	Joshua	76,000
88.	Moses	84,000	97.	Max	75,500
89.	Timothy	83,000	98.	Lloyd	75,000
90.	Maurice	82,000	99.	Warren	74,500
91.	Gilbert	80,500	100.	Roger	73,500

It must be remembered that the above lists are only estimates for the United States as a whole, and are not accurate for any particular area of population or age group. This list will vary greatly when compiled for a particular age group, particularly among the girls' names.

Research has uncovered the fact that people with common surnames are only two-thirds as likely to choose common Christian names for their children.

It is also interesting to note, in the above list of girls' names, the relative popularity of such forms as *Jean, Jane, Joan, Jeanne, Joanne; Anne, Ann* and *Anna; Marion, Marian; Katherine, Katharine, Kathryn* and *Catherine; Caroline* and *Carolyn.* With the boys, *Fred,* a short form of Frederick, is very common. Both *Henry* and *Harry* appear high on the list, as well as *Frank* and *Francis.* Among male names there are fewer forms of the same name. It is interesting to note, however, that *Lawrence* and *Augustus* are the preferred forms of those names.

The longest girls' name on the list is the ten-lettered *Jacqueline,* but there are many of nine letters. The shortest is *Ann.* Boys sport the eleven-lettered *Christopher* and *Roy, Leo, Guy* and *Max* contest for the shortest name.

How and When Surnames Originated

But the French and wee termed them Surnames, not because they are names of the sire, or the father, but because they are super added to Christian names, as the Spaniards call them Renombres, as Renames.
—CAMDEN: *Remaines*, 1605

THAT surnames have not existed since the time of Adam is known by everyone who is familiar with the Bible. People who have claimed that they could trace their family name back through the Middle Ages to the time of Christ are more than a trifle imaginative.

Exactly when the first hereditary surname or family name originated it is impossible to say. Not everyone adopted surnames at one time, and the surname period covers several centuries. Camden, in his *Remaines of a Greater Worke Concerning Britaine*, which was first published in 1605, said,

About the yeare of our Lord 1000 (that we may not minute out the time) surnames beganne to be taken up in France, and in England about the time of the Conquest, or else a very little before, under King Edward the Confessor, who was all Frenchified.

His estimate of the time certainly is not far from accurate, although, as Camden himself states, no instance of a hereditary family name is found in England before the Conquest. It was not until a hundred years or more after the Conquest that hereditary surnames were found in any great numbers. The first to use surnames were, of course, the lords and more important franklins and others who took as surnames the names of their estates which descended to their sons along with the estate.

The absence of surnames in very early records is not reliable proof that they did not then exist. Custom favored the font-name and thus there was a tendency to omit the surname.

Not until the latter part of the thirteenth century are hereditary surnames found to be the rule rather than the exception. For several centuries afterward, nay, not until well in the seventeenth century, could it be said that hereditary family names were upon a sound and firm basis and not subject to change at the slightest whim of the individual.

At first only the great nobles felt the need of a surname, and then it seemed a disgrace for a gentleman to have but one name as the meaner sort had. The daughter of Fitz Hamon, a great lord, when King Henry I wanted her to marry his base son, Robert, is said to have refused, at first, saying:

> It were to me a great shame,
> To have a Lord with outen his twa name.

Whereupon the king, to meet her objections, gave him the surname of Fitz Roy, meaning "son of the king." He was afterward Earl of Gloucester. Today, we are apt to consider that a Mr. Brown is called William to distinguish him from the other Browns, but formerly he was only called Brown to distinguish him from the other Williams.

The rise of surnames was stimulated by the paucity of personal names in general use after the Conquest. The Norman list of names brought over by the Conqueror was really a small one, yet it took possession of the whole of England and drove out the larger number of old Saxon names. Out of every hundred men there would be twenty *Johns* and fifteen *Williams*. The rest were called *Thomas, Bartholomew, Nicholas, Philip, Simon, Peter, Isaac, Richard, Robert, Walter, Henry, Guy, Roger* and *Baldwin*. Consequently, to identify persons, nicknames or bynames were necessary as well as descriptions, which gradually developed into surnames and hereditary family names.

To understand the origin and rise of English surnames, one must first know something of the organization and state of society in Norman times, after William defeated the Saxons at Hastings, in 1066, and through the thirteenth century.

After the Conquest the entire population of England has been estimated to have been only about two million. And this was about all that the land could support as it was then worked. Much less than a tenth of the people lived in the towns such as London, York, Bristol and Coventry. Only some half dozen towns had a population above

5,000, and there were then only about ten important towns in all England. London itself had less than 35,000 inhabitants.

The rest of the people lived in the *hams* or *tuns*, the villages, under what is known as the manorial system. The manors differed from each other in many respects, and our knowledge of them is faulty because of the fragmentary and one-sided records that have come down to us from medieval times. Nevertheless it is necessary, in order to understand the origin of family names, to get a bird's eye view of the everyday life of the peasants and others who lived there.

No two village communities were exactly the same, and each had its special customs which had the force of law against both lord and tenant alike. In general, however, we can say that a manor consisted of the rude houses of the peasants, grouped about the manor house, or hall, as it was often called, the parish church and the village green. The habitations were surrounded by open fields of arable and pasture land, wasteland and woods which extended away to the boundaries of the neighboring manor. The houses were not isolated or separated from one another by surrounding fields as they are so generally found in modern times, but were grouped in villages which were often, but not necessarily, coextensive with the manor. Only the mill, and sometimes the church, were detached from the main group of buildings.

Of the people of the manor, the overwhelming majority in the eleventh century were the villeins and the *servi*, or slaves, and they were bondsmen who could not leave the soil and seek better conditions of life elsewhere. If they ran away, they could be brought back by order of court and returned to the lord's service. Permission from the lord to remain away in a town could be bought only by the payment of a periodical sum known as head money. The medieval peasant could not even sell his cattle or anything else without the lord's consent, which could be bought only at a price.

The better-class villeins cultivated approximately thirty acres of land divided into acre or half-acre parcels and equally distributed in each of the open fields, in long, narrow strips, with rights in the common land. They each owned two or more oxen. The poorer-class villeins farmed five or ten acres or less, or, in some cases, held only a cottage, and they were designated as cotters. Few villeins were wealthy enough to own eight oxen, the usual plow team; so they had to co-operate among themselves to plow their holdings. In early Norman times villeins constituted about seventy per cent of the total population of England.

Lower than the cotters were the slaves, constituting about nine per cent of the population, who worked chiefly in the households of the lords of the manor. Slaves were bought and sold in the market and exported to the Continent. Less than a century after the Conquest the slaves disappear and merge with the cotters, so it is unnecessary here to describe them further.

Above the villeins was a growing class of free tenants who cultivated larger amounts of the arable lands and who paid the lord either in money or in kind or both. The more substantial of the free men were the franklins, who often had twice as much land as the more important villeins. For their lands the villeins paid by working for the lord of the manor two to four days a week and paying certain dues. The cotters, by reason of their smaller holding, often worked for their lord only one day a week. This work may be divided into week-work, which consisted of plowing or reaping or other agricultural labor for the lord, and boon-day work, which was rendered whenever required by the lord, although the number of boon-days in a year was limited by custom in each particular manor.

When not working for their lord, the villeins tended their own land. The cotters, having less land and more time to spare, frequently worked for others for hire. Indeed, from the cotters sprang the distinct wage-earning class who lived almost entirely on wages. Some money and farm produce were also paid to the lord. By the fourteenth century the lord paid many of his servants in cash.

Each manor had three or six (but sometimes only two) fields, and they might be named with reference to the direction in which they were situated from the houses of the village, as the West Field or North Field. The forest land was owned by the lord although the tenants might have certain rights to collect fallen branches for fuel and turn their swine there to pick up what food they could. The lord always had a close on his demesne, which was a portion of land set off and enclosed and which he would let separately at a higher rental. The chief tenants might also have close land. From time to time new land might be brought under the plow by clearing a part of the forest or wasteland, either permanently or temporarily. The land so reclaimed was called *assart* land or, in the North of England, *riddings*, and a rent was paid to the lord of the manor for the right to cultivate this land.

The lord of the manor, above the freemen and villeins, was either the king himself, a bishop, abbot or other ecclesiastical official, an earl or

other noble, or a knight, esquire, or merely a freeman. The resident lord of the manor was often the mesne tenant of a greater lord. If the lord held only one manor, he was usually resident thereon; if more than one, he was usually represented by a steward who traveled from manor to manor.

The chief manor officials, in the absence of the lord, consisted of the seneschal or steward, a man of rank or standing, whose duty it was to preside in the manor courts, inquire as to services and rents, of suits to the lord's courts, markets and mills and as to alienation of lands. He must see that the land was properly arranged and that the lord's plows were in good repair. The steward looked after all his lord's land. If a lord had more than one manor, each had its reeve to do the actual work of the steward, instead of his regular duties, and the reeve's overseer was the lord's bailiff.

The bailiff, who was always a freeman, was the official in charge of the manor, in consultation with the steward. In many cases he was in charge of more than one manor and had to travel constantly from one to another. While he was absent from the manor, the reeve did his work. The bailiff also presided at the manor courts in the absence of the lord and steward.

The position of the bailiff was emphasized by the fact that, as an outsider, he dwelt in the manor house where he could keep a sharp eye on the manorial servants who lived in the outbuildings attached to the manor house. Among these were the deye (in charge of the dairy), carter, akerman (plowman), carpenter, or woodwright, and wheelwright.

The sergeant appeared to be an official found now and then with a status between the bailiff and the reeve. Sometimes the word is used with the meaning synonymous with that of bailiff and other times with that of reeve. The work of the bailiff and the reeve overlapped in many manors, and many manors did not have both, but only one or the other. Oftentimes we find that the titles of bailiff, sergeant, reeve, beadle and hayward are bandied about by a scribe in such a way as to indicate to us how hazy he was as to their precise meaning. One entry may give a man the title of reeve, and in the next the same man may be referred to as a sergeant.

The reeve (in the north, called the grave) to some extent represented the peasantry, but his duties consisted mostly in seeing that the interests of the lord were properly handled. He was generally chosen for a year at a time, generally at Michelmas (September 29), when the harvest was over and the new year of husbandry was about to begin. While he was usually elected by the villeins, we may be sure that it was always with the tacit approval of the lord. The reeve was generally responsible for the management of the lord's demesne and especially for getting out and overseeing the work services owed by the villeins.

During the time that a villein served as reeve, he was relieved of all or a large part of the services he was required to perform and the payments he had to make, and was often, in addition, paid a stipend and given various perquisites, such as keeping his horse or ox in the lord's pasture and eating at the lord's table during harvest. That the reeve's task, however, was hard and thankless is disclosed by the efforts of villeins to avoid the office even at the expense of onerous fines. The duty of serving as a reeve became one of the tests of villeinage.

Petty officials of the manor were the messor or hayward, the beadle or constable, the woodward, the forester and parker, and also the beekeepers, swineherds, goatherds, shepherds, cowherds and oxherds, all mostly elected by the tenants. Many of these latter were often manorial servants rather than petty officials. It is a mistake to suppose that every manor had each of these officers or that the duties of a particular official were the same in every manor. While the reeve and the hayward usually came from among the more substantial villeins, the others were drawn from the cotter class.

The hayward, who was in charge of sowing and gathering the crops, was next to the reeve in importance, and his privileges and compensations were similar. He was, as the word implies, the warden of the hays or hedges, and his duty was to protect the fields not only against cattle but also against men trespassing, and watch to prevent theft from the fields after the crops were ripe. His horn, his badge of office, was used to give warning that cattle or other trespassers were in the corn (English for *grain*, especially wheat, rye, oats and barley). Little Boy Blue was a hayward. The old rhyme read:

> Little Boy Blue, come blow your horn;
> The sheep's in the meadow, the cow's in the corn.

The hayward presented to the manorial court all cases of straying animals and trespassing men so that the guilty ones might be amerced.

The beadle, or bedell, was the policeman of the village and also a court officer. He made all summons ordered by the court (sometimes he was called a summoner), and levied distresses, made attachments and collected fines. The woodward safeguarded the lord's woods. The

forester watched over the lord's deer and his rights of chase. (Middle English *deer* meant any wild animal.) The parker had charge of the lord's parks. The swineherds, shepherds and oxherds took care of the swine, sheep and oxen, not only those belonging to the lord, but those belonging to all the villagers, and received their pay from everyone. Cows were leased by the lord to the *deye* or dairyman, who then sold some of the milk to the villagers.

Every community required a smith to make and repair the iron-work of the plows and other farm implements, a carpenter or wright, a miller and a baker. These were villeins, or, more often, freemen, who rendered no other service for any holdings they might have by reason of their official obligations to the lord, which were carefully set out in the manor records. They were entitled to charge for work done for the villeins or for extra work for the lord. A chance weaver or other craftsman was sometimes found.

The priest of the parish house enjoyed quite a bit of freedom because of his position and learning, although his origin may have been as a humble villein. In most manors he also cultivated land and was thus a peasant in competition with the villeins. During early medieval times marriage in the priesthood was by no means rare and he often had a family to keep.

Life on the medieval manor was hard. But the habit of living in a small village must have given opportunity for social contacts which distinguished it from the loneliness of life in the isolated farms of later times. The intermingled strips of holdings in the open fields, the neces-sary co-operation in the performance of their daily labor, attendance at the parish church and attendance and action in the manor courts developed a close social relationship between the inhabitants. But this close organization tended to prevent change and inhibited inter-course beyond the manor. The villages were separated by many miles of bad roads through forests, sometimes infested by highwaymen, so that, in Norman times, there was very little communication between them. In relation to everyone except the lord, the villeins were perfectly free citizens.

The manor house or dwelling of the lord was, of course, the largest and best house in the village and was called the *hall*. Here the manor courts were usually held. When the lord did not live on the manor, the bailiff or steward would live in the hall. The early Norman houses of the villeins and freemen were crude and sparsely furnished, but con-sisted of from one to four rooms.

When a villein died, he was succeeded in possession of the holding by the person who was his heir, according to the custom of the manor, upon payment of the fine to the lord. The heir was usually the eldest son, although sometimes it was the youngest; in some manors the father chose the son he wished to succeed him. Daughters often held jointly. Commonly, when the son who was to succeed to the holding became of age, the fine was paid to the lord and the father relinquished the holding to that son upon his agreement to maintain him for the rest of his life. Upon receiving possession of the land, the heir paid the lord for license to marry. He did not marry before obtaining the land.

The sons who did not inherit either left the manor to seek their fortune in the nearest borough, or married an heiress, or became churchmen, or else stayed on the land to work for, and be supported by, their brother. In the latter case they could not marry. Landholders married; landless men remained single. The fate of the daughters of the house was parallel to that of the sons. Thus the land descended from generation to generation without ever being partitioned, and the population did not increase very rapidly. Besides the single brothers and sisters of the heir, the villein's household might include various single men and women servants and undersettles, that is, married couples who occupied a small cottage in the curtilage and who tilled an acre or more of the villein's land in return for rendering part of the villein's services to the lord. Sometimes an undersettle was merely one who leased a cottage from the holder of a tenement.

In Scotland, Ireland and Wales, in place of the manorial system and parallel in time with it, was the tribal or clan system with its inferior septs. A sept consisted of a number of actual or reputed blood relations bound together by artificial ties such as common liability for the payment of blood fines. The septs were divided into separate families of varying degrees of wealth, partition of land being among the males in a similar scatter field system as prevailed in the English manors. All were clustered around the chief, whose surname almost everyone in the sept used. When a chief died, a new chief was elected, the office not being hereditary.

Next, let us look briefly at the life of the less than ten per cent of the people of Norman England who lived in the towns. The earliest towns were only more thickly populated than the village communities; they were more stricly organized forms of the village, or perhaps a group of manors owned either by one lord or several. A town might be under

the protection of some great noble, prelate, or of the king himself, who would finally grant it a charter.

Some towns grew in the shadow of a great abbey or monastery; others around the country houses of the king or some earl, or as market towns, while others grew because they were situated at a port or other natural trading center. Towns with cathedrals, and therefore the seats of bishoprics, were called cities. London was a town apart and was the only one with an advanced civic constitution in all England in early times, and so, of course, it was the center of national life. However, not before the fifteenth century did most towns advance to any certain status with definite privileges. The nobles parted with their manorial rights over the towns chiefly to get money to fight wars against each other, and to take part in the Crusades.

Another powerful factor in the growth of the towns was the rise of the great merchant guilds and the craft guilds. The merchant guilds were associations of the merchants or tradesmen, at first, for social purposes. The craft guilds in the smaller places included all the members of various crafts; in the larger towns each craft had a guild of its own. The guilds, with their strength through numbers, had many important privileges that made others anxious to join their ranks. For instance, membership in a guild for a year and a day made a villein a free man; thus all the free men belonged to guilds as proof of their status.

The craft guilds tried to secure good work from the members and keep out irresponsible persons. The system of masters having apprentices arose from a desire to train a limited number of young people in the particular industry of the craft guild. The guild also exercised some moral control over its members, but might go to the rescue of its members imprisoned elsewhere.

The presiding officer of the guild was usually known as the alderman, while other officials were called stewards, deans, bailiffs, chaplains, skevens and ushers, the duties they performed varying from town to town. There were no separate shops, and every craftsman worked in his own home or in a room adjoining.

Some of the most important craft guilds were the goldsmiths, dyers, fishmongers, weavers, glovers, girdlers (makers of girdles), skinners, white tawyers (those who prepare skins), fletchers (arrowmakers), bowyers (bowmakers), stringers (makers of bowstrings), bakers, smiths, carpenters and masons. By 1340 there were about forty different craft guilds in London.

The craft guilds at one or more times during the year held great feasts, which varied in luxuriousness according to the wealth of the group, and also engaged in other social, charitable, philanthropic and religious activities. We often find them taking entire charge of the series or cycles of mystery plays which were produced in various towns and based on some scene of biblical story, so arranged that the whole Bible narrative might be given in consecutive plays. Guild meetings were held in the great guild-halls of the towns.

After the Conquest, many Flemish people came to England and settled in the towns and engaged in the craft of weaving. The manufacture of wool was by far the most important industry in the towns for the first century or more after William's battle at Hastings, and a great deal of fine woolen cloth was exported.

Now, after this brief inspection of the people of medieval England, let us see how they obtained their surnames. For a long time after the Conquest each peasant was known in the village, or in the borough, only by his given name. He was John or William or Robert or Thomas or Henry or Walter or Richard. After the Conquest, the Christian names of the Normans almost completely replaced the older English font-names, but there were not so many of them. The women were Alice or Agnes or Lucy or Mabel or Margery or Maud.

The lords, who traveled more, earlier felt the need of a surname, or family name, to distinguish them from others with the same font-name. Again, the lords and the knights had been on the crusades and had observed the rise of surnames in France and other countries. They tended to take the names of their lands and estates as family names.

But what of the peasants? Did they "take" surnames? The life of the peasant was firmly ruled by custom, and, never having had a family name, it did not occur to the rude villein that he needed one. For a long time after the Conquest only the lords and knights had surnames, and the peasant, if he thought about it at all, considered an additional name merely as another badge worn by "his betters."

There were occasions when the clerk of the manorial court had to list the villein's name in the court records, as a matter for all to know. A fine might be assessed and a memorial would have to be made. When he paid the lord for license to marry, the fact would have to be written down. When the villein died, a heriot, which was the best domestic animal or other chattel the deceased had possessed, had to be given to the lord and the parish priest would claim a mortuary, usually the second best animal. All such occurrences must be faithfully recorded in the hallmote, and the man must be clearly identified.

If the peasant was the reeve, the clerk naturally so described him and listed him as John, the reeve. Similarly with hayward, woodward, shepherd and all the other petty officials. If he was the smith, miller or wright, he was so designated. Chaucer gives a good list of village officials and occupations in his *Canterbury Tales*.

Perhaps he was not an official but was merely an ordinary villein or cotter. If his father was then living, particularly if he was at all prominent by reason of ability or personality, the clerk might refer to John as "Robert's son," or if he was the son of a prominent widow, it might be as "Emma's son." His residence might be near a pond or lake, and the scribe would write *atte water* or *lake*. For one reason or another he might live in or very near to the manor house or hall, and this would identify him. Again his home might be near the west field and the two words would be run together as a surname. If it was near the village green, the description of *at the green* would be natural. He might reside near the isolated mill and thus have that, or *milne,* the early spelling, after his given name.

The villein might have red hair and thus be inserted as *reed* or *reid* (early spellings of red), or be short of stature and have *short* added to his name. Any prominent personal peculiarity would quickly identify him.

The next year when the same John had ceased to be the reeve, he might be listed by the clerk in the court rolls with some other description. A different clerk might write the name at the next hallmote and use some different description, or even if it were the same clerk, he might not remember or care what descriptive words he used before, and use the first ones that came into his mind in connection with the person he was noting in the records. Each time it became necessary to give a man a surname to differentiate him from others in the same group, a descriptive word was added to his Christian name. Whether the same word was used each time the necessity arose to describe him depended on how soon the need arose and on whether that word was then the best descriptive term that could be used. As the need arose for naming him, more and more often the same word was used, and he came generally to be known by that surname. When his son grew up and became prominent, the same or a different word might be employed as a surname. When the same word was used as a matter of course, it then became a hereditary family name.

Hereditary surnames originate through disregard of the meaning of some descriptive term.

The manorial court rolls were written, not in English, but in Latin, and thus the descriptive words were translated by the clerk into Latin, and for reeve he put *præpositus*; for smith, *faber*; for baker, *pistor*; miller, *molendinarius,* etc. The Christian names were also given their Latin forms as *Johannes, Willelmus, Ricardus, Alicia, Angnes* and *Mabilia.* Since English was the language commonly used by the people, few Latin forms of surnames have survived, and those that have are sometimes ones translated by the bearers into Latin in a comparatively late period.

The surnames that have come down to us are the English words commonly used by the people in the ordinary affairs of life. Although we have many manorial court rolls of the twelfth and thirteenth centuries which seem to give a surname, such surnames were not used by the peasants themselves until the fourteenth or even a later century.

The Statute of Additions, passed in the first year of Henry V (1413), provided that not only the name of the individual but his calling and the place of his abode should be inserted in every writ or indictment. This proved to be a potent force for the adoption of surnames and also stimulated occupational and place surnames. Names were also perpetuated and standardized by the parish registers which were established in 1538, by Cromwell in England. Civil registers have been kept in England and Wales by statutory enactment since the year 1837.

The reader will observe in the last few pages that the word used for the surname does not have the initial letter capitalized. Certainly the clerk when writing the word did not give it an initial capital, but he had no reason either to capitalize or not to capitalize. The point, which cannot be too strongly emphasized, is that the clerk when he wrote these descriptive phrases after the villein's name was not consciously giving a surname. He was merely adding a descriptive word so that there would be no question of mistaken identity.

Now that we have traced, to some extent, the origin of the early descriptions used to identify men, the next step in our examination of surnames is to consider how and when they became hereditary or family names, that is, where used as surnames by all the legitimate sons and unmarried daughters. We use the word *hereditary* here really in the sense of birthright, that is, the right to the name comes at birth of the person, not at death of the ancestor, and the right to use the name is not a sole right but a joint right with that of brothers and sisters.

It is impossible to say just when surnames became hereditary family names, but in England, particularly during the thirteenth and four-

teenth centuries, the bynames of the people gradually crystallized into hereditary family names. The process was a very slow and irregular one. It came first among the most consequential families, those that were proud of their achievements and whose descendants wished to parade their paternity, and the hereditary quality, slowly over five or six centuries, filtered down through the most humble classes. Surnames are not of a hereditary nature until they have ceased to describe the bearer. When William *Robertson's* father was not named Robert, and John *Cook's* occupation was other than that of a cook, and Thomas *Hall* did not live in or near the manor house, and Richard *Reid* did not have red hair, then these surnames could be said to have become hereditary.

This is amply shown by the plurality of descriptions found among families. For instance, Ewen describes, from the *Visitation of Cheshire* (1580), William Belward of Malpasse, who had two sons, David de Malpasse and Richard; David had three sons known as de Malpasse, Gogh, and de Golborne; Richard's five sons were described as de Cotgrave, de Overton, Litell, de Hampton and de Coddington; Gogh had a son called Egerton and a grandson, Wigland; Golborne's second son acquired de Goodman as a name; Litell had a son, Kenen le Clark, and a son of Hampton was called Houa Bras. No dates are given, but the family probably flourished in the thirteenth century. The common use by the scribes of such words as *filius, de* and *le* before the descriptions is an indication that the surnames used are descriptive of the person and are not hereditary family appellatives. As the names became somewhat hereditary, these auxiliary words dropped away in most cases.

While historians have complained of the paucity of materials on the life of the peasantry during the medieval period in England and elsewhere, it is strange that little or no effort has been made to attack the problem from the surname angle. Instead, the historians have relied almost entirely upon manorial court rolls and a few contemporary poems, the most important of which is the *Vision and Creed of Piers Plowman*.

There is considerable relation between the numbers of men following certain occupations and numbers of officials and the proportion of persons living now who bear those words as surnames today. But anyone attempting to elicit medieval facts from present-day surnames must be fully alive to the many pitfalls. For instance, the more prestige an official or occupation has, the more likely a man will see to it that he continues to use it as a surname. Conversely, the very commonness of surnames of office or occupation in our present day is evidence of their prestige or position in early times.

The position of lord's steward was a powerful and enviable one, and thus the *Stewards, Stewarts* and *Stuarts* today are numerous. If there had been a steward in every village in England, the name would today rival or surpass Smith. Many bailiffs were proud to continue the name *Bailey*. Sergeant was an honorable position, and we find *Sargent* today. We also find *Freeman* and *Franklin,* which must have arisen when most of the peasants were serfs.

On the other hand, positions which people did not fancy were unlikely to produce many surnames lasting throughout the years. Cotter and villein designated a servile class, and people resented being so called. There are manorial court records of persons being fined for libel in referring to villeins as such, the truth being no defense. Consequently, although cotters and villeins were numerous, few now bear these words as surnames. Similarly as reeve indicated villein status, this office did not surname so many people as one would expect. Names like *Sargent, Stewart* or *Steward* and *Franklin,* representing highly respectable men, are today slightly more popular than the numbers of these men in medieval times would otherwise warrant.

In the last century in England the most numerous occupational or official names are the *Smiths, Taylors, Wrights, Walkers, Turners, Clarks* (early pronunciation of clerk), *Coopers, Wards, Bakers, Cooks, Parkers* and *Carters.* In general, these became the most popular of occupational surnames because there was most likely to be one, and only one, in each village or small town. Each manor probably would produce at least one *Smith, Wright, Clark, Cooper* and *Parker.* The absence of *Miller* from the above list is surprising when we know that most manors must have had at least one miller. The popularity of *Miller* in America is due to the German influence of *Mueller.* The reason for its weakness in England is probably due to the hatred toward millers, engendered by their tendency to cheat the villeins who were compelled to have their grain ground at the lord's mill. A medieval riddle illustrates the miller's reputation when it asks, "What is the boldest thing in the world?" and gives the answer, "A miller's shirt, for it clasps a thief by the throat daily." Official names like *Bailey* and *Stewart*, while not so popular as the ones above, still are common and their bearers are known to everyone.

Popular names derived from locality are *Wood, Hall, Green, Hill, Moore, Shaw* and *Lee.* Probably few manors at one time or another

did not describe their inhabitants with these words to designate their residence near such topographical elements. Many of these originally had *atte* (at the) before them, but as the words became surnames, the prepositions fell away, particularly by the latter part of the fourteenth century. Few of such names originated in the towns. *Brown* and *White* are the two common nicknames designating the dark-skinned persons and the light ones.

We know the most common men's given names during the medieval or surname period because they have produced the most surnames. On this point the extreme Welsh influence must be taken into account. These surnames are *Jones* (Welsh pronunciation of John), *Williams, Davies, Thomas, Evans, Roberts, Johnson, Robinson, Wilson, Hughes, Lewis, Edwards, Thompson, Jackson, Harris, Harrison, David, Martin, Morris, James, Morgan, Allen, Price, Phillips, Watson, Bennett* and *Griffiths*. Note that those ending in *-son* were least affected by the Welsh influence. Thus we can confidently say that the popular Christian names of medieval England, as actually used by the people in their everyday life, are *John, Robin, Will, Tom, Jack, Harry* and *Wat* (nickname for *Walter*). Of these, all but *John* are pet forms.

The early inhabitants of the towns were likely to feel the need of surnames long before the villager ever recognized his lack of an identifying designation. There would be, of course, more strangers in a town, and the other townspeople were likely to identify them by the town or manor from whence they came. A large city would not surname people in proportion to its population because several were likely to come from the same large city so that other means of identifying them had to be found. One coming from a small place would not be troubled by competitors. Thus *London* is an uncommon surname, while *Middleton* is more often found, coming as it did from thirty-three small localities so named. *Weston* is the name of eighty-three tuns.

The many occupational names which are not among the most popular were more likely to come from the boroughs where population was more dense. Names like *Taylor* and *Weaver* came from the towns because in the villages each villein or his wife made their own clothes and produced their own cloth. Conversely, names like *Husband*, a tiller of the ground, and *Farmer*, are names originating in the town and not in the village. Most of the occupational names can be definitely classed as referring to either village or town occupations.

By the end of the fourteenth century, when most of the work service had been commuted to a rent payable in money, the lord had a large body of paid servants. The king and more important nobles had great castles where they naturally felt the need to employ a great number of menials to do the work. Also the large ecclesiastical houses necessarily had to have many servants and minor officials. All of these occupations gave surnames to those who followed them.

Many nicknames expressing personal characteristics originated in the cities. Some of this class of names arose when it was necessary to distinguish between two smiths or two fishermen living or working near each other, and temporary occupational descriptions were dropped in favor of nicknames. Thus one smith might be called *Young* because of his age and a fisher labeled *Brown* from his complexion or hair. In many cases nicknames were used when the surname did not sufficiently identify the man, even as they are used today, but in early times the nickname then came to replace the surname.

That there were so many names reminiscent of religion and the Church is not to be wondered at when we note the important part played in the life of the Middle Ages by clergymen and the Church. Originally parishes and parish churches were coeval with the manor, although in later times the boundaries of one or the other changed. In the thirteenth century there were about, 9,500 parishes in England, each serving an average of about 300 persons.

There were about 60,000 clergymen, or one for every fifty of the population. Today, there is only one clergyman to each thousand of the population. Those in the thirteenth century consisted of the secular clergy and the monks, canons and friars.

The secular clergy were the rectors and vicars, chaplains in charge of outlying chapels, and parish priests in the diocese governed by the bishops and archbishops. In addition, in the parishes there were archdeacons, deacons and subdeacons. In each parish the humblest, but by no means the least important, member of the staff, was the clerk, who, although his regular stipend might be very small, was quite secure in his position.

As the Church played such an important part in the life of medieval England, it is not surprising to find that it also influenced our surnames. Naturally the parish clerk, or priest, or deacon, or rector, or vicar, would be so known in the community. But some will object that since the clergy were celibates they could not pass their names on.

However, in England, clerical marriages before the Norman Conquest were quite common. Mr. John R. H. Moorman, in his *Church*

Life in England in the Thirteenth Century, points out that attempts to abolish clerical marriages were only partially successful throughout the twelfth century, especially in the North of England where old habits died slowly. Several bishops of Durham, and at least one archbishop of York, had legitimate families. Throughout the thirteenth century, and even later, some of the lesser clergy married; others had illegitimate children, some of whom took the name of their father's office as their surname.

Thus the surnames *Bishop, Priest, Rector, Vicar, Chaplain, Deacon* and, from the monasteries and friaries, *Monk, Friar, Canon, Prior* and *Abbot* have become permanent surnames. But if marriages were not uncommon among the lesser clergy and quite rare among bishops, abbots and priors, why are the surnames, *Bishop* and *Abbot,* so much more common than their subordinates? The reason is that the bishop and abbot, because of their administrative work and travels in the diocese and throughout the country, had quite an entourage of servants. A bishop's entourage might be composed of forty men or more. These might consist of squires or armigers, valets, clerk of the chapel, carters, a porter, a messenger, a huntsman, a butler and a larderer, besides pages and several general servants. Some of them would become known as "the bishop's man" and, in time, the word *man* dropped away and only *Bishop* remained as the surname. This was also true, in a lesser degree, of the Priors.

Thus, surnames reflect the life of the Middle Ages, the work of the people in the medieval manors and towns, and the work of the Church, a most potent factor in the life of the individual. And in the names of the men of today are mirrored all the struggles, ambitions and aspirations of the villagers of the Middle Ages, all of the activities and work of the townsmen as well as the daily life of the noble and ecclesiastical prince.

CHAPTER III

The Classes of Surnames

In foord, in ham, in ley, and tun,
The moste of English surnames run.
—VERSTEGAN: *Restitution,* 1605

ATTENTIVE readers of the last chapter will have noted that, in connection with the question of origin, all the surnames mentioned fall into one of the following four classes:

1. Local
2. Occupational
3. Patronymical
4. Descriptive (Nickname)

These four classes originally identified men by answering one of the following questions:

1. *Where does he live or where is he from?*
2. *What does he do?*
3. *Who is his father?*
4. *What is his most prominent peculiarity?*

Every man might have all four types of surnames in early times. Thus he might be John, the son of William, a miller, living near the west field, of dark complexion, thus being known as John *Williamson,* John *Miller,* John *Westfield* and John *Brown.* At different times in his life he might be known by each of these names.

One might have two or more surnames and be as well known by one as another. In such cases he might be listed as John Westfield *alias* Brown. This style may remind us of the way men wanted by the law are described in the posters put up in our local post offices.

Ewen divides these four classes of surnames into twenty-eight sub-classes, but such minute classification is not necessary to obtain a comprehensive view of the subject. In general, surnames in all countries originate in one of the above four ways if they are not consciously adopted. It is possible, in some cases, for the same name to originate in more than one of these classes. Ewen asserts that most surnames may be derived from more than one source.

Let us examine the homonymic name *Bell*. Perhaps its most usual derivation is local, from residence near "THE BELL," an inn sign; also it is local from Flemish, *Belle*. Next, many Bells originate from *the bel*, or handsome one, and is a nickname. As a patronymic it refers to the "son of Bell," a hypocoristic form of Isabel. A few Bells represent a shortened form of *Bellringer* or *Bellmaker* and are thus occupative in origin.

Without tracing a name to its origin, it is thus difficult, if not impossible, to give the derivation of any particular surname. Numerous other names have two or more explanations, as *Hull*, a place name from the English town, local variants of Hill and Hall, and, in Lancashire, a font-name. *Smith* may not always be the worker in metals; he may be "the smooth" as in *Smithfield* in London, formerly "the smooth field." Some names while pronounced alike may proclaim their diverse origin by their spelling. Thus *Hughes* and *Hewes* sound alike, and some conceive these forms merely to be different or phonetic ways of spelling the same name, which may be true in some instances. *Hughes*, of course, refers to "the son of Hugh"; *Hewes* is a genitive form of the Old English *hew*, a servant.

Harrison, besides being the "son of Harry," is from *hérisson*, "hedge-hog." *Wills*, besides indicating descent from Will, is a variant of Wells. *Knight* may not always be from the chivalrous fighter; it sometimes is from Old English *cniht*, a servant.

Common names thus swallow up unusual names and no one is the wiser. Names, the origin of which are not easily understood, are most commonly perverted.

Before spelling became stabilized as we know it today, the alteration and mutation in names was to be expected. When a word is changed ever so slightly, it becomes more like another word. It may then be changed more until it actually becomes that word in form.

It is not always possible to classify correctly any given surname. For instance, one who mended his own boots might be nicknamed "the shoemaker"; another who spoke like a priest might be called accordingly; and their names would forever after be considered purely occupational. Another name might be imagined to be obviously patronymical in its beginning yet have a local origin for the particular family bearing it.

The story is told of the man revisiting the town of his boyhood and asking, "Who lives at the Williams' farm now?"

"Joseph Williams and his family."

"But I thought that the Williamses sold out and went away?"

"Oh, so they did, but these are Polish people who bought the farm. They had some sort of outlandish name, but of course we didn't use it."

One reason for the irritating difficulty in classifying surnames was that a particular name might be derived from an unusual occupation, a presently unknown town, an unusually odd nickname, or a very rare Christian name, or a corrupt spelling of any of them. Or, again, these difficult names might come through any other language, yet look like Old English words or names.

Some occupations are little known to us at the present time. Take the surname *Smoker*. It is not "the man who smokes." Smoking was not introduced into Europe until the sixteenth century when Sir Walter Raleigh popularized it. It is from the Old English *smoc*, a woman's undergarment, and designates "one who makes or sells smocks." Again *Poker* does not refer to poking but is from Middle English *poke*, a bag. Everyone remembers the phrase, "a pig in a poke." Mr. Poker was thus "the maker of bags."

Many English surnames are from French words because surnames arose in the Middle Ages when French was the language used by all educated people in England. In addition the scribes wrote in Latin, and some Latin forms persisted as surnames. Also they sometimes translated the English forms into French.

LOCAL

Local names form the largest class, although more individuals bear occupational names. About half of all English surnames are of this class. Scarcely a manor, town or city in England, or place in France and the low countries, has failed to provide English surnames. Camden says, "Neither is there any village in Normandy that gave not denomination to some family in England." Comparatively few surnames of this class originated in Wales or Ireland, however.

The nobles and important men, returning from the Crusades, early adopted the name of their estates as surnames, after the French manner. As these estates descended from father to son, the names of the estates quickly became true hereditary family names. But a local surname indicates that one's ancestors were lords of that place in an extremely small percentage of instances. In most cases it means that the ancestors were vassals of the lord of that place.

In general, the eldest sons of families took their surnames from the principal estates. The second and sometimes the third son adopted surnames from the lesser estates belonging to the family. The landless sons were likely to receive and transmit to their progeny descriptive and patronymical surnames. In the towns where trade was carried on the men received designations derived from their trades.

Local names are divided into two very important classes: (1) from place-names, i.e., the name of a village, city, county or country; and (2) from topographical features such as *gate, hill, shore, tree* or *barn*. The latter are given to natives while place-names are applied to newcomers. With reference to the first class, a man might be lord of a particular place or the name might be associated with him in some particular way. English local surnames may designate either English or Norman towns. The prepositions used are not always conclusive of nationality, as the Latin *de*, for example, is found in both England and France.

When a man went to a town or city from a small village or hamlet, or from another town, it was only natural that his new associates would dub him with a surname taken from his late place of residence, as *Sutton, York* and *Middleton*. Those who would identify bynames, or additional names, of this type, are referred to Ekwall's *Dictionary of English Place-Names* and the excellent volumes issued by the *English Place-Name Society*. When a peasant came from a different county, the name of the county might be applied to him, as *Dorset, Kent, Norfolk* and *Surrey*. This propensity was especially strong when the stranger came from another country. Surnames like *Scott, Walsh, Fleming* and *French* are found everywhere. They designate the men from Scotland, Wales, Flanders and France. Ewen, with some reason, prefers to classify these latter names as "characteristic," the term he uses in place of "nickname."

Many difficulties arise in identifying local surnames from place-names because the surnames, arising as they did at some distance from the place-name, often tended to change in orthographic form along divergent lines. The surname might arise in London, for instance, and change in spelling according to English principles, while the place-name might be in Normandy and its spelling be influenced, since medieval times, by French principles of orthography. With early local names the question comes up whether the first bearer actually wore it as a surname or whether the name was only an address affixed by the scribe.

Surnames from topographical features, sometimes called toponymical surnames, are very numerous and very common. In this classification are such names as *Wood* or *Woods, Green, Moore, Shaw, Lee* and *House*. Unlike place-names used as surnames, these names arise from present residence (or, in a few instances, place of work) near such a topographical feature.

The man in each village who lived closest to the woods, mill or green would be likely to be so alluded to and surnamed. If he lived on, or near, a hill or moor, he would be so identified. If he lived or worked in or near a particular kind of building, he would be so known as *Castle, Church, Hall, House, Mill, Millhouse,* or *Woodhouse*. Names of trees are often seen, as *Ash* and *Nash* (atten Ash), *Birch, Holly, Maple, Oaks* and *Noakes* (atten Oaks) and *Yew*; there is also the plain name of *Tree* or *Trees*. In the same way, names of rivers, as well as the plain word itself, have surnamed many men.

There are various suffixes which clearly indicate the local type of surname, such as *-bank, -combe, -don* (town), *-edge, -field, -ford, -house* or *-hus, -hurst* (a wood), *-ing* (meadow), *-land* (cultivated land or field), *-law* (hill), *-ly* or *-lee* (meadow), *-ness* (headland), *-ridge* or *-rig, -thorp* (village), *-thwaite* (a clearing), *-tree, -well* (well, spring or stream), *-wood* and *-worth*. All these are also found alone as surnames. In some few cases, these and similar local words may be a description of one's land holdings rather than a word signifying place of residence or work.

Most of these local names originally had a preposition, such as the French *de,* or the English *at, a, of, in* and *under,* which were gradually dropped, principally during the fourteenth century. When the byname was associated no longer with the original place, there was a tendency to drop the preposition. Some were left out as a result of the carelessness of the recording clerk. In some cases the preposition blended with the following word, and we still have with us *à Becket, Atterbury, Atwater, Bythesea, Delafield* and *Underwood*.

In early times the preposition, article and noun sometimes coalesced to form a long, proletarian name, such as *Douninthethoune* (down in the town), *Abovethenbroc* (above the brook), *Atthedichende* (at the ditch end) and *Overthewatere* (over the water). Mr. *Bisouthethe-*

cherche lived "south of the church." Mr. *Binethetheweye* could be found "beneath the way," while "under the hill" could be located Mr. *Hunderpehulle*. All of these are real names, but naturally they were radically shortened before our day, as is shown by a comparison of our modern surnames with the many long, awkward, descriptive names found in early times.

The question may arise in some minds as to why there is a final -*s* on many topographical surnames like *Banks, Dykes, Holmes, Parks, Styles, Woods, Yates* and many others. In a very few cases it is a patronymical ending referring to the son of the man living near the place named. But generally the -*s* is merely a meaningless excrescence, the addition of a terminal sibilant, not uncommonly developed among uncultured peoples.

There are two types of toponymical surnames which are curious because, at first glance, they appear to be occupational names. First, there are some that terminate in -*er*, such as *Broker, Haller* and *Streeter*, that is, one who lives at or near a brook, hall or street. There is the same idea when we speak of the Londoner and the New Yorker. Secondly, some surnames end in -*man*, such as *Brokman, Crossman* and *Wellman,* denoting "the inhabitant who lives near the brook," "the dweller near the cross" or "the man who lives near the well."

In the early surname period few people, other than the clergy, could read. Therefore houses were not numbered as they are today. Places of business and many houses (usually the place of business and residence was the same), had pictorial signs outside to identify them to the illiterate passers-by. Taverns were required by law to have a sign-board. Many inns and taverns had representations of animals and birds as a hanging signboard outside. As one who worked in and owned a place of business, set off by a distinctive sign, would be referred to as John *atte* (at the) *Boar's Head* or Wat *Oliphant* (Elephant), it cannot be doubted that many of our family names came from shop and tavern signs. This is a prolific source of many of our animal and bird names such as *Bear, Hart, Roebuck, Wolf, Cock, Crow, Eagle* and *Peacock*, although each of these has other origins. Besides animals and birds, many other things or objects were used as signboards, such as *Ball, Cross, Crown, Devil, Prince, Millstone, Green Man, Hand* and *Whitehorse*. Löfvenberg, while agreeing that many names are derived from signboards, puts the finger of caution on the matter, and points out that most of these local surnames have other interpretations.

The origin of many surnames which designate common objects

(except those appellations which arose in other ways and were then changed in spelling to equalize to common objects) may be looked for in some odd, or little known, shop sign. While signboards were so common in the Middle Ages, comparatively few have come down to us at the present time. However, distinctive signboards not containing words are sometimes seen in American cities, and more often in England and on the Continent. Conclusive evidence of names derived from shop signs is rather scarce. Three balls to designate a pawn shop and a striped pole to indicate a barber shop comprise our principal survivals of the old shop signs. Formerly a bush designated a place where wine was sold, from whence we get the proverb, "Good wine needs no bush." The reader who wishes to know more of the intricate science of old signs could not do better than consult Larwood and Hotten's, *History of Signboards*.

OCCUPATIONAL

Some onomatologists have divided occupational surnames into two main classes, occupational and official, but it is often hard to distinguish between occupation and office. Some are clearly on the official side as *Reeve, Bailiff, Constable, Parker, Steward, Sumner* (the summoner), and *Sheriff*; on the occupational side we have surnames such as *Chapman* (merchant or trader), *Fuller, Walker* and *Tooker* (those who full cloth), and *Potter*; but on the borderline we have names like *Baker, Miller, Smith* (in some cases), where the original bearers were often petty officials of the lord, king or churchman.

That it is natural to use a man's occupation to help identify him is illustrated by our disposition to refer to people today by their occupations. We speak of the postman, the milkman, the doctor or the druggist. In earlier times men usually learned their fathers' trades, and important trade secrets were retained in a family for many generations, being passed down from father to son. This feature of father and son following the same trade gave impetus to the word, first applied merely as one of description, developing into a true hereditary family name.

Occupational surnames sometimes supplant local bynames. When a craftsman came from a city and settled in a small village, he might first be known by the name of the city and then acquire a trade name. This is another reason why *London* is such a rare surname.

Occupational surnames often have the agential suffix *-er* or *-ier*, as *Carver, Cowper* (i.e. Cooper), *Chaucer* (breeches maker), *Lawyer* and

Sawyer, or the feminine *-ster* as in *Webster*, *Baxter* (Bake-ster) and *Brewster*. In the Middle Ages women often performed the same kind of work as men. While undoubtedly femi..ine in origin, the suffix *-ster* gradually became only an emphatic form of the masculine *-er*, and was used indifferently for men and women. To sit and spin, however, was an occupation felt to be essentially feminine, and a *spinster* thus continued to designate a woman distinct and apart from a man.

An important group of occupational names are those consisting of Christian names plus the termination of *-man*, as *Harriman* and *Watman*. Others have this ending with names of occupations as *Smythman* and *Kingsman*. The early meaning of Anglo-Saxon *mann* was "a servant," and these names refer to the servant of Harry or Wat, or of the smith or king. A woman's name might arise by reason of service in a queen's or widow's household. Sometimes *-man* is corrupted into *-nam*, as *Putnam*.

Occupational words compounded with such second elements as *-herd*, *-maker*, *-man*, *-smith*, *-ward*, and *-wright* are quite common, as in *Shepherd*, *Oxherd*; *Shoemaker*, *Bowmaker*; *Sherman* (one who shears woolen cloth), *Ironman*; *Arrowsmith*, *Goldsmith*; *Milward*, *Woodward*; and *Cartwright*, *Wainwright*. Of course each of these suffixes and many more have numerous variant spellings and forms. The author has made a collection, over a period of many years, of compound names with *smith*, as the first or last element, and has found more than 470 actual surnames ranging alphabetically from *Ainsmith* to *Zugsmith*, not all of them being occupational.

There are English surnames referring to every important occupation. The number of persons bearing a particular surname is some index of the importance of that occupation in the late Middle Ages. If there are few men named from the furniture trade, for instance, you can be sure that the houses of the people were sparsely furnished.

The many surnames denoting specialized trades in medieval times brings our attention to the surprising fact that occupations were more specialized in those times than they were afterward, although when our complex, modern factories arose, the trades again became greatly specialized. One reason for the early specialization was the desire of workmen to improve their output and produce really superior work. They not only fabricated the article but they sold it. In some instances a man might have had an incidental occupation along with his ordinary trade, but be known by the side work, perhaps, because it would better distinguish him from his fellow craftsmen.

A fascinating feature of official surnames comes from mock office. The medieval drama, with its miracle plays lasting sometimes for days, was one of the most important recreational and religious features of the town or village, looked for with anticipation every year. Principal players acquired the names of the characters they portrayed. This is one explanation of such names as *King, Queen, Angel* and *Devil. King* and *Queen* of the May were elected for a year. These names might well be classed as nicknames. Other surnames derive from military rank, as *Knight* and *Squire*.

PATRONYMICAL

Next to local names in number are the patronymical names. These are surnames indicating that the person is the son of his father. While the number of popular font-names in early times was limited, the variations in them were almost unlimited and they had numerous pet, or nursery, forms. Also, the same Christian name had variations in form in different countries, and in different parts of the same country.

The oldest patronymics are those with the Old English *-ing* suffixed to the name of the father, in which cases the father's name is usually Anglo-Saxon or Old English.

As a partial explanation of how this class of names arose, Verstegan, in 1605, wrote,

It hath also somtymes hapned, that diuers youthes coming out of the countrie to serve in the citie of London, have not bin able to tell their own surnames, but beeing demaunded how they had heard their fathers called, could only tell that they had heard them called *Iohn*, or *Thomas*, or *William*, or the lyke, as their proper names might bee, or otherwise after our vulgar use of clipping, *Iac, Tom*, or *Wil*, whereupon they came easely to bee surnamed, *Iohnson* or *Iackson*, or otherwise according as they said their fathers were called.

Ewen calls this class of names genealogical surnames, the better to include the rather unimportant classes of metronymics, or mother names, and surnames from personal names of other relatives. Other relationships, as *Cousins, Brothers*, and *Eames* (from Middle English *eme*, uncle), are not rare cognomens. Names like *Watmough* and *Elysmagh* designate Wat's brother-in-law or Ellis' brother-in-law respectively. A long surname is *Thepundersstepdoghtre* (the punder's step daughter, the punder being the keeper of the village pound).

Professor Ekwall in his *Variation in Surnames in Medieval London* calls attention to the fact that many London apprentices in the thirteenth and fourteenth centuries dropped their fathers' surname and became known by their masters' surname. This change to the master's surname is not particularly surprising if we remember that when the boy became an apprentice, he left his father's home and lived with the master. Naturally, then, as he grew in importance in the master's home, he became known by the master's surname rather than his own. When he finally left the master, after a long apprenticeship, to pursue his trade on his own account, acquaintances knew him by the name of his former master rather than that of his father with whom he had not been identified for seven or more years. If, as a journeyman, he continued to labor for the same master, the long period during which he was affiliated with the master's household would be very likely to influence the surname used by others.

The surname of a girl is the same as that of her brother even though it ends in -*son*, as *Wilson* or *Johnson*. That this incongruity proved a difficulty to our forefathers is evident from the entries in the registers of the thirteenth and fourteenth centuries, where many names like *Margaret Wilkesdogthter* and *Nan Tomsdaughter* are found. As would be expected, these names did not survive because the girls lost their surnames upon marriage. These names were probably entered in the parish registers by purists who did not like -*son* for a girl. Many are found localized in certain hundreds in Lancashire. In like manner, *Avice Mattwife*, i.e., Avice, the wife of Matt, is found at the same period.

The patronymical names of all countries are comparatively easy to recognize because they usually have the patronymical word meaning "son" as part of the name. A rather comprehensive list of these patronymical forms in the various countries is given in the chapter on "Names in Other Countries" (page 124).

With the patronymical surnames we may, for reasons of simplicity, include the few metronymics found. These are the surnames from the personal name of the female parent, as *Beatson* (son of Beatrice) and *Sisterson* (son of Cecelia). The old theory that a feminine surname indicated illegitimacy is not true. Where the wife was from the dominant family, her name was sometimes taken instead of the father's name. This would be particularly true where the surviving parent was the widow. Some come into existence by virtue of service in the household of a queen or other great lady. Part of the names which appear to be feminine are actually men's names, either because the name was originally masculine, or because it was one which, in early times, was common to both sexes.

The patronymical word will sometimes be found added to the father's occupation rather than to his Christian name, as *Cookson*, *Clerkson*, *Smithson*, *Taylorson* and *Wrightson*. Other patronymical words will also be added to the occupation, as the Gaelic *MacGowan* (son of the smith).

The suffix *-son* does not always signify a patronymical name. In some instances it is a foreign word with another signification. In many cases it is a corruption of *-ston*. Thus *Johnston* (or John's tun) slides into *Johnson*.

Many patronymical surnames consist only of the Christian name as *John*, *Edward*, *Henry* and *Thomas*. Generally in these cases the patronymical prefix or suffix has been dropped.

DESCRIPTIVE (NICKNAME)

Nicknames as family names, while the smallest class, is probably the most interesting. Surnames of this group represent nicknames given practically spontaneously to the original bearer because of his appearance, character, physical attribute, habit, condition, kinship or other peculiarity. Persons inheriting this type of name actually know the most prominent characteristic of a remote male ancestor living at the time surnames became fixed as hereditary family appellations.

Ewen claims that very few nicknames have survived as family names, and most of those that appear to have done so are anything but what they seem to be. Many surnames, which appear to be of the nickname class, are really imitative spellings of other classes of family names. Surnames which seem to be of the nickname variety must be regarded with great caution. This is because of the propensity to respell foreign names to make them as nearly like English words as possible.

In considering the meaning of many surnames which, to all appearances, consist of ordinary English adjectives, one should check the meaning of the word in Chaucer and his contemporaries; and then it is often found that the meaning was in early times much different from what it is today. *Silly* or *Silliman* means "the innocent one"; *Sadd* was originally "sedate or steadfast." *Stout*, now used euphemistically for fat, is cognate with German *stolz* (proud), and possibly with Latin *stultus* (foolish). *Sly* and the variant *Sleigh* once meant "skilled." Middle English *Lyte*, now often spelled *Light*, meant "little." From *crum,* meaning "crooked," we have the names *Crum* and *Crump.* *Grace,* as a surname, is usually from the French *le gras,* "the fat."

The most popular nicknames are the color names, *Brown* and *White,* both of which refer to the color of skin or hair. (*Green* generally refers to the village green.) *Reid, Reed, Rede* and *Rod,* early spellings of *red,* usually refer to the color of the hair. This latter name we can understand quite easily as everyone has friends or acquaintances who are known as "Red," because of the ruddy color of their hair. Other color names, in order of frequency, are *Gray, Black, Pink, Blue, Lavender, Orange, Red* and *Purple.* Also, from appearance, there are *Fairfax* (fair hair), *Campbell* (wry-mouthed); *Short* and *Long* are well known.

From character come the modern surnames of *Noble* and *Savage.* From physical attributes we get names like *Armstrong* and *Cruikshank* (crooked leg). A man with some prominent habit might have it attached to him, as *Humble* or *Meek.* Even a single act could give rise to an epithet. Else how could Hugh *Hoppeoverhumbr* have become so known unless it was by his jumping over the Humber River in the early part of the thirteenth century? Condition or quality gives rise to names like *Elder* and *Newman.*

A particularly large group of names, many of which can be classed in the nickname group, are those compound names consisting of a verb and a noun, as *Drinkwater, Lovejoy* and *Makepeace.* Compare the nickname of *Sawbones* for a surgeon. There was John *Neverathom* (never at home) applied to some medieval gadabout. Some of this type of names are occupative rather than of the nickname or descriptive class.

A few surnames have, no doubt, been acquired by knights in the Crusades performing some meritorious act and receiving a surname from the king as a mark of recognition. The desire of families to relate a story explaining their surname, even though the story is an obvious legend, is the basis of most of these family names.

Without batting an eyelash, the Guthries will tell you of the Scottish king, David II, who, his boat being overtaken by a storm, landed, after great tribulation, weary and hungry. Approaching one who was gutting fish, the king requested that one be prepared for him. The hospitable answer was, "I'll gut three."

Dropping into rhyme, the grateful monarch quoth, "Then gut three, thy name shall be," and straightway granted suitable lands. While truth may be stranger than fiction, it is not that outlandish, as Guthrie is from the barony of that name in Angus, Scotland.

The Lockharts affirm that their progenitor was a follower of James, Lord Douglas, and accompanied him to the Holy Land. There the master died, his last request being that his heart be returned to Scotland. It was not unusual for the hearts of kings and nobles, dying abroad, to be conveyed home. The heart might be returned in a locked casket. The Lockhart family bears in its arms a heart clasped by a padlock.

An unusual variety of nicknames are those applied because of the habit of swearing acquired by the bearers. Swearing in early English times was not at all uncommon. While the French were not averse to the practice, still they professed to be shocked by the Englishman's facility for cursing. Their nickname for the English was *Jean Goddano*, or, translated, *John God Damn*. Berry and Van Den Bark, in their *American Thesaurus of Slang*, still list *Goddam* as a synonym for an Englishman. Surnames commemorating this pernicious habit are *Godbode* (God's body) and *Godsowle* (God's soul). Our modern *Pardews* and *Pardoes* are, in some cases, forms of the old *par Dieu* of the Middle Ages, in the same way as *Bigod* or *Bygot* is sometimes an English oath.

The great majority of the surnames in most countries can be classed in one of the four main classes mentioned in the beginning of this chapter, but the proportion in each class varies widely among different nationalities. Nearly all Welsh family names are patronymics. Many Russian and Polish surnames, as well as Scotch and Irish surnames, also have reference to one's father.

Most of the examples given are common words and are self-explanatory. To find the class of other lesser known names, it is usually only necessary to learn the meaning of the word in the language from which it came. This puts the problem rather simply, but the difficulty arises in being sure of the translation or present meaning of a word which may be long obsolete. The difficulty is multiplied when the name has, during the years, undergone arbitrary change. Many foreign names have received changes in spelling to make them the same as common English words and thus less strange to English ears. To suppose that they now have the derivation we ascribe to these common English words is to fall into the trap that the study of onomatology so well presents.

These four groups classify the family names that were *applied* to people and became hereditary. Chosen names are usually either patronymics or place-names. When one consciously adopts a name, it may be one of the usual family cognomens, but it will usually have no meaning in itself. It may be, in a few cases, a manufactured name and have no significance. Surnames applied to foundlings generally have reference to the place or circumstances under which the child is discovered.

Probably the largest class of persons who have deliberately adopted surnames are the European Jews. They have acquired surnames within the last one hundred and fifty years. Many of the names they selected will not fall within any of these classes as they were chosen for their pleasant sound or associations. Some Indians and Negroes in America have also selected surnames which do not slip easily into our classifications, although many appear to do so.

Ecclesiastics, theatrical people, criminals, authors, artists, refugees, aliens, servants, and manumitted slaves are among those who, for one reason or another, consciously selected a surname different from that to which they were born.

The importance of identifying a person by a reference, in some way to his father, is the basic reason for family names becoming hereditary. Other causes consist of the fact that when the father lives near an outstanding landmark, the children also live there and thus acquire the same name in the same way as their father. In estate names the son who inherited the estate would, of course, inherit the surname. As sons would naturally learn the trade of their father, they would continue with his surname, but it would then not be hereditary, but continue to be descriptive. Nicknames and patronymics were the last among surnames to become fixed. Surnames became fixed in the South of England a half century before they did in the North, probably because of the more direct influence of Europe. For three hundred years hereditary and nonhereditary surnames existed side by side in England.

Family names are subject to the same distortions and phonetic changes as words. Indeed, because of the truly intimate and personal character of one's surname, it is more subject to arbitrary and peremptory changes than ordinary words since each bearer in the past had no scruples in corrupting it. There has always been a tendency to alter surnames to significative words, particularly foreign names that seem to have no meaning. It is only in late years that universal education, and the full development of printing, have operated to freeze the spelling of family names. Most names, odd to the eye, can be explained as corruptions of quite ordinary forms, although many odd names may also have their face value.

In the old registers we find the same names spelled in many different ways. In an early record there is the sentence, "On April 23, 1470, Eliz. Blynkkynesoppye, of Blynkynsoppe, widow of Thomas Blynkyensope, of Blynkkensope, received a general pardon." Here are four variations in one sentence by the same hand. The poor scribe started well and the first five letters are uniform but he floundered after that. There are said to be 137 variants of *Mainwaring* and over 400 of *Cushion*, all to be found in family archives.

Many popular names have settled down to one principal form and that different from the word from which it was derived. The surname from the trade of tailor is spelled *Taylor*; that derived from the office of clerk is *Clark* and *Clarke*. Terminal consonants are often doubled in surnames.

Besides the spelling, the pronunciation of names has made for corruption. Very often the short form persists separately, especially in America, where we find *Posnett* and *Poslett* for Postlethwaite and *Beecham* for Beauchamp. *Snooks* is a contraction of Sevenoaks. The termination -*house* is often shortened to -*us*, and we find *Malthus*, *Loftus* and *Bacchus* for Malthouse, Lofthouse and Bakehouse. In the past, long surnames have shown a marked propensity to become shorter due to their clipped pronunciation in ordinary use.

Many terminations become altered. The diminutive ending -*kin* sometimes was corrupted into -*kiss*, -*kes* and -*ks*, hence the origin of *Perkes*, *Purkiss* (Peter); and *Hawkes*, *Hawks* (David). The ending -*in* often took a *g* or a *gs* to become -*ing* or *ings,* as *Tippings* and *Collings* (Theobald and Nicholas). The suffix -*head* frequently becomes -*et* or -*ett*, and -*thwaite* evolves into -*white*. To list all the changes of this type would be out of place in a work of this kind.

The termination -*man* is quite common in English surnames. It is also found as a corruption of *mond* or *mund* (from Old English *mund*, "protection"), of *munt* and *mont* (from Old French *mont*, "a hill"), of *min* or *myn*, of *nam, nham* and *ham,* i.e., "home" or "enclosure," and of several other name-elements.

From the more or less simple words and expressions heretofore mentioned in this chapter innumerable names are evolved in a host of ways. Additional letters or syllables are added at the beginning or end or inserted in the middle, or altered, all in accordance with rules of change well understood by philologists. Other changes are, of course, arbitrary and without ascertainable reason. Chance intermingling of languages plays a part. Many modifying words, such as diminutives or augmentatives, are instrumental in building names of families. In this book we can only hint at the various elements and forces that influence the evolution of surnames. Ignorance and error have also exerted considerable force in multiplying surnames.

Ever since surnames first became part of a man's full name they have been changed, corrupted and multiplied almost beyond number by bringing to bear upon them many diverse influences. The chief causes of the corruption of surnames are:

a. By the early use of the Latin and French languages in writing—the scribes indited almost everything in Latin—as *Faber* for Smith.
b. By slight individual variation in spelling due often to petty vanity.
c. By change to the singular or plural forms, as *Wood* for Woods and *Smiths* for Smith.
d. By change in national or local pronunciation.
e. By synonymous employment of letters, as *e* and *y*.
f. By ignorance of foreign languages.
g. By dropping or adding an initial letter, as when *Wood* becomes *Ood* and then *Hood*.
h. By abbreviation, in writing, as *Thom̄* for Thomas, and lingual abbreviations as *Spark* for Sparrowhawk.
i. By carelessness in writing.
j. By translation and transliteration from other languages.
k. By arbitrary change.
l. By synonymous change, i.e., change by adoption of a synonym for all or a part of the name.
m. By indiscriminate use of vowels and of some consonants, as when *e* is substituted for *a* or *i* and *h* for *v* and *c* for *k*.

Hyphenated names are employed in English, usually to keep alive the surname of the mother after marriage, particularly when she comes from the more important family. When Emanuel Julius, publisher of Little Blue Books at Girard, Kansas, married the writer and actress, Marcet Haldeman, he prefixed Haldeman to his surname to become known as E. Haldeman-Julius.

The laws of some states provide that in divorce the court may order that the wife shall thereafter resume her maiden name. One couple took advantage of this to cause a decree to provide that the child of the couple would thereafter bear the surname *Martens-Hughes*, the maiden surname of the mother and the surname of the father. Some look with disfavor upon a hyphenated name thinking that it manifests snobbery. H. L. Mencken observed that hyphenated names of divorcees in this country quickly succumbed to the national gift for ribaldry. Three and more hyphenated surnames are not unknown in England. An Admiral in the British navy supports the appellation, Reginald Aylmer Ranfurly *Plunkett-Ernle-Erle-Drax*. Ewen has found Mr. *Temple-Nugent-Brydges-Chandos-Grenville*.

CHAPTER IV

Your Name and You

What should be in that Cæsar?
Why should that name be sounded more than yours?
Write them together, yours is as fair a name;
Sound them, it doth become the mouth as well;
Weigh them, it is as heavy; conjure with 'em.
—SHAKESPEARE, *Julius Cæsar*, Act I, Sc. ii, 1599

OUR system of nomenclature is very simple. Each person has a family name which he inherits and a given, or Christian, name which is bestowed upon him at birth. In addition, most have a middle name which is of relatively little importance and is usually only another forename. With such a simple system of naming it would appear at first blush that there is little that is interesting or exciting about personal names. But after hundreds of millions have borne names in daily life, the complexities of the matter are enormous and make a fascinating story.

In early times, when life was simple, one name sufficed. Later two names were required for identification, particularly in the cities and congested districts. Now in our large cities, with our complicated lives, and particularly with the traveling we do, three names and an address are usually necessary for complete identification.

A man's name is his most prominent feature to others than his most intimate friends. It is also his most vulnerable point. An old Roman maxim runs, "*Sine nomine homo non est* (Without a name man is nothing)." A man's name is his signboard to the world. It is one of the most permanent of possessions; it remains when everything else is lost; it is owned by those who possess nothing else. A name is the only efficient means of describing a man to contemporaries and to

6̱

posterity. When one dies it is the only part that lives on in the world.

Language is all names. Nouns are the names of persons or things; adjectives and adverbs are the names of qualities; verbs are the names of actions. Thomas Carlyle said, "All poetry is but a giving of names." Ancient philosophers believed that the nature and character of things were condensed and represented in their names. Naming, in one form or another, has been asserted to be the earliest of all intellectual accomplishments.

In early times and among all peoples, personal names, in their original invention and imposition, had a definite and appropriate significance. It is true, in our present age, that some names have been invented by grouping letters to make an agreeable sound without any reference to meaning, but this practice is relatively rare.

The reader must understand that while a great deal is known about names in general, very little may be known about any particular name. The origin and derivation of many surnames can only be guessed at, and the meaning of a certain surname may be discovered only by the use of much theory and conjecture. Given names, being much older, are likewise explained only with much difficulty and mental reservation. A single name may have several distinctly independent origins.

Names which seem very odd to us are often, upon closer inspection, really very simple and ordinary names. For example, *Booze* does not refer to vile liquor but is the "bowe-hous" and designates the one who lived in the house by the bow or bend in the river. Sometimes this name comes from other languages and thus has a different meaning. *Handsomebody* is the handy or dexterous person, the word *handsome* having changed in meaning from "handy" or "skillful" to "beautiful." *Honeychild* refers neither to honey nor to child; the last five letters are from the Scandinavian *kelda* meaning "spring," while the first part is a corruption of *Huna*, the name of the man who lived by the spring. Only a few of these puzzles can be explained in a book of this size, but the reader is introduced to the problem and a few hints are given as to how to solve the mysterious origin of a particular name.

The disagreement over the name *Shakespeare*, which has been studied intensely by competent scholars, accentuates the difficulty in the study of surnames and places the finger of caution on the whole subject.

The ignorant derivation of names may reach truly absurd heights. For example, the derivation of *William* has been evolved from Will by the supposed answer of one so named, who, on being asked his name, replied, "Will I am." The name of *Mary* has been given at least seventy different interpretations in a frantic effort to get away from the Biblical signification of "bitterness."

When the average magazine writer sits down to dash off a pecuniary piece about names, he can't resist the temptation to entitle his opus, "What's in a Name?" or to commence with some reference to Shakespeare's popular quotation. It is astonishing how contemplation of the study of names causes one to remember the words of the bard of Stratford-on-Avon, and many think this settles the question. An anonymous writer of the middle of the last century came forth with:

A rose is supposed to be capable of exerting the same titillatory power to produce sensations of pleasure under any other cognomen; as Shakespeare has erroneously but beautifully observed.

Tiring of the intricacies of names, a few authors have suggested the substitution of numbers. At birth each one would receive a number. The number would be tremendously large if not intermixed with letters. Would little R7468X32 be cute with such a darling number? Would anyone like to be summoned to dinner by his social security number? Those who cannot remember their auto license would be in the position of not remembering their own names. Montana, the first state to do anything about the matter, has enacted a law providing that, commencing January 1, 1949, each baby, at birth, will receive a number which will not change during his lifetime, and which will be discarded only at death. In the course of time, probably most of the other states will follow suit.

Names are of much concern to the custodians of books. When librarians must make an alphabetical card catalogue of their books, they nearly go crazy trying to be consistent in keeping authors' names in proper order. The use of pseudonyms in this country they take in their stride and enter them under the real name of the author. Then up pops a Hindu or a Japanese writer, and the conscientious librarian tears her hair. In some parts of India, and in certain other countries, the patronymic is placed first, and what is one to do? Some Chinese do and some don't. Portuguese family names come after the more important given name and just which one of many is the surname, anyway?

A title is not part of the name in America. *Lord* and *Lady* are not used in the United States, although *Lady* was heard in the early days of the Republic. *Sir* and *Madam* are not heard so much as formerly. The universal titles of respect and courtesy in this country are *Mr.*,

Mrs. and *Miss*, the first two being abbreviations of *Master* and *Mistress*. The abbreviations are pronounced *Mister* and *Misses*. *Colonel* and *Major* are common American honorifics in the South and have little reference to military prowess. *Cap'n, Boss* and *Judge* are freely used as titles of respect by the lower classes.

Hon. for *honorable* is used for public men of the higher echelons. *Esq.* for *esquire*, following the name, is not often used in America except for professional men, and officials not entitled to *Hon.* For a woman of dignified position both *Hon.* and *Madam*(e) are used. *Dr.* for a medical practitioner is the universal custom. A dentist is addressed as *Doctor* in America but as *Mister* in England. Many who hold nonmedical doctoral degrees are addressed as *Doctor*. All sorts of quack schools grant a doctorate after a few months' attendance. The tendency in America, in addressing professors, at least among themselves, is to drop the title.

The question of when a person adds the abbreviation, *Jr.* to his name is puzzling to some. Correctly, one is a *junior* only when he has either a living father of the same name, or a living grandfather of the same name who has no living son of the same name. When a grandson bears *Jr.* his cousins, born later and given the same name, are *2nd*. There may be more than one *2nd* of the same generation. One is never a *Jr.* unless his father's or grandfather's, name is exactly the same. If the father is James Whitney Burch and the son is James William Burch, the son does not add the suffix, *Jr.*

When the father, or grandfather, dies, the *Jr.* is dropped. If John Smith has both a father and a grandfather of the same name, he is John Smith III; when the grandfather dies, the *III* becomes *Jr.* Commodore Allen George Quynn lists a son, Allen George VIII, in his sketch in *Who's Who in America*, although he refrains from alluding to himself as VII. If John Smith's father is William Smith and his grandfather is John Smith, but the grandfather has a living son, John Smith, the grandson is John Smith II, and not *Jr.* The English always use *2nd* or *3rd* in the belief that *II* or *III* is the prerogative of royalty. When one is named for an uncle he is *2nd* or *II,* and never *Jr. Junior* always denotes a descendant. The terms *Jr.* and *II* seldom mean the same thing and can be used interchangeably only when a man is the only one named after the grandfather.

When a father dies leaving a widow and the *Junior* son also has a wife, the widow adds *Senior* to her name and the son drops the *Jr.* Emily Post, however, says that if the widow is much younger than her late husband and is unwilling to add "Senior" to her name, the son may be obliged to keep the suffix, *Jr.* The wife of John Smith, Jr., is always Mrs. John Smith, Jr.

When a girl has the same name as her mother she does not use the term *Junior*, because that has a connotation of "my son." Usually the question does not arise because in social intercourse one is *Mrs.* and the other *Miss.* But if they are both professional workers, it may be necessary to distinguish between them. Then it is correct for the daughter to add *the Younger* or just *Younger* to her name. The abbreviation, *Yr.*, is all right, but it suggests "year," and is not sufficiently popular to be generally recognized.

A woman who is divorced puts her maiden name in place of her husband's given name, particularly in England. Mrs. Henry Jones, who was formerly Mary Smith, becomes Mrs. Smith Jones upon being divorced. If her husband's name is distasteful, she may take her mother's maiden surname and prefix it to her maiden surname to become Mrs. Johnson Smith.

Spelling has been known to get a little tangled up, as the following story from Lancashire, England, illustrates:

Judge: "Spell your name for the reporter."

Witness: "O, double T, I, double U, E, double L, double—"

Judge: "Not so fast. Begin again."

Witness: "O, double T, I, double U, E, double L, double U, double O—"

Clerk: "Your honor, this man should be committed for contempt of court."

Judge: "What is your name?"

Witness: "Your honor, my name is Ottiwell Wood and I always spell it, O, double T, I, double U, E, double L, double U, double O, D."

On the other hand, B. E. Bee of Washington, D.C., and Bob Bobo of Macon, Georgia, write their names using only two letters of the alphabet.

Anthony Ogsodofchik of Albany, New York, found the spelling of his name so difficult that he had it tattooed on his arm for ready reference.

Because there are so many ways of spelling surnames that are pronounced alike, compilers of very large indices of names are now beginning to index by sound and not by spelling. The Social Security Board finds this the best way. There are, for example, about forty-six ways of spelling Baer but the name is pronounced by all of them in about the same way. There are *Baer, Baar, Baare, Baear, Baehr, Baehre, Baehoar, Bahar, Bahor, Baere, Baiar, Baier, Bair, Baire, Bairr, Bare, Barr, Bayer, Bayeur, Bayor, Bayre, Beaher, Beahr, Beair, Beaire, Bear, Beare, Beer, Beere, Behar, Beher, Behr, Beier, Beir, Beirr, Bere, Beyar, Beyer, Biar, Biare, Bier, Bohaer, Byar, Byer, Byher, Byor.*

This soundex system finds that there are thirty-seven ways of spelling Burke, thirty-one of spelling Snyder. Abramowitz is spelled in twenty-six different ways. Even Smith is listed in thirteen spellings. Indeed, all the common names may be found with varied spellings.

In early times each spelled his name as he pleased and his pleasure might change from day to day. Attention to detail in the spelling of one's name is entirely modern. In the sixteenth century four brothers named Rugely executed a legal document and each spelled his name in a different manner.

Perhaps, in the strictest sense, proper names of individuals have no plurals. But when mention is made of several persons with the same name, the designation becomes in some degree common and admits of the plural form. Grammarians and careful writers give proper names the effect of a plural by following an established and logical rule of adding either *s* or *es* to the name, the latter being added when the name ends in *s*, or the sound of *s*, as *Ajax*.

We speak of several *Johns* or *Williams* without much thought about the matter. We refer to *Miller* and his wife as the *Millers* or to Mr. and Mrs. Brown as the *Browns*. It is correct to say that the *Joneses* have left New York or that the *Williamses* and the *Briggses* will attend the party. Forms like *Atkins'* (when the possessive is not intended) or *Atkinss* are improper.

If there are three men named John Brown, the proper designation is the three John *Browns,* not the three *Johns* Brown. Grammarians have formulated the rule that the principal name is generally pluralized. An exception is in the case of the three Misses *Brown*, which many prefer to the three Miss *Browns*, but they naturally say the three Mr. *Browns* or the Lieutenant *Browns*. The plurals of James and Charles are *Jameses* and *Charleses*; the possessive plurals are *Jameses'* and *Charleses'*.

There is some uncertainty in respect to the plurals of names ending in *i, o, u* and *y. Ptolemies* is the correct plural of Ptolemy. Some grammarians indorse the view that proper nouns follow the same rule as common nouns, while others, particularly some of the later ones, seem to prefer to consider each case separately. Thus the plural of Henry used to be written as *Henries*, while the modern usage seems to prefer *Henrys*. Some ending in *o*, as *Cato*, becomes *Catoes* in the plural. Others follow the rule for the plurals of the language in which they arose.

An old Welsh refrain ran:

> I was go down to Pwllheli,
>> I was mingle in a dreadful melée
> I was very near get crushed to jelly,
>> With the people standing on my toes.
> There was forty thousand William Williamses,
>> And sixty thousand Robert Robertses,
> But how many millionses of Johnny Joneseses,
>> Dewch anwyl; there's nobody that knows.

The pronunciation of names is interesting. Some families, particularly among the upper classes in England, have adopted fanciful pronunciations and we frequently see lists of them. *Ayscough* is pronounced *Askew*. General Auchinleck is called *Affleck* by those who know him. Perhaps when the introduction took place it sounded like *Barf* but it was spelled *Barugt*. Mr. *Beaulieu* calls himself *Bewly*. *Farquhar* is heard as *Farker*, while *Mohoun* is contracted to *Moon*. The Saints are particularly eccentric. *St. John* Irvine is well known as *Sinjun* Irvine. *St. Leger* is *Sillinger*. The English pronounce *Sawbridgeworth* just as it is spelled; they used to call it *Sap-sed*, but gave it up. But nothing will stop *Cholmondeley* from being referred to as *Chumly*. Mencken gives a long list of these English surnames with strange pronunciations in his *The American Language: Supplement II*.

This practice is not entirely English, however, although it is not so marked in America as in England. The famous old American baseball name, *McGillycuddy*, is clipped into something like *Ma-clik-uddy*. But the prize American pronunciation is the *Enroughty* family that lived in Henrico County, Virginia, and insisted on the pronunciation *Darby*. They actually bore two names, *Enroughty* in writing and *Darby* in speech. Various legends are current in Virginia to explain this name.

Ridiculing this snobbish habit was the Englishman who signed himself in the hotel register as John Phtholognyrrh and affirmed that it was to be pronounced "Turner." Upon being pressed a bit he pointed out that the *Phth* was sounded as in "phthisis," the *olo* as in "colonel," the *gn* as in "gnat" and the *nyrrh* as in "myrrh"; and with our failure to reform the English language no one could say him nay. Then there was Jones who spelled his name "Jolquhones," erroneously relying on "Colquhoun" as his authority.

The late Samuel G. Blythe, the eminent writer, observed of the full name of Major Archibald Willingham DeGraffenreid Clarendon Butt, then the president's military aid, that it sounded "like a cookstove falling downstairs."

Some people ask, "What is the correct way to pronounce my name?" The only answer possible is: The way it is pronounced in your immediate family. In one family the proper pronunciation is one sound; in another family with the same name it is different, but *correct* in both cases. So, in general, the "correct" pronunciation of a name, in polite society, at least, is that adopted by the bearer of the name. The "correct" spelling of a name is the way the bearer of the name spells it. Among the fundamental rights of a man in America are spelling and pronouncing his own name as he pleases.

Aristotle mentions the mispronunciation of a man's name as one of the most disagreeable of insults. Nationalities clash when one incorrectly enunciates the names of the other. Probably Goethe and his works would be much better known in this country if the pronunciation of his name were not so difficult. When a foreign name which is difficult is used in America, its pronunciation may really get mixed up, as the following poem on Van Gogh illustrates:

V-A-N G-O-G-H

(*Pronounced* Van Gogh)

Today his paintings are the vogue;
And all the world salutes *Van Gogh*.
But there are folks, not bright enough
Correctly to pronounce *Van Gogh*.
Perplexed, bewildered, all agog,
They venture, haltingly, *Van Gogh*.
Or hem or haw or grunt or cough,
And hastily suggest *Van Gogh*.
Or cough or grunt or hem or haw,
And then, inspired, blurt out *Van Gogh*.
While others, with deep furrowed brow,
Determine that he is *Van Gogh*.
And some there are, content and smug,
Who are convinced he is *Van Gogh*.
And do not smile and think it gauche

If someone states he is *Van Gogh.*
Or if a haughty lass says, "Bosh!
The artist's name is clear, *Van Gogh.*"
Or Herr von Schnauzer cries out, "Och!
Der painter's namen iss *Van Gogh.*"
But since I also do not know,
I nonchalantly say *Van Gogh.**

         —Ilo Orleans

* By permission. From *Word Study,* copyright, 1941, by G. & C. Merriam Co.

The nurses in a hospital in Fargo, North Dakota, contended that a three-day-old baby in the hospital could pronounce her surname. Skeptics departed hastily when they learned that the parents were Mr. and Mrs. Albert *Waa.* This is much like the man whose dog was so clever that it could pronounce its own name, but the dog's name was *Bow-wow.*

Then there was the man who was always addressed correctly, even by strangers. His name was *Hey,* the first part of "Hey, there." A lady, of Honduran ancestry, named Woollomoolloo Munox de Cleaves, has a name that is really not difficult to pronounce if one can keep his balance. Pronunciation might be easier if one had the forethought first to fill the mouth with hot, mashed potatoes.

Even a churchman notices the mispronunciation of his name. Once, at dinner, Cardinal Gibbons was seated next to a lady of another faith who was not noted for her tactful consideration of others. Perhaps only to make conversation, she inquired if he *really* believed in the infallibility of the Pope. The Cardinal quickly silenced her and won the verbal tilt when he replied, "Well, when he greets me in Rome he addresses me as 'Jibbons'."

The beauty of a name is similar to the rhythm of verse. As the fundamental beauty of verse is a matter of art and not chance and depends upon the skillful employment and disposition of words of harmonious and expressive sound, so the euphony of a name is due to its content of pleasant vowel sounds and agreeable, delicate consonants. A name has poetry in its sound and meaning, an innate quality that clicks with our personality.

Names in comic strips have had an evolution all their own. Because the artist is faced with the requirement of great condensation, he utilizes the names of his characters to tell something about them or as a means of providing atmosphere. Bombastic or incongruous names and high sounding titles are good for a chuckle, as *J. Pierpont Dingle* and *The Duke of Camembert*. The successful comic artist is extremely skillful in his choice of character names. An outstanding user of apt or descriptive names is the American cartoonist, Al Capp (Alfred Gerald Caplin) in his *Li'l Abner*.

Much may be learned from the inspection of another's name. If the first names are James Aloysius or Francis Xavier, he is undoubtedly a Catholic. Or at least his parents were Catholic. The given name may sometimes provide a clue as to the pronunciation of the surname, as when Mr. and Mrs. Kiam name their son Omar.

Some may inquire as to the object of the study of names. The answer is that it aids in checking and verifying knowledge uncovered in other fields. History, anthropology, ethnology, philology, biography, literature and genealogy owe much to the work of the onomatologist. The study of names directs the attention of the historian to many errors. Anthropologists add the information derived from names to the figures obtained from body measurements and description. Names often call the attention of lexicographers to archaic and obsolete words, or bring forcibly to their scrutiny the fact that the words were in common use long before the time they have ascribed to them. To philologists, names are the language of another era frozen for all to see. Much can be learned of the structure of language when the personal names contain verb-inflections. The biographer and genealogist of medieval families owe much to their knowledge of surnames and their origins, and are often prevented from arriving at absurd conclusions by this knowledge.

The casual student of names obtains much useful information. A half-hour's study of a telephone directory or an ambulatory observation along the street will provide pleasure and recreation. National history is revealed in the names of people.

The study of names often provides a clue as to whether a certain author wrote a particular work. For example, Walter Franklin Prince, in the *American Journal of Psychology*, sought to prove by the proper names chosen that Joseph Smith wrote the *Book of Mormon*. Inspection of names in early writings gives us a hint as to whether the manuscript is fact or fiction. The practice of giving label-names to fictional characters is strongly exemplified in the allegories and allegorical dramas of the Middle Ages. The characters in Bunyan's *Pilgrim's Progress* are known to everyone. Fiction, especially the more vulgarly humorous, tends definitely to employ names evolved from words which serve to suggest the character named. The cartoon feature *Bringing Up Father* brings in many characters with such names.

Onomatology, or the study of names, is important in many fields of learning. The inspection of the names of persons—both first names and surnames—provides many an additional clue to our knowledge of the stream of history—facts which are unlikely to be uncovered from any other study. The degree of fame enjoyed by great personages and rulers may often be accurately measured for any given historical era by the names the people bear. This contribution to history, which is made by a detailed examination of nomenclature, is so important, suggestive and interesting that the scholar cannot but be surprised at the neglect of such an inquiry by our historians. Names have been called history's footnotes, also fossils of history. If we had a well-arranged catalogue of the names of each period, we could construct a rather complete history of the world from the beginning, including prominent characteristics, social conditions, and habits of each people.

The anthropologist and the ethnologist must take cognizance of the names of primitive people to round out their study of the customs and habits of early cultures. To an ethnologist an old name is as valuable as a fragment of pottery. Mr. Charles Hill-Tout, the eminent Canadian ethnologist, suggested that the study of names be treated as a separate department of anthropological study under the term "nomenology."

To the student of comparative religion the examination of the names of gods and the names borne by primitive peoples is especially invaluable. Names record accurately the intensity of a group's religious fervor. People have adopted theophorous names, i.e., names which contain as an element the name of a deity, in the eras when they were most intensely religious. The names the people bear point to the status of the civil government of the age during which they were used. The poetical and artistic imagination of the original bearers is elucidated. Names mark the beginning and end of various religious and social movements. Mormons name their children from the Book of Mormon —*Nephi, Lehi* and *Moroni*. Primitive gods and their attributes are sometimes kept alive only through names.

The scholars concerned with ethnology are aided by a detailed inspection of the names of the people who lived in a given locality; and by the names they have given to places, the migrations of ancient tribes and races can be traced. Clues as to the boundaries of ancient cities and countries can be brought to light by paying attention to names and thus help in the study of ancient geography.

Howard F. Barker made an extensive study of national stocks in the United States as indicated by surnames in the census of 1790. He considered nomenclatural evidence to be the most satisfactory and comprehensive for this purpose.

Personal names are a prolific source of new words in our language. Some last only a few years and others continue as a part of the permanent language and the source is forgotten. *Zany*, for example, comes from John through the Italian *Giovanni*. Vidkun Quisling of Norway, by his traitorous collaboration with the Germans in 1940, brought into existence the common noun, *quisling*. Whether it remains in our language, as a synonym for traitor, only time can tell. Each word derived from a personal name is a story in itself.

The study of surnames is important in the study of the language of the Middle Ages. Our family names are in many cases merely a frozen or petrified form of the words used in the times after the English Conquest.

In the same manner many of our Christian names present to us, in a disconnected outline, the language of early times in various countries. The continual change and permutations of Christian names and surnames present a pictorial view of the slow growth and decay of language. Nomenclature is the part of a decayed language which is kept alive the longest. Linguists have not given sufficient attention to the study of names in their investigation of various tongues, as witness the neglect of names in the compilation of the English dictionaries.

Names among primitive peoples, without a pre-existing stock to draw from, must, if given at all, be drawn from the spoken language of the people by whom they are first imposed. All personal names were originally nicknames in that they are descriptive in some way of the person so named. In modern times, only the Puritans gave new names with meanings.

A dictionary of surnames both current and obsolete should be compiled with all the care the philologists lavished on the great Oxford dictionary, tracing each name back to its original form and citing authority whenever possible. In the many cases where there were several origins they should be listed in order. Such an undertaking, however, would require the same superior type of scholarship that produced the *Oxford English Dictionary* and the *Dictionary of American English*. Weekley has criticized the Oxford dictionary, pointing out that it could have been made more accurate and complete by citing the earliest appearance of a surname where it appeared centuries before any record we have of the word composing it.

It would be of great benefit to the sum total of knowledge if a society could be formed for the study of personal names somewhat on the lines of the scholarly English Place-Name Society. Perhaps an American Name Society should also include the student of place-names. Such a group could produce works on the subject, perhaps through a serial publication. While a place-name society is necessarily limited to one country, a group studying the names of people would include both English and Americans and, indeed, all other nationalities, since they all come together in the great American melting pot.

CHAPTER V

Nicknames

Father calls me William, sister calls me
Will,
Mother calls me Willie, but the fellers call
me Bill!
—Eugene Field, *Jest 'Fore Christmas*

WHEN the beasts were brought before Adam, he gave to each a name in accordance with the characteristics he observed in each (*Genesis* ii, 19-20). There is something of the Adam in every one of us and it emerges through our propensity to give nicknames to people, that being the most forceful way we can express our inherent sense of the significance of names.

Nicknames are called upon to supply defects in names—defects in identification and defects in description. In some cases sobriquets are an absolute necessity, as when there are ten John Joneses in a single locality or seven William Johnsons in one village.

Nicknames are not new, University of Chicago Egyptologists have discovered. Pepiseshemsenefer was the royal treasurer in Egypt 2600 years before Christ. When he died, the Ancient Egyptians put his name under his likeness on his tomb and added that he was called *Senni* for short. The early Latin inscriptions sometimes listed a man's nickname, preceded by appropriate descriptive words, after his real name. Nicknames are older than Christian names or surnames; the earliest appellation applied to the most primitive man must have been a descriptive nickname.

In the past almost every man who forged ahead in any line of endeavor was dubbed by a title which marked some trait in his character or peculiarity in his personal appearance or preserved the memory of some outstanding achievement. An old Chinese proverb asserts: "If a man has no nickname, he never grows rich." Few national leaders have escaped having at least one nickname appended to them.

Because of the prevalence and importance of nicknames in the Philippine Islands the election law in the Islands had to provide that "certificates of candidacy shall not contain more than one nickname of the candidate." Many cases have been brought before the courts to construe this provision of the law.

A nickname may be defined as a name added to, or substituted for, or used alternately with, the proper name of a person, place or thing, given by others in contempt, derision, ridicule, sportive familiarity or affection. Nickname is a corrupt form of *an ekename*, which, being misdivided, became *a nekename*. Ekename, now obsolete, merely means an additional name. It usually describes physical or mental characteristics or actions of the person designated.

Originally it might be said that all surnames started as a form of nickname, being names added to the person's real name generally from a practical point of view, that is, for the purpose of identification. All personal names were originally nicknames in the sense that they were significant and descriptive. Nicknames are sometimes used now as a means of identification, as when they are used to distinguish between two persons with the same name; but, in general, nicknames as discussed in this chapter are clearly distinct from family names. Nicknames correspond with the old Roman *agnomen* (see page 131). Sometimes nicknames entirely displace a person's original name and become the real name by which he is known.

The story is told of the attorney's clerk who was professionally employed to serve a process on someone in a small town where everyone was known chiefly by his nickname. The instrument contained the man's real name with deadly, legal accuracy. After much fruitless inquiry, the clerk was about to abandon the search as hopeless, when a young woman, who had witnessed his efforts, kindly volunteered to assist him.

"Oy say, Bullyed," cried she to the first person they met, "does thee know a man neamed Adam Green?" The bull-head was shaken in token of ignorance.

"Loy-a-bed, dost thee?"

Lie-a-bed's opportunities of making acquaintance had been rather limited, and she could not resolve the difficulty.

Stumpy (a man with a wooden leg), Cowskin, Spindleshanks,

Cockeye, and Pigtail were severally invoked, but in vain. The querist fell into a brown study, in which she remained for some time. At length, however, her eyes suddenly brightened, and slapping one of her companions on the shoulder, she exclaimed triumphantly, "Dash my wig! Whoy he means moy feyther," and then turning to the searcher, added, "You should'n ax'd for Ode Blackbird."

In an English coal district there was a postman who had so completely forgotten his own proper name, having so long identified himself with his nickname, that he carried a letter correctly addressed to himself for a fortnight, making inquiries all the time for the party for whom it was intended.

In certain village districts in Scotland the variety of names is limited, and the people are forced to resort to *tee* names (Scotch for bynames or nicknames) to identify their neighbors. The story is told in *Blackwood's Magazine* for March, 1842, of a stranger who had occasion to call upon a fisherman named Alexander White. Meeting a girl, he asked:

"Cou'd you tell me fa'r Sanny Fite lives?"

"*Filk* Sanny Fite?"

"Muckle Sanny Fite."

"*Filk* muckle Sanny Fite?"

"Muckle lang Sanny Fite."

"*Filk* muckle lang Sanny Fite?"

"Muckle lang *gleyed* Sanny Fite," shouted the stranger.

"Oh! It's Goup-the-lift (stare at the sky) y'ere seeking," cried the girl, "and fat the deevil dinna ye speer for the man by his richt name at ance?"

All races at all times have made an extensive use of nicknames, and many times the nickname entirely replaces the original name. Nicknames drive out given names as bad money drives out good, according to Gresham's Law. While a few men have exercised a choice in the selection of their surname, almost none have had anything to say about the nickname applied to them by others. Good or bad, particularly the latter, nicknames have a tendency to stick and the hardest job one can undertake is to try to shake an opprobrious nickname. An old proverb admonishes us, "A nickname is the heaviest stone that the devil can throw at a man."

Nicknames were popular among the early Greeks and Romans. From the latter we observe ones such as *Crassus*, "fat," *Varus*, "bowlegged," and *Cincinnatus*, "curly." Pericles was called *Onion Head*, from the shape of his head. Some have figured in history only by the nicknames conferred upon them. *El Greco*, i.e., "the Greek," the foremost Spanish painter of the sixteenth century, is known chiefly by his nickname, which arose from the nation of his birth. One of the early Roman emperors received the nickname *Caligula* (little boots) from the soldiers because of the military shoes he wore in his youth, and by that title he has been known ever since. The great Greek philosopher is known to history by his nickname *Plato* meaning "broad," first bestowed by his wrestling instructor in reference to his big shoulders. Plato so replaced his real name, Aristocles, that he is not even cross-indexed in reference books under his former name.

The early Hebrews were not above bestowing nicknames. With the Celts, Welsh and Manx, nicknames have always had a strong hold upon the people, and whole villages have designated their inhabitants by descriptive terms. Fantastic nicknames are rather common among Italian- and Spanish-speaking peoples, particularly among the lower classes.

Just why some nicknames adhere so tenaciously is difficult to learn. Positive proof that they are false or malicious has little or no effect in dislodging them. Epithets that stick are usually due to pure chance, a joke or a whim, and their origins are often obscure, not only to the persons who first applied them, but to the persons to whom they were first applied. Many continue because they are so apt and appropriate that they are quickly called to everyone's mind by the sight of the person involved. This is particularly true when they signify a bodily defect. One low in stature is likely to be called *Shorty* by utter strangers as well as by friends. One inclined to be slender may be addressed, independently, by different people as *Slim*.

Another reason for the rugged life of an apt nickname is that there is some concealed humor in the term which will be grasped by all and be long remembered. A nickname is the most stinging of all species of satire because by its very vagueness it admits of no reply. A nickname excites a strong idea without requiring any proof. It is not logical but takes the place of logic and may be used effectively without the trouble of thinking when ordinary argument fails. Napoleon is supposed to have asserted, "No one can afford to overlook nicknames."

Many nicknames have no clear or definite meanings, but it is enough if the sound seems to suggest some imperceptible wrongdoing or if there is a tinge of the ludicrous which is felt to be appropriate. Nicknames are definitely masculine in that they are more common among men than among women. Men just seem to be more nicknamable than women; perhaps men are less reserved and do not resent them so much; they also get out among people more.

Some terms or epithets, originating in a compliment, have become most damaging by being sarcastically associated with ridicule. For example, Harold Ickes was originally called *Honest Harold* by his admirers, but was later designated by the same name by his political enemies in a tone which belied the meaning of the words. Men dislike being continually reminded of one virtue by their fellow men, or having to listen continually to the endless changes which may be wrung on one great action or daring deed.

In general, nicknames are either derogatory, complimentary, or affectionate. Derogatory nicknames may be either opprobrious or contemptuous. Complimentary epithets may be merely respectful or admiring. Affectionate appellations may have been derogatory in their origin; they are pet names or terms of endearment. Additional names may be useful as when they serve to describe or identify; mischievous when they are odious; and harmless when they are merely trivial.

All nicknames are either descriptive in their nature or are pet forms. For purposes of analysis of origin and meaning, although it may sometimes be difficult to classify a given nickname with complete accuracy, and some may fall in more than one class, all added names may be arranged as follows:

I. Descriptive Nicknames:
    (a) Personal characteristics, as *Schnozzle* and *Blondie.*
    (b) Peculiarity of dress, as *Redcap* and *Baggypants.*
    (c) Action or deeds, as *Itchy* and *Gabby.*
    (d) Social position, as *Bridget.*
    (e) Attribute of proper name, as one rhyming with the surname.
II. Nursery or Pet Forms:
    (a) Diminutives, as *Johnny* and *Billykins.*
    (b) Abbreviations of Christian names, as *Geo.* and *Al.*
    (c) Terms of endearment, as *Honeybun* and *Snookums.*

To subdivide more minutely would not be difficult, but for our present study the above is sufficient for a full understanding of the classes of nicknames. The German language has a term for every shade of an added name or nickname, as *Spottname,* derision; *Scherzname,* fun; *Ekelname,* disgust; *Spitzname,* teasing; *Scheltname,* reproach.

DESCRIPTIVE

People easily call a man a name which expresses what they see of him. The Duke of Wellington was called *Old Nosey*, because of his nose. Thus nicknames descriptive of the most prominent personal characteristics form by far the largest group. They are descriptive either of the body, mental processes or moral attributes. Nicknames that describe the bearer are really just surnames written in English.

The hair often determines the nickname. Besides *Red* there is *Bricktop, Carrots, Rusty* and *Sandy* for the redhead. *Curly* is sure to name the curly-headed man. *Baldie* denotes lack of hair. *Blondie* is feminine for the blonde. A fat man or boy is called *Big Boy, Chub, Fat* or *Fats, Fatso, Fatty, Jumbo, Pudgy, Tiny* or *Tubby* while the opposite is known as *Skinny* or *Slim* or perhaps as *Ribs, Scarecrow* or *Spider*. A fat and hearty boy is *Buster*. A tall or lanky person may be *Daddy Longlegs, High-pockets, Lanky, Legs, Lofty, Shanks* or *Slats* while his short brother may be dubbed *Half-pint, Shorty, Sawed-off, Tom Thumb* or *Warty*. Physical nicknames often go by contraries, as when a burly football tackle is known as *Tiny* and tall men are dubbed *Shorty*.

Nicknames based on appearance are often picturesque. One with shining eyes may be *Bright-eyes*; with a prominent nose, *Schnozzola*, or with a hooked nose, *Hook-nose*; or with a freckled face, *Freckles* or *Spec*. One who limps is often called *Gimpy* or *Step and a Half*, while if he has lost his leg, he may be *Peg-leg*. If he is a hunchback, *Humpy* describes him. *Bull Frog* or *Frog* sometimes describes the deep voiced individual. The dark-complexioned boy is invariably *Blackie*; while one with a pink complexion may be dubbed *Pinkie*.

Weaklings are called by girls' names as *Betty, Ethel*, or *Molly*, also as *Cream-puff, Fancy-pants, Lacy-pants, Pansy, Panty-waist*. The opposite are labeled *Buck, Bull, Butch, Spike*, or *Spud*, and are thus popular with young boys. An old person may be *Old Man* or *Father Time*, while a youth is *Growing Pains*, in the slang of the day

Prominent mental characteristics bring on nicknames such as *Boob, Dizzy, Dopey, Goofy, Sap, Dumb Dora* for dull-witted people; *Molasses, Sleepy, Weary Willy* for slow or lazy persons; and *Breezy, Hot-Shot, Lightning* and *Speedy* for fast or energetic people. The disposition of a person is enough on which to hang a nickname; a cheerful person is *Hap, Happy* or *Sunshine*, while a gloomy one is *Old Poker Face* or *Sour Puss*.

Indeed, every common disposition has its special nickname to distinguish it, as *Puck* for a lively or mischievous child; *Splutterfuss,* one who splutters and fusses, and *Kayo,* a fighter. The nickname becomes ambiguous sometimes when it outlives the characteristic.

Moral characteristics appear when we call the pious person *Holy Joe. Fingers* denotes the skillful pickpocket. *Fagin* points out the crime teacher.

Every reader will be able to think of dozens of other nicknames conveying the same meanings. From time to time some famous personage or pen character gives his name to a characteristic which in turn nicknames numerous persons all over the country. In the past we have had *Bluebeard, Don Juan, Doubting Thomas* and *Peeping Tom.*

Peculiarity of dress is the peg on which many nicknames are hung. In modern times dress has not been so prolific in producing nicknames as in the past because men now generally dress alike. Among boys temporary nicknames come from attire. The author, as a boy, remembers his pride in a new fur cap until another boy saw in the cap a false wig. The well dressed man is a *Beau Brummel,* while the boy who sports a fancy outfit is called *Little Lord Fauntleroy.*

Nicknames which have a peculiar adhesive quality are those which arise from deed or action in the past. One of the commonest situations causing the application of a nickname arises when one makes some egregious blunder, perhaps in pronunciation, or makes some important error in his school recitations. Indeed, an error in school may be disastrous due to the remarkable capacity of children to take advantage of it via the nickname route. The nineteenth-century English proverb, "Sticks and stones can break my bones, but names will never hurt me," was not quite accurate. Beyond being a defensive retort or comforting phrase for children to fling back at their tormentors, it has no other use.

Lower tells of the parish clerk of Langford, England, being called *Red Cock* for many years before his death, who after having slept in church one Sunday, and, dreaming that he was at a cock-fight, bellowed out, "A shilling on the red cock." A very talkative person often acquires the appellations of *Big Mouth, Gabby* or *Windy.* The excessive use of an exclamation, or the intemperate use of an oath, may cause the person to be so nicknamed.

Sometimes a nickname results from a child's imperfect attempt to pronounce a word or name. Thus we all know that *Boz* was an infantile attempt at Moses, Dickens' pet name for one of his younger brothers. Professor Weekley says that a relative of his was called Bob, which was short for Libob, a childish effort at Elizabeth.

Hannah Clifford, of Cornish, Maine, when a child, could not pronounce Hannah, but said "Haha." The name stuck to her throughout her life. She married Ranger Wood who died shortly afterward. In her grief her terse telegram to her father read, "Ranger is dead. Haha." The small town telegrapher, who knew Mr. Clifford but not his daughter, was rather shocked at such seeming levity.

Social position or pseudo-social position, particularly the latter, produces appellations. We have *Duke* as an example. Nicknames are given to trades or occupations, as *George* for a pullman porter and *James* for a chauffeur. In Germany, *Johann* is a name for any servant; in Holland, *Jan* is equal to "waiter."

In the Middle Ages one's condition as a free man or serf was constantly in the minds of his associates, so that nicknames or bynames indicative of position were by no means uncommon. In our day, when everyone's political status is the same, it is a difficult peg on which to attach nicknames. Back in 1355 Stephen, son of Thomas, claimed damages from Ralph Grayfe for calling him by his nickname in court. But Ralph replied that he was better known by his nickname than as *fitz Thomas* and the jury agreed.

Some descriptive nicknames delineate the name of the bearer in some manner rather than his person or actions. Thus John Keats' name was telescoped by his friends into *Junkets,* a nickname he hated. Disraeli was contracted into *Dizzy.* Other nicknames are suggested by some subtle sound of the proper name in relation to some characteristic or peculiarity of the person.

Many times the nickname is a word which rhymes with the Christian name or surname as when Arthur E. Gehrke was nicknamed *Turkey* by his youthful playmates. In some instances the nickname is a translation of the real name of which the most famous example is *The Little Flower,* sobriquet of New York's former mayor, *Fiorello* H. LaGuardia. A nickname may be given because of its affinity with the proper name as when Sir Robert Peel was dubbed *Orange Peel* by the Irish foes of the House of Orange, or when Sanders, the foul-mouthed libeler of Queen Elizabeth, was given the title of *Slanders.*

Many times the initials of the nickname describing the bearer in some manner are made to correspond with the initials of the Christian names as when N. P. Willis was called *Namby-Pamby* Willis and U. S. Grant was nicknamed *Uncle Sam, Unconditional Surrender,*

Uniformed Soldier, Union Safeguard, United States, Unprecedented Strategist and *Unquestionably Skilled*. In other instances the Christian name is converted into a word with a similar sound; Ulysses S. Grant was also called *Useless*.

In many cases the nickname a man bears consists of the initials of the Christian names or Christian names and surnames. This type of nickname is sometimes called initialism. In recent years the best example has been the familiar *F.D.R.* for Roosevelt. Sometimes writers are well known by their initials, as *G.B.S.* for George Bernard Shaw, *F.P.A.* for Franklin Pierce Adams, *G.K.C.* for Gilbert Keith Chesterton and *B.L.T.* for Bert Leston Taylor. Important business men, particularly those who are just a little too eminent to carry a pet name gracefully, are, by their associates, often referred to by the initials of their forenames. The late Mitchell D. Follansbee, the distinguished Chicago lawyer, was known even among his younger associates as "M.D."

NURSERY OR PET FORM

That some years back most given names had their hypocoristic, or familiar pet, form is shown by Sam Weller's replying that Job is the "only one I know, that ain't got a nickname to it." (Dickens, *Pickwick Papers*, Chapter XVI). In general, a hypocoristic form is such a transformation of the real name of a person as is intended to give it a more familiar, intimate, affectionate or playful sound. It speaks from the point of view of the family, nursery or inner circle of friends. This, however, holds good only at the time the name is formed. Later it may entirely supersede the normal name and be used by everyone. John and William, when altered to *Jack* and *Bill*, are now understood by everyone.

The pet names parents call their children are important. No matter what a boy's name is, he may be called *Junior* in the home. Many boys in their teens are embarrassed when their parents continue to call them *Sonny*. Continued use of a nickname suggesting dependent childhood is unfair to a teen-ager who is striving hard to grow up. It sounds odd when the practice is continued until one is well past middle age, but by that time the man is seeking to recapture his youth so that he does not mind.

The popular girls' names of *Mary, Margaret* and *Elizabeth* have produced a truly amazing array of variations and pet forms, many of which have developed into Christian names in their own right. In fact, many girls' names obviously were originally pet forms but separated from the parent name so long ago that we are not now just sure which one is the original form. We can conjecture that *Ada* is short for Adela; *Eda* for Edith; and *Ella* may in some cases come from Ellen; *Etta* may come from Esther or Henrietta; *Lina* may be either from Adeline or Caroline. Many medieval forms replaced the full name in early times and few clues have been left to enable us to connect them. It is only by patient search to find the same person indifferently called by two forms that we are able to come to a decision.

The simplest way of providing a pet form for a familiar Christian name is by shortening it to its first syllable. Thus there is *Di* for Diana and *Vi* for Violet; *Pen* for Penelope and *Marge* for Margaret. Cuth-wulf, a king of the West Saxons in the seventh century, was known as *Cutha*. Oftentimes the pronunciation is slightly altered and we have *Kate* for Katherine; *Jim* for James; *Wat* for Walter, although some-times this is a clue to early pronunciations of the name. *Rick* for Richard is evidence that it was often pronounced Rickard. Many times one shortened form does for several forenames as *Ed* for Edmund, Edward, Edsel, Edwin, etc., and *Al* for Albert, Alfred, Alvin, etc. Sometimes more than one syllable is taken, as *Alex*, for Alexander and *Eliza* for Elizabeth. Sometimes the pet form arises from a middle syllable, as *Sandy* for Alexander, *Liz* from Elizabeth, and *Seph* from Josephus. Then many times the last syllable is used as a nursery form, as *Trude* from Gertrude, *Beth* for Elizabeth and *Tony* from Anthony. This loss of the first syllable is called *aphesis*. In other cases no precise portion of the name is used, as *Babs* from Barbara, *Molly* from Mary, *Chuck* from Charles and *Hank* from Henry. The same pet form may be from the first or last syllable, as *Bert* from Albert or Herbert, or from Bertram.

In the north of England and in Scotland pet forms were made by adding *-ie* or *-y*. Thus there is *Johnnie* and *Johnny, Georgie, Jimmie* and *Jimmy* and many others. This suffix is also added to other pet abbreviations; there is *Bessie* and *Jackie*. Indeed, all the diminutive endings have been added to abbreviations and pet forms to produce a bewildering array of nursery forms.

The trick of rhyming produces curious results in pet names. From Richard there is the archaic *Rick* on which were rhymed *Dick* and *Hick*. Today we have all but discarded both Rick and Hick and re-tained Dick as a common alias for Richard. In the same manner we have kept *Bob* for Robert and we still refer to *Rob*; but *Hob, Dob* and *Nob* are obsolete, although their appearance in popular surnames of

Hopkins, Dobbins and *Nobbs* proves their early popularity. Roger gave gave us *Dodge* and *Hodge*. *Bill* arose from William by this rhyming method, although it is quite modern, as shown by its absence from common surnames. Margaret produces *Meg* from which comes *Peg*; Mary gives us *Molly* and *Polly*, possibly sometimes *Dolly*. Other nursery forms are developed by the prefixing of *N-*, which has given us *Nan* for Ann, *Nell* for Ellen or Eleanor, *Noll* for Oliver, *Nam* for Ambrose and *Ned* for Edward.

In other cases the nickname seems to bear no other relation to the Christian name it stands for except agreement in initial letter, as when *Jack* designates John and *Chuck* refers to Charles. In many cases persons carry nicknames like *Bobby* or *Pat* when their given names are not Robert or Patrick.

Most pet-names have letter changes which imitate the halting pronunciation of infants. Thus, *l* is lisped for the *r* which the baby can't pronounce, as in *Sally* for Sarah, *Dolly* for Dorothy and *Hal* for Harry; central consonants are doubled, as in Sally and Dolly; there are vowel changes to make the name more easily sounded, as *Jim* for James, *Kitty* for Katherine; and *p* is more easily formed than *m*, as in *Patty* for Matilda and *Peggy* for Margaret. Combining the above principals in a single name, we can observe that Mary becomes Polly in the following order: *Mary, Maly, Mally, Molly, Polly*. There are other changes which the child learning to talk makes, and they are all found in these nursery names.

Sometimes diminutives or pet forms represent surnames rather than Christian names. The most common is, of course, *Smitty* for the ubiquitous Smith. Then there is *Mac* for all the *Mc-* and *Mac-* surnames. *Whitey* for White and *Blackie* for Black are well known. Many family names ending in *-s*, as Binns, Briggs, Jones, and Sparks carry the pet forms *Binnsey, Briggsie, Jonesy,* and *Sparksy. Hutch* is for Hutchins and Hutchinson and *Mitch* for Mitchell. *Van* represents the van names, *Wally* those beginning Wal-, and *Woody* those commencing with Wood-. In England anyone surnamed Clark is called *Nobby*; Mr. Parker is *Nosey*, Mr. Walker is *Hookey*, Mr. Green is *Dodger* while Mr. Martin is *Pincher*.

Some parents tax their ingenuity to invent a name for their children that will defy nicking or abbreviation. With Southey's Doctor Dove they think, "It is not a good thing to be Tom'd or Bob'd, Jack'd or Jim'd, Sam'd or Ben'd, Neddy'd or Teddy'd, Will'd, or Bill'd, Dick'd or Nick'd, Joe'd or Jerry'd, as you go through the world." With life getting more and more complicated there seems to be a tendency for modern children to prefer the use of their full names instead of diminutive forms.

A man who detested nicknames is said to have determined that none in his family should have them; so, after much thought, he named his sons, Edgar, Edwin, Edmund, Edward, Edson and Egbert. But his system failed. They were known among their fellows as *Eddie, Chuck, Bim, Snorkey, Muggins* and *Pete.*

Many do not like the nursery or pet form of their Christian name. Perhaps the reason is that the hypocoristic form connotes a certain lack of dignity or contains a faint suggestion of inferior status. One is not sure of the reason—he just doesn't like the name. On a trip west with President Truman in 1948, his daughter, Margaret, appeared at a train stop where some one called out, "How about a date, Maggie?" "Nobody that calls me Maggie gets a date," she shot back. "I hate that name."

Thomas Heywood, after observing in *The Hierarchie of the Blessed Angells* that Shakespeare and many of his contemporary dramatists were called by pet names continued,

I for my part
(Thinke others what they please) accept that heart
Which courts my loue in most familiar phrase;
And that it takes not from my paines or praise.
If anyone to me so bluntly com,
I hold he loues me best that calls me *Tom.*

People give nicknames to conceal their feelings—as when they apply a pet name to one they love or reverence.

While most pet forms are really abbreviations, this classification is reserved for those names which are written in a short form but pronounced fully. There are not many well-known abbreviations. We do have *Wm.* and *Jno.* for William and John. And there is *Geo.* for George, *Jas.* for James, *Jos.* for Joseph, *Robt.* for Robert, and *Thos.* for Thomas. Less common is *Hy.* for Henry and *Aa.* for August.

Somewhat different from the usual pet names are the terms of endearment applied to children, particularly girls, which sometimes stick to them throughout their life. These are infinite in number but some of the more popular (frequently prefaced by "my" or "little") are: *Angel, Babe, Baby Doll, Birdie, Bud, Bunny, Chickie, Cutie, Dovey, Ducky, Dumpling, Fuzzy-Wuzzy, Honey, Honeybunch, Honeychild,*

Lamby Pie, Lollypop, Lovey, Ootsie-Wootsie, Peachy, Piggy, Precious, Pretty, Puss, Snookey, Sugar, Sweety, Toots, Turtledove and *Za-za.* General forms addressed to older girls are *Babe, Dearie, Kid,* and *Toots.* Pet terms of endearment for a boy are *Bub, Bud, Buster, Chic, Skeeter, Skippy* and *Skeezix.*

Men in the United States call their wives *Darling, Baby, Honey, Snookums, Sweetheart, Precious* and *Dearest.* Not only in the funny papers, but in real life some call them *Sweety Pie* and *Lamikins.*

Among political orators the most powerful and the most feared are those who can apply apt and telling nicknames—epithets that will catch the imagination and the memory of the populace and will cause one's opponent to shrink back, branded for all time. The mob takes hold with alacrity as a telling nickname saves them from the onerous effort of thinking. An insignificant man may succeed in fastening a ludicrous or degrading nickname upon his superiors. "Give a dog a bad name," says the proverb, "and you hang him." You cannot properly hate a man until you have labeled him with some unpleasant epithet.

If the group who opposes one can be saddled with an odious or ridiculous appellation, the battle is half won. Sometimes, it is true, a group can over the centuries bring respect to an otherwise opprobrious sobriquet. The names of *Quaker, Liberal, Christian, Methodist* were all first applied with malice. Many important factions have received their names from their enemies in pure mockery and have made them honorable, thus turning the tables on their detractors. Dictators know very well that Napoleon was hitting the nail on the head when he is said to have declared that, "It is by epithets that you govern mankind." Hazlitt said that nicknames, for the most part, govern the world.

The Institute for Propaganda Analysis, Inc. has found that the first tool in the propagandist's kit for fooling the public is the "name calling" device. It warns that the propagandist "appeals to our hate and fear by giving bad names to those individuals, groups, nations, races, policies, practices, beliefs and ideals which he would have us condemn and reject."

Some people have a peculiar facility for giving apt nicknames to people. Queen Victoria, it is said, had this habit. Franklin D. Roosevelt dubbed many of his faithful followers. Thomas Corcoran became *the Cork,* Henry Morgenthau, *the Morgue,* and Harry L. Hopkins, *the Hop.* These nicknames of the Rooseveltian era are now fast fading from memory. That a nickname is vague is not important so long as it suggests some blemish or wrongdoing. Indeed, if it is not clear, there is little chance for reply or denial. In this generation in America General Hugh S. Johnson, Senator Huey Long, Fr. Charles E. Coughlin and Secretary Harold Ickes have been particularly feared as coiners of troublesome nicknames.

Public men are especially likely to be referred to by various nicknames in this country. From the beginning, important statesmen in the United States have usually rated eulogistic titles. Shankle in his *American Nicknames* lists twenty-four for Grant, Webster with twenty-three and Lincoln twenty-one. He finds that Grover Cleveland had nineteen nicknames while Theodore Roosevelt and Van Buren had fifteen apiece, and Washington and Samuel Adams thirteen apiece.

To women in public life there appears to be a tendency to apply the nickname *Ma*. Thus *Ma* Ferguson was governor of Texas and *Ma* Ross once occupied that position in Wyoming. *Ma* Perkins was the first woman cabinet member in the United States. The Hon. Mabel Walker Willebrandt, who was assistant Attorney-General of the United States from 1921 to 1929 in charge of prohibition enforcement, was commonly referred to as *Ma*.

In England, Frey found rulers and writers had the most nicknames. Cromwell, he finds, had twenty-six and Queen Elizabeth (*Good Queen Bess*) nineteen. It takes the English to apply nicknames in profusion to their authors, although some were given by admirers only after death. Thus Frey in his *Sobriquets and Nicknames* lists thirty-one nicknames for Shakespeare and twenty-six for Dr. Johnson. Scott comes next with twenty-five, followed by twenty-four for Gabriel Harvey. France gave seventeen nicknames to Louis XIV and sixteen to Napoleon, according to Frey.

It is not the man with a great number of nicknames but he who is known to everyone by a single nickname whom one thinks about when considering nicknames of well-known men. In this classification we are likely to find commanding generals. Indeed, military commanders have been the recipients of nicknames more than any other respectable class. Almost every general has received one or more. In the First World War Pershing was known both to his men and the public as *Black Jack*. General Winfield Scott was widely known as *Old Fuss and Feathers*, comparable to General *Blood and Guts* Patton in World War II. Those who read history are familiar with *Old Hickory*, the popular sobriquet for Andrew Jackson, given to him by his soldiers. Many know *Stonewall* Jackson, but would not recognize Thomas J.

Jackson. In the last war General Eisenhower was constantly called *Ike* and McArthur *Mac*, due chiefly to the efforts of the press to refer to the most eminent of men in a free and easy manner, and also to the necessity for a short designation to fit into headlines.

The most common nickname—rather, we might almost refer to it as a title—is that commencing *Father of*. There are Fathers of Angling, Burlesque, Poetry, Chemistry, Comedy, History, Inductive Philosophy, Medicine and hundreds of others. Shankle catalogues 147 American "Fathers" of this and that. The one most easily recalled by Americans is *Father of His Country*, the appellation bestowed on George Washington. But many would be surprised to learn that this title has also been given to many others in the world including Cicero, Julius Caesar, Cosmo de Medici, Henry I and Frederick I, both of Germany, Andrea Doria, Genoese admiral, and Suger, French statesman.

Many of the nicknames given to public men are of the ponderous type found in print but almost never used verbally. Thus Shankle lists twenty-six nicknames beginning, *Sage of*—and twenty-five *Hero of*—. Naturally, sobriquets of this nature are not used familiarly. There is a class of nicknames commencing with an adjective like *Big, Black, Boy, Bull, Fighting, Good, Great, Little, Old, Red,* and *Uncle,* which are extremely popular in application to famous men. Shankle lists ninety-eight nicknames of famous men in this country which start with the word *Old* and thirty-five with *Little*.

Men active in amateur and professional sports seem to have a tendency to acquire picturesque nicknames. As baseball is our leading sport in America, so baseball's stars are given nicknames by sports writers or others, by which they are known to the public. Everybody remembers *Ty* Cobb, *Honus* Wagner, *Babe* Ruth, *Dizzy* Dean and a host of others, but few can recall their real Christian names.

Stars in the entertainment world pay attention to nicknames. Their press agents make strenuous efforts to fasten onto them highly laudatory nicknames. In late years we have had *The Voice* for Sinatra, *The Body* for Marie McDonald, *The Beard* for Monty Woolley and *The Torso* for Johnny Weissmuller, besides the usual pet forms of names.

Most Hollywood actors are known among their close friends and co-workers by nicknames. Humphrey Bogart is *Bogey*; Ronald Colman is *Ronnie*; Brian Donlevy is *Briney*; Gary Cooper is *Coop*; Claudette Colbert is *Satch*. Claudette didn't have a nickname until she made *So Proudly We Hail*. During that film she was called *Satchel Pants* by the other Bataan nurses because her khaki coveralls fit so loosely. The director began calling her *Satch* and it stuck; she liked it well enough to have *Satch* lettered on the door of her dressing room.

Many prominent stars use nicknames professionally, as *Jack* Benny, *Bing* Crosby, *Jinx* Falkenburg, *Kay* Francis, *Bob* Hope, *Al* Jolson, *Bert* Lahr, *Ginger* Rogers, *Red* Skelton, *Sonny* Tufts, *Rudy* Vallee, to name only a few.

Kings have been prolific in attracting outstanding or bizarre nicknames to themselves. For example, all the French King Charleses have been known by descriptive sobriquets and there were Charles *the Hammer, the Great, the Bald, the Fat, the Simple, the Bad, the Sage, the Idiot, the Dauphin, the Bold,* and *the Foolish,* in that order from 714 to 1483. No popular king in any country has ended his reign without an apt nickname. King Richard *Coeur de Lion,* i.e., the "Lion-Hearted," was one of England's most romantic rulers. Richard III's nickname was *Dickon.* William IV of England, the uncle and predecessor of Queen Victoria, was called *Silly Billy.* Malcolm IV of Scotland was surnamed *the Maiden. Bastard* has not been such an opprobrious nickname but what kings have been so nicknamed. William the Conqueror was known as *the Bastard.* Darius II (d. 404 B.C.) was surnamed in Greek, *Nothos,* i.e., "bastard." Many ancient Roman and Greek sovereigns were known by nicknames.

Political candidates of today are anxious to acquire good nicknames. If they are warm and strong like *Old Hickory* or *Honest Abe,* they are very helpful. A shortening of a baptismal name may give a homey, affectionate feeling for the man, as *Teddy Roosevelt.* When Robert Taft was attempting to secure the Republican nomination for President, he pleaded, "Don't call me Senator; call me *Bob.*"

Next we might turn our attention to the criminal element. In his heyday *Scarface* Al Capone was known all over the country. Since then *Baby Face* Nelson and *Pretty Boy* Floyd have been brought to justice. Other modern well-known criminals have been referred to as *Knifey* Sawicki and *Bugs* Moran. Basil *the Owl* Banghart's highly arched eyebrows with lines between them, pale, staring eyes, peculiar hairline and stray tufts of hair gave him an owlish appearance.

The lawless element are peculiarly adept in applying crudely descriptive nicknames to their members, names which explain the man in a word—his weakness, his racket, how he works, or some characteristic. Female criminals, as well as men, acquire baldly blunt nicknames. Men with a police record are extremely reticent about disclosing their "working names." Either they are too embarrassing or they give the law-enforcing officials too much candid information.

The pen-name, or *nom de plume*, that writers use arose from the French *nom de guerre*, which at first meant simply "war name," but later came to mean any name assumed to conceal identity. Years ago when failure to serve in the army constituted a capital offense, the frequent necessity of concealing one's identity caused the *nom de guerre* to be extensively used. The *nom de plume* was first used for the same practical reason—protection. In early times the liberty of speech was greatly restricted, and if an author's works happened to offend a ruler or a priest, his life might, and many times did, pay the forfeit. The use of the *nom de plume* dates from the Middle Ages.

Nicknames have found their most complete use in designating groups or classes of people. The people of every state in the Union have a nickname, some better known than others, as *Hoosiers* for the men of Indiana. People of important cities are sure to have sobriquets. Peoples and governments of nations are personified in a name. In this country *Brother Jonathan* has given way to *Uncle Sam*. The Government of England is cartooned as *John Bull* and that of China as *John Chinaman*; the French use *Jean Crapaud* (toad, since the Kings of France used toads in their heraldry) for the nation and *Jacques Bonhomme* for the simple French peasant, although American cartoonists generally employ the feminine *Marianne* for the French. The German people are satirized for their lethargy and credulity with *Deutscher Michel*. *Ivan Ivanovitch* facetiously denotes the typical muzhik found all over Russia.

Every nation has numerous nicknames, usually derogatory, for the nationals of other countries. For instance, the Americans dub Mexicans *Greasers* and are, in turn, called by them *Gringoes*. The French Canadian may be called a *Canuck*; a Frenchman, a *frog*; a German, a *kraut*; while a Spaniard may be called a *Don* in allusion to the dignity of bearing proper to the type. The Italian is contemptuously called a *Wop*. In England, *Taffy* represents a Welshman, being a corruption of David, while *Paddy* from Patrick designates the Irish. To give all the derogatory terms each nationality saddles on those of other nationalities would fill a book. In fact, Dr. A. A. Roback has collected them in *A Dictionary of International Slurs* (1944), and has attempted to measure the hate of one group for another by the odium of the slang terms used. The demarcation between nicknames and slang is often nebulous.

Closely akin to nicknames are the various, modern distorted or minced pronunciations of the names of God and of Jesus Christ, employed by people who desire to use colorful expletives yet are unwilling to violate openly the third commandment. Distortions and softenings for the name "God" are *Cock, Dashed, Dod, G, Gad, Gar, Gawd, Gawsh, Ged, George, Godfrey, Gog, Gol, Goles, Golly, Gom, Gord, Gos, Gosh, Got, Gud* and *Gum.* Representing "By God" are *Adad, Adod, Bedad, Begad, Begar, Begorra, Dash, Ecod, Egad, Icod* and *Igad.* Some of these latter are of Irish extraction. *Great* or *Good* is sometimes used with other words in the same manner, as *Great Guns, Great Scott, Great Horn Spoon, Great Snakes, Good Grief, Goodness Gracious, For Goodness Sake* and *Thank Goodness. Dear Me* is possibly a pronunciation of the Spanish *Dios Mio.*

For "Jesus" there is *Gee, Jeez, Jiminy* (or *jeminy*), *Jemina, Jerusalem, Jehosaphat, Gee-whizz, Gee-whillikens* and *Gee-whittaker.* "Christ" is represented by *Cripes, Crickey, Christmas, Cracky* and *Christopher.* "Jesus Christ" may be recognized in *Jiminy-crickets, Judas Priest* and *Judas Christopher.*

Among the English-speaking peoples perhaps the best known proper name for the Devil is *Satan* meaning "the adversary." Other familiar names used in the Bible are *Asmodeus, Beelzebub* and *Lucifer*, besides many descriptive terms and phrases such as "the prince of the world" and "the prince of the power of the air." The English language has numerous other aliases for the devil, perhaps more than in the argot of any other country. Often there is no clear distinction between the devil and his demons. Other countries use other names, as *Mephistopheles* in Germany, *Duyuel* in Holland, *Devas* (bad spirits) in India, *Pooka* in Ireland, *Nikke* in Norway and *Tchort* in Russia. Most of these terms really mean an evil spirit but are now proper names.

Because to name a person is to evoke him or render him present, the devil is seldom named. All sorts of general and ingenious locutions are used as *the Evil one, the Black Man, Old Horny, Old Hairy,* or *Harry, Black Bogey, the Bogey man, Old Nick, the Deuce, Old Scratch.* The venerable prefix "Old," used by the English with various words and names to refer to the devil, is not found among other nations. On the other hand, many people have referred to the devil by flattering names like *the Good man, the Good Fellow, Gentleman Jack, his Most Christian Majesty,* and *his Satanic Majesty,* just to be on the safe side in the event the reference gets to his keen ears.

Political parties are known by their nicknames and, in fact, their "real" names usually arise via the nickname route. The Republicans are the *Grand Old Party,* shortened to *G.O.P.* Church groups are not exempt, and we recognize the difference between a *Hard-Shell* and a *Soft-Shell* Baptist. The athletic teams of a school or university are nothing without a nickname, and the team sobriquet, or another, is sometimes applied to the whole student body. The first group of advisers which surrounded Franklin Delano Roosevelt in his early days as President was denominated the *Brain Trust.*

The only defense to, or cure for, a hateful nickname that has stuck, besides leaving town in the hopes of never meeting a former acquaintance, is to accept it graciously, and take care to propagate it. Cecil William *Runt* Bishop, representative from Illinois, inserted his nickname in his official biography in the Congressional Directory in 1942. Maybe *Runt* was better than Cecil. The Italian singer, Lucrezia Agujari (1743-1783), was known as *Bastardella* or *La Bastardella* (the little bastard) and some of her concert programs so listed her. Reference books even now cross-reference her under this nickname.

Perhaps this remedy appears a bit drastic, like withholding hay from the horse until he gets used to going without food and happens to die in the process; but if one can conquer his own aversion to the horrible misnomer, he has won much more than half the battle and he will silence the contemptuous laughter and confound his enemies. Perhaps this drastic cure is worse than the disease. And some think this is a disease for which the doctors have not yet discovered a satisfactory specific. Any cure which serves to aid the mind to overcome the antipathy towards the sobriquet has served its purpose. Big men must learn to be thick-skinned, as no one can be long in the public eye without being the recipient of a telling epithet.

CHAPTER VI

American Names

Oh, what was your name in the States?
Was it Thompson or Johnson or Bates?
Did you murder your wife
And fly for your life?
Say, what was your name in the States?
—Old Western Miners' Song.

THERE are, by far, a greater variety of surnames in the United States than in any other country because every other country in the world has contributed most of its surnames to our melting pot. If a dictionary of all surnames in America could be compiled, it would be sufficient to serve as a reference book for the names of most other countries. Not only are almost all the important family names of all civilized countries found in the United States, but there is a bewildering mass of variations of foreign names which would be unrecognizable to the inhabitants of the countries from which they have come.

In the early days in our land the names of settlers from all countries were misspelled by ignorant clerks and distorted out of all recognizable shape and then crystallized by the rapid advance of education. In later years the tongue-twisting names of people from eastern and southeastern Europe were altered and changed when Americans could not handle them. The number of alterations and changes in the family names from a single language group are almost endless, and every modern language group of the world is well represented with us. Many of these immigrants, in more recent years, were not well educated and they were responsible for some of the unwitting alterations. The flowing together of all races in the United States has produced an immense number of cognominal riddles.

93

Just how many different surnames there are in America can only be surmised. Guppy found that there were 32,818 in current records in England. Some have attempted to estimate the number of different surnames in this country, but the highest guess has been 100,000. A count of one twenty-fifth of the pages in the Chicago telephone directory, evenly spread throughout the book, indicates that there are approximately 154,750 different surnames in the Chicago telephone book alone. Many unusual surnames are not found in Chicago. The different nationality groups in cities like New York, Milwaukee, Minneapolis and Boston produce surnames that are not in Chicago. The author has compared the Chicago list with various other lists. While even a careful estimate is little more than a wild guess, the author estimates from the above and various other counts and comparisons that there are approximately 350,000 different surnames in the United States. There is a much greater variety among surnames than among forenames.

In making such an estimate, the slightest variation in spelling was considered to constitute a different surname. Without going to this extreme, there was no place to draw the line between a simple variation in spelling and a totally different appellation. On the other hand, many thousands of names have two or more derivations, although each is spelled alike. *Black,* for example, may be a nickname from the color of the hair, complexion or costume, and means "black" if from Old English *blac,* or "white" or "pale" if from Old English *blác,* or may even mean "yellow" in the North of England. One here really can't tell black from white. They are actually different names but of course are not counted as different names in making the above estimate.

The common names in America are not uniform in popularity throughout the country. This is also true of the common names in England, as a glance at Guppy's *Homes of Family Names in Great Britain* will show.

Smith is the most popular surname in both England and the United States. Due to the Scandinavian influence, *Johnson* leads *Smith* in Chicago and in the Twin Cities of Minneapolis and St. Paul. Indeed, in the Twin Cities, besides *Johnson,* one finds that *Anderson, Nelson* and *Peterson* also lead Smith. *Anderson* is third in Chicago. With its Irish population Boston lists *Sullivan* second to Smith, and *McCarthy, Murphy* and *O'Brien* are within the first ten. In Cincinnati, *Meyer* is in third place, while *Schmidt* and *Weber* are high on the list. Milwaukee groups *Krueger, Meyer, Mueller, Schmidt, Schneider, Schroeder* and *Schultz* within its top ten.

Jews in the United States have concentrated in New York City to such an extent that the ten most popular family names there include *Cohen, Friedman, Goldberg, Goldstein, Levy* and *Schwartz*. Only *Smith* leads *Cohen*. *Levy* is second in New Orleans.

Since the cities of America, with their diverse foreign populations, cannot agree as to the most popular surnames, the important list is that of the most common names for the country as a whole. Therefore, from the Social Security files of the Government, the following list of the fifty most popular surnames in this country has been compiled. The estimated number of persons in America bearing each of these names has been made. Because of the number in the Government files these estimates are much more accurate than the estimated figures in connection with Christian names.

COMMON SURNAMES IN THE UNITED STATES

Rank	Name	Estimated Number	Rank	Name	Estimated Number
1.	Smith	1,258,010	26.	Baker	213,490
2.	Johnson	938,880	27.	King	210,400
3.	Brown	701,940	28.	Roberts	199,370
4.	Miller	663,850	29.	Phillips	182,760
5.	Jones	663,420	30.	Evans	180,620
6.	Williams	660,160	31.	Turner	170,340
7.	Davis	532,960	32.	Rogers	156,820
8.	Anderson	448,470	33.	Edwards	155,280
9.	Wilson	399,590	34.	Bell	141,500
10.	Taylor	357,220	35.	Bailey	131,910
11.	Thomas	354,910	36.	Fisher	129,950
12.	Moore	352,760	37.	Bennett	128,400
13.	Martin	337,960	38.	Brooks	122,650
14.	White	337,010	39.	Foster	117,380
15.	Thompson	328,110	40.	Butler	116,590
16.	Jackson	308,680	41.	James	102,470
17.	Harris	289,080	42.	Cohen	102,200
18.	Lewis	256,980	43.	Jenkins	100,750
19.	Allen	243,450	44.	Ellis	91,940
20.	Nelson	243,370	45.	Jordan	90,740
21.	Walker	243,020	46.	Burke	89,360
22.	Hall	242,170	47.	Elliott	86,030
23.	Robinson	231,980	48.	Johnston	84,570
24.	Green	220,430	49.	Black	80,720
25.	Adams	216,400	50.	Owens	78,670
				Total	14,095,720

These fifty names, it will be seen, surname about ten per cent of the people in the United States. It has been calculated that about 840 common names in America account for about half the volume in the average American directory. In England, Guppy found that the fifty commonest names covered eighteen per cent of the population. About 150 names designate half of the people in Scotland.

It will be noted that practically all of the names on the foregoing list are either English, Irish, Scotch or Welsh. It is not greatly different from the list of the fifty most popular English names, but different linguistic groups have increased the popularity of certain names. For instance, the Scandinavian element in the country has pushed *Johnson* up to second place and has contributed greatly to the list of *Andersons*. *Johnson* is also stimulated by the Scotch *Johnstons*. The Germans have been largely responsible for the high standing of *Miller*. Many of the occupational names have been increased by translation from the many languages that have gone into the huge melting pot known as America.

To narrate all the alterations and variations which surnames of the different nationalities have undergone in America would be very tedious and would be of little real value in a work of this type. Nevertheless, a few of the more outstanding changes will be mentioned to give one the feel of what the English reader considers to be foreign names.

Before the Revolution the alteration and changing of German, Dutch and French names were not dictated by ascendancy of the English but came about in a casual manner. The rough life in the New World, where men paid little attention to spelling, brought about many name changes or rather an amalgamation of surnames tending to produce the dominant English type. Names circulated mostly by word of mouth and took on an Anglo-Saxon sound and then were spelled phonetically. There was a tendency to trim long, cumbersome, English names and even to clip many that were not awkward. President *Polk's* ancestral name was *Pollock*. The British names of *Harrison* and *Davies* have tended to become *Harris* and *Davis* in the United States.

As for given names, America also presents a composite picture of the names of all nationalities, as well as of regional variations. The mountaineers in the Southern Appalachians are in the habit of giving droll names to their children. After the birth they are in no hurry to name the child and may take as much as three months or even a year in deciding upon a name. In the meantime the baby acquires an original pet form which may be retained as the permanent name. Names like *PeeWee, Poke* or *Cap* are found in this region. Hypocoristic forms of short names seem to predominate for girls, as *Snowie, Cornie, Coba, Tullie, Hallie, Onza, Monie, Tella.* Boys' names are also short, as *Esco, Oder, Creed, Osie, Irby* and *Cam.*

In the United States odd Christian names are not at all unusual. Obviously invented given names abound in the Southwest. The center of this practice is Oklahoma. Texas and Arkansas produce more than their share of odd forenames. In these states given names are colorful, fanciful and sometimes highly imaginative. James Stephen Hogg, Governor of Texas from 1890 to 1895, named his only daughter *Ima.* He had three sons with ordinary names. The persistent report that he named another daughter *Ura* was the result of writers attempting to make a good story better.

In Oklahoma names of girls like *Bevelene, Bytha, Deatha, Donovea, Gala, Juhree, Rulema, Veroqua* and *Zazzelle* are not Negro names. *Moneer, Raysal* and *Flay* are names of white boys. Unlike in other parts of the country, this kind of name is borne by white college students and the children of families of wealth and position. Mencken, in *The American Language, Supplement II,* sets out an extensive list of these queer names.

Besides the odd, invented forenames, the use of pet names, diminutives, nicknames and clipped and hypocoristic forms of the popular Christian names are common in the South, and are also found in the North. In the faculty of the University of Oklahoma are three professors whose first name is simply *Jack,* two named *Joe,* one *Sam,* one *Gus,* and a female educator, *Margie.* Ministers of the gospel are common whose formal Christian names are such as *Sam, Tommie* and *Phil.* In the use of these pet names as forenames little effort is made to distinguish sex. Girls are named *Tommie Joe* or *Bobby Lee.* Many have masculine middle names like *Betty Bill* and *Dorothy Jim* to commemorate their male parent. Boys may be called *June, Doris, Voline,* etc. The incongruity does not seem to occur to the Southerners.

One reason for the prevalence of these fancy, illogical forenames in the South and Southwest is the strength of the Baptist Church where the minister has no part in the giving of the baptismal name, and thus cannot exert that conservative influence considered so important in other churches. The parent is left free to individualize his children for all time, without a sobering thought.

In the last century in the South it was customary to refer to anyone by the first part of his forename, as *Clem* for Clement, *Newt* for Newton, *Gid* for Gideon, *Barb* for Barbara, *Marg* for Margaret and *Marth* for Martha. On the other hand, girls, particularly among the gentry, were often given two names, as *Sarah Lou* and *Lucy Belle* and they so remained on all occasions. Girls received surnames for Christian names and were sometimes named *Henry, Frank* or *George* after their fathers.

In America middle names gravitate toward a pattern. The common names like *John, Robert* and *Elizabeth* are often found as middle names. Of late years there has been a decided disposition to use, particularly for girls, the popular one-syllable names like *Lou, Mae* and *Jean*. In the backwoods in America favorite affixes to girls' names are *Jane* and *Ann*. Sometimes these middle syllables are affixed to the first name to form one name, as *Maryjane* and *Emmalou*. Others are shortened corruptions of double names as *Olouise* (Olive and Louise) and *Maybeth* (May and Elizabeth). *Lee* is popular as a middle name for girls in the South, from General Robert E. Lee.

An oddity in American surnames is the capitalization of a letter in the middle of the surname, although not of the patronymical type, like *FitzHugh* or *MacDonald*. Examples are: *FlaHavhan, GaNun, KenMore, KleinSmid, ReQua, RiDant, SaCoolidge, SeBoyar, VirDen* and *VisKocil*. Some of these medial capitals are inserted to aid pronunciation, others from misapprehension as to the correct foreign form of the name, while a few are deliberately altered to produce a bizarre or fancy effect. In the Southwest capitals are likewise inserted in Christian names, such as *ArLette, DuWayne,* and *VeRee*. Some other American surnames are parted in the middle and the second part capitalized as *Be Gole, Bel Geddes, Boyn Ton, Do Ran, Dos Passos* and *Le Hew*. Part of these simply consist of two names without a hyphen. This custom by no means originated in this country. In England in Shakespeare's time and later it was not unknown. The great dramatist was often styled *Shake-Spear*. The famous philologist was listed as *Holy Oke*.

Many foreign language groups in America have frowned on the changing of names and have ridiculed their countrymen who have altered their patronymics. This attitude has retarded the gradual Americanizing of their names by these groups. Among them are the Bohemians who fiercely resent change of names by their compatriots.

Very difficult foreign surnames are slowly disappearing from our directories. But much faster is the disappearance of odd, foreign given names. After the immigrant arrives in this country he is quick to give his children American-sounding Christian names, if not in the first generation at least by the second. If the child does not receive a given name he can proudly flaunt before his companions, he will adopt and use some well-known pet form to the exclusion of the name given him at birth. This seems to be true of all nationalities.

When a national group lives together in America there is little change of names. The greatest change from foreign names to English-sounding names is in the cities and not in the country or in small towns. Foreign names are steadily decreasing in the telephone books of our cities.

Interesting examples of the way the Americans altered the forms of German and Swiss names may be seen in eighteenth century lists of the names of foreigners who took the oath of allegiance in Pennsylvania, published in the official *Pennsylvania Archives*, Second Series, Volume XVII. There the names of the settlers and the boats in which they arrived are tabulated. In many instances two lists are given, one an "original list," which was apparently made by an English-speaking person upon hearing the names given orally. These double lists cast considerable light on the spelling and pronunciation the German and Swiss names received in America.

Examining these duplicate rosters, one sees many of the odd names known in America and recognizes their original forms. The immigrants were assigned changed names even before they landed on these shores. As examples *Albrecht Graff* was registered in the boat list as *Albrake Grove*. On the same ship *Jacob Graff* was merely booked as *Jacob Grove*. A brief scanning of these lists shows that scarcely a name is exactly the same on both rolls.

It is in the Pennsylvania cities that one may see the most radical changes in names. Mr. *Whitsell* was originally Herr *Weitzel*. *Schumacher* becomes *Shoemaker* and *Slaymaker* does service for *Schleirmacher* and *Wanamaker* for *Wannemacher*. The spelling and phonetic changes follow certain definite patterns, but there is not space here to list them all and it would merely tire the reader to set out all the recognized vowel and consonant changes. The short German names are formed by dropping the second stem, leaving Hein from *Heinrich*, Ott from *Ottmann* and Traut from *Trautman*.

The first Germans who came to America cared little how their names were spelled and readily allowed others to Anglicize them. *Rockefeller* came from the *Roggenfelders* (ryefielder) of the lower Rhine. *Grosskopf* changed to *Grosscup*; *Westfall* came from *Westphal*; *Cronkhite* derived from *Krankheit*. The *Jungs* became *Youngs*.

It is surprising how many of our familiar English surnames are really Englished forms of difficult German family names. *Studebaker* is from *Studebecker*; *Pound* comes from *Pfund*; *Westinghouse* was *Wistinghausen*; *Sunday* was *Sonntag*. President *Hoover* descended from German *Hubers*; General *Pershing's* ancestors were surnamed *Pfoersching*. Difficult German names are usually mispronounced in America and this leads to alterations. The umlaut in *ä, ö* and *ü* generally disappears in this country, leaving *a, o* and *u*.

The Dutch lived together and were slow to Americanize their names. Many of their important family names survive to this day and are well known, for example, *Schuyler, Stuyvesant, Ten Eyck* and *Van Rensselaer*. The Dutch *Wittenachts* became *Whitenecks* in Kentucky. *Kuipers* became *Coopers*; *Nieuwhuis* is now *Newhouse*; *DeJong* changes to *DeYoung*. *Van Kouwenhoven*, by a series of transformations, became *Conover*. Even their given names were strictly of Dutch formation until the nineteenth century, and they thus contributed quite a few forenames.

Professor Joseph G. Fucilla, of Northwestern University, who has made an extensive study of Italian names in America, says that the principal modifications of Italian names in the new world are translations, dropping of final vowels, analogical changes, French influences, decompounded and other clipped forms and phonetic respellings. The Italians in general do not change to English names or seek deliberately to conceal the Italian character of their names.

Many of the Italian surnames that are patronymical in form have equivalent American baptismal forms and it is easy to alter the form to concur with the English name, the preposition *di, de* or the article *la* being retained, as *De George* and *La Frank*. Nicknames are translated. Sometimes the translation is far from accurate.

As Italian names are generally most easily recognized by the final vowel, it is natural to expect many to eliminate this badge of foreignness since it may be accomplished so easily. In the same way we have analogical changes when the *i*-ending of many Italian names becomes *y, e* or *ie*, terminations common in English.

The French custom of merging the name with the particles has been followed by some Italians and we have *Dadario, Dellaquila, Deluca, Dimatteo, Larocca* and the like. Sometimes this is only partially done as *De Larocca* and *De Lorto*, again comparable to French habits. In Italy the preposition or article is invariably separated from the principal part of the name.

The practice of shortening foreign names is so common in America that we need not specifically notice the Italian practice except to point out that either element may be retained. The same is true of phonetic respellings. People who are sensitive to the American mispronunciation of their surnames will make it easy for the natives to get them right.

Polish surnames in the United States present an almost overwhelming obstacle to the average American. Many are short and are often not recognized as Polish. Indeed, it takes the *-ski* termination to stamp one indelibly as a Pole in America. This ending to one's name was indicative of a certain standing in Poland, because kings often awarded honor to their subjects by granting them the right to add the suffix to their names. Many, therefore, on emigrating to America, seized the opportunity to increase their social position among their compatriots, and the termination is thus relatively more common among Poles in America than among natives of Poland. The second and third generation of Polish-Americans, not feeling such sentiment for their names, and often not recognizing the honor attached to them, wish to change to simpler cognomens.

Considering the extreme difficulty that Americans experience in handling Polish surnames compared to the names of other countries, the immigrant Pole seems to be extremely tenacious in clinging to his family patronymic, as a glance at *Who's Who in Polish America* will illustrate. Most Poles in this country, however, bear non-Polish forms of given names.

Listening to a Pole pronounce the names of his countrymen calls attention to the fact that the sounds he makes are not at all harsh, but are really suave and quite musical. The names shorten up a lot from their printed aspect; the sibilant sounds *s, z, sh* and *zh* either disappear or behave with pleasing mildness. Well, maybe one could have a nice cozy chat in a corner with Mr. Szczyszek and Mr. Gwzcarczyszyn!

Although Polish names seem to contain an imposing array of consonants, each has a certain sound singly or in groups, and when this is learned, pronunciation is not at all difficult. There are no silent letters in the Polish language. In America the Polish feminine ending *-a* is not used in surnames of women.

The Russian names received little sympathy in America even before Stalin achieved his unpopularity. Scholars have never agreed upon the transliteration of the Russian alphabet. Thus the termination of many Russian surnames in this country may be either *-offsky, -ovsky* or *-owsky*. Russians usually tend to change their names to English names which seem to resemble their native names in sound or spelling. Some translate their names, however. Feminine forms disappear.

Among English-speaking peoples the Czech names are particularly difficult. Pronunciation is choked when the eye catches some of the shorter ones which do not contain any vowels, as *Chrt* (greyhound), *Krč* (stump), *Prk* (a goatish smell), *Smrt* (death), *Srb* (Serb), *Srch* (trickle), *Srp* (sickle), *Vlk* (wolf). Czech names like *Lámar* (twisting) or *Dudek* (little bagpipe) have been mistaken for French, especially by persons whose knowledge of the latter language does not go much beyond the articles. Among the Czechs migrating to the United States were many with German names, some of them partially Bohemianized. Many Bohemians have been confused in this country with Germans and Austrians because of their names.

Nevertheless, Czechs in America stoutly resisted the pressure upon them to change their names. A generation ago they considered alteration of the family name as almost criminal. Farmers in one county refused to patronize a banker who translated *Novák* to Newer (Newman is now more commonly substituted for this name). When a Nebraska politician named *Lapáček* announced himself as *La Pache*, a storm of protest arose. Now it is not unusual for Czechs, particularly in the Middle West and South, to take a newcomer aside and urge him to get rid of a cognominal impediment such as *Drbohlav*, *Křivohlávek* or *Trpaslík*, although a few old-timers still go into paroxysms of holy wrath when a younger Czech modifies his patronymic. Some who failed to change voluntarily woke up to find their names supplanted by uncharitable American versions.

The first ones who became bold enough to change took the new form because of some real or fancied resemblance to the sound or spelling of the original: e.g., Bunch for *Bunceš* or *Bochňák*, Birch, Berry or Barry for *Bareš* or *Bureš*, Cover for *Kovář*, Roberts for *Robot* or *Robota*, Leech for *Liška*, Knott or Knox for *Hnát* and Molly or Marley for *Malý*, *Maliček* or *Moláček*.

Because Czech family names can be classified in exactly the same way as English names, the most natural alteration, when that is practicable, is translation of the substantive or adjective: *Kovář* to Smith, *Krejčí* to Taylor, *Pekař* to Baker, *Mlynář* to Miller, *Truhlář* to Carpenter, *Mráz* to Frost, *Svec* to Shoemaker, *Kopecký* to Hill, *Cerný* to Black, *Hnědý* to Brown, *Zelený* to Green and *Zlatý* to Golden. When a literal translation was not satisfactory, some adopted current American names suggested by the Bohemian appellation: *Sládek* (sweet) to *Sweetman*, *Jablečník* (*jablko*, apple) to *Appleton*, *Nádherný* (elegant) to *Prout, Bělohlávek* (a tow-headed person) to *White, Whitney, Whitman* and *Towe, Hruška* (pear) to *Pearson.*

Different individuals have proceeded along different lines, as when one *Beneš* (a shortened Czech form of Benedict) becomes Bennett while another likes Banes; one *Mužný* translates correctly to *Manly,* while another prefers the sound of *Music.* There is also the freak type like *O'Hare* for *Zajíc* (rabbit).

The change of stress in these foreign names produces odd results at times. An Eastern college professor was walking on the street in Iowa City when a stranger asked, "Where is the office of Joan of Arc?" Just as the professor was about to say that he didn't know, he looked up and saw the sign of the well-known lawyer of Bohemian orign, JNO. NOVAK. So he just said, "There," and walked on.

Monsignor J. B. Dudek in the *American Mercury* of November, 1925, tells of the Bohemian *Záchod* (whose name originally signified a bypath, then euphemistically, and now exclusively, the little outdoor building so important in more primitive times), who fondly imagined that the German, *Bachaus,* would escape the American interpretation, "backhouse." But it didn't, and a quick transition to Bakehouse failed utterly to remove certain first impressions.

The Irish who had names which could not be pronounced easily by the Americans changed them to avoid ridicule, particularly when they were names of minor clans of little fame in Erin's history. Many made guess translations into English. Some of the Irish Anglicized their names before coming to America.

The more unusual of the Irish Christian names have disappeared in this country. Thus Celtic names like *Aodh, Aneslis, Diarmuid, Fergus, Finghin* and *Morlagh* are almost unknown. Even an English form like *Bridget* is now becoming unusual. Of the many Gaelic Christian names only *Eileen, Nora, Owen, Brian,* and *Patrick* seem to have survived in general use today.

The newspapers on November 6, 1946, reported that Federal Judge Michael L. Igoe, freed an admitted car thief named Robert B. Murphy with the remark, "I hate to see a man with a good Irish name get in trouble." Perhaps there were other reasons for leniency, but the Irish name did help.

Because Scotch names are so very much like English names, the Scotchman in this country has no problem in respect to change of name. By the middle of the twelfth century, the speech in the southern counties of Scotland was like that in England in most respects.

The Norwegians, particularly the great majority who have come to this country from the rural sections of Norway, have had to alter their customs of naming. When they left Norway, they had both a farm name and a patronymic, that is, the father's given name, with the word -*son* (-*sen* in Norway) or -*datter* added. In conforming with the customs in America, the Norwegian immigrant first had to choose either the patronymic or the farm name. The Norwegians are the only group entering this country who had a free, although limited, choice of surname.

As the patronymic fitted best in American patterns, and the farm name marked him as a foreigner, the large majority chose the patronymic. Some were known to their American neighbors by their patronymic surname, but to their Norwegian neighbors by their farm name. Farm names, if taken, were sometimes altered to fit American pronunciation; the longer ones were shortened.

If the farm name was an important one in Norway, and so recognized by his Norwegian neighbors, the Norwegian would adopt the farm name as his American surname for social reasons. Some Norwegians, in order to be as much like the Yankee as possible, would take a common American surname. Because of this necessity for choice of a permanent surname in America and the several choices available, each member of a family might take a different surname. Some of the names which implied a low social position were discarded as undesirable. For that reason they might be used by the man's Norwegian neighbors as nicknames. Since Norwegian farms were generally given descriptive names, the farm name often described the kind of farm from which the immigrant came. Thus, *Bakke* was a hill, *Berge*, a rocky mountain, and *Flaam*, a small flat piece of land on a mountainside.

The invariable Americanization of Norwegian names occurred in this country, and *Fjeld* became *Field*, *Kvaale* became *Qualley*, *Kvammen* became *Quammen*, *Sjautveit* became *Shutvedt*, *Skjelstad* became *Shelstad*, *Tveten* became *Tweeten* and *Ygre*, *Egre*.

The Swedish surnames, like the Danish and Norwegian, have become so firmly established in this country that they have lost any aspect of "foreignness," and name changes among Swedes are infrequent, although some were changed because they were difficult to American vocal organs, as *Sjögren* which became *Shogren*, *Schugren*, *Segren* or *Seagren*. The combination with *j* sometimes causes trouble, as in *Hjelm* and *Kjellstrand*. The *Hjelms* solved the difficulty by dropping the offensive letter to become *Helm* while the *Kjellstrands* changed to the phonetic *Chilstrand*. In a similar manner the *ki* names become *chi*.

The poetic Swedish custom of making surnames out of natural objects has a parallel only among the Jews in Eastern Europe. The names often become incongruous looking when they are translated, as when *Sjöstrand* becomes *Seashore* or *Fagerdahl* becomes *Fairvalley*. Usually this type of name is only half translated as when *Stenberg* becomes *Stoneberg* or *Östlund* becomes *Eastlund*. The umlaut is generally dropped from the *o*. Swedish-Americans often change the spelling to the English sound rather than translate, as when *Ljung* (heather) and its combinations *Ljungberg, Ljungdahl, Ljunggren,* etc., become *Young, Youngberg, Youngdahl* and *Younggren*. Or *gren*, meaning "bough" or "branch" becomes "grain" or "green" and *blad* (leaf) becomes "blade." *Qvist* (twig) generally becomes *quist* in this country; in the old country it may be either of these or *kvist*.

Some Swedes in this country, when in need of a surname, have created one by adding *-ing* to the name of their birthplace, as *Bergling, Cassling, Widing, Nordling, Glemming, Hemming* and *Erling*. An interesting one is the rather common *Fremling* (stranger). Perhaps the distracted immigrant became so accustomed to introducing himself, *Jag är en fremling* (I am a stranger), that finally with grim humor he used the word as a surname.

Next, some attention might be given to the priest names and soldier names which are important among Swedes in America. The priest names are easily recognized by the terminations *-us* and *-ander*, for example, *Geselius, Marelius, Ringius, Renius, Tunelius* and *Bolander, Neander, Fornander, Rosander*. Although not all with priest's names are or were clergymen, such names have a class distinction and a Swede with a priest name does not often change it. As more fully explained in the chapter on "Names in Other Countries," the soldier's names are those conferred by the military during the man's conscription period in the Swedish army and are often warlike, as *Stark* (strong), *Modig* (brave) and *Rask* (daring).

The reader may note that the patronymic names ending in *-son*, thought to be so popular among the Swedes, are not so universal as popular jokes would have one believe. The universal change of these names in this country is the dropping of the possessive *s* as when *Larsson* becomes *Larson*. *Johnson* is not a Swedish name, but the American form of the Swedish *Jansson*, and *Johansson*.

Among the Finnish-Americans, business and professional men have altered their names and some few have abandoned them entirely. The situation has been different among those Finnish immigrants whose work has not brought them into much close contact with others. The majority of Finns in America have steadfastly resisted all temptations to modify their names. This is due to the strong national feeling among the New World Finns, and their separate churches, fraternal lodges and brotherhoods have contributed to their success in retaining their original family patronymics.

Most of those who did change accomplished it by simply clipping either a prefix or a suffix, thus retaining their unmistakable Finnish identity; for example, *Kangasniemi* became *Kangas* or *Niemi*. Some changed the spelling to correspond with the pronunciation, as when *Penttinen* became *Bentinen*. Many Finns bore Swedish or Norwegian patronymics and these found the problem much simpler; some assumed these Scandinavian names after arriving in this country, *Johnson* being by far the most popular.

Finns' family names are outstanding in America because of their musical pronunciations produced by accenting the first and last syllables of three part names, the chief stress being on the first syllable. Names like *Eckonen, Heikkinen, Hokkanen, Lamminen, Nieminen, Seppänen* and *Westola* trickle from the tongue in a pleasing manner.

Spanish and Mexican names are found mostly among the Spanish-speaking peoples in the Southwest. Also there are numerous Mexican workers living in the large cities. Many illiterate Mexicans work on the railroad right-of-ways. Little effort is made to get their names straight. The Mexican given names are the Spanish forms of the day-saints or events in the Catholic ecclesiastical calendar.

Among Spanish-speaking peoples the use of the colloquial, or nickname, form of the baptismal name is common. As these colloquial forms vary greatly they are a puzzle to most Americans. For example, to take a very popular Christian name, the Spanish-Mexican form of *Joseph* is *José*; the more important colloquial and diminutive forms are *Che, Chepe, Chepito, Josecito, Joseito, Pepe, Pepillo* and *Pepito.*

Other familiar forms are quite as misleading. *Pocorro* is a pet form of *Francisco,* but there are also *Chico, Chito, Curro, Frasco, Paco, Pancho, Paquito* and *Quico,* among others. Girls named *Francisca* would have the same familiar forms except that they would terminate in *a* instead of *o*. *Concepción* may be either a boys' or a girls' name. For a boy the pet form would be *Chon,* but for girls *Chona, Chonita, Choncha, Chonchita, Cota* or *Cotita* would be appropriate.

Spanish surnames in America are often recognized by the *y* connecting two names and the frequent use of the particle *de*. The more popular Spanish surnames like *Fernandez, Garcia, Gomez, Lopez* and *Ruiz* tend to preserve their forms in America. Others suffer slight modification. *Señor* is equivalent to the English *Mister*. *Don* connotes more dignity and is similar to the English *Sir*. *Don* is only used preceding a forename and thus sometimes aids in distinguishing the baptismal name.

Among the uneducated French in the lower Mississippi valley the old French family names are characterized by a fine disregard for spelling. For instance the name *Kiercereau* is also found spelled *Kiercerau, Kiersereau, Kersereau, Kesserau, Kiergereau, Kiergereaux, Kiergero, Quiercero, Tiercero* and in a host of other ways. Difficulties in pronunciation increase the uncertain orthographies.

Common among the French is the use of *dit* names, that is, additional surnames or nicknames previously applied to grandparents or other remote ancestors, preceded by the word *dit* which may be translated, "called." Dropping the *dit* adds confusion. Sometimes the *dit* name was reversed, as when we discover that Joseph *Michel dit Taillon* and Joseph *Taillon dit Michel* represent the same man. Either surname or both, with or without *dit*, are employed in a casual manner which makes identity difficult. Other *dit* names originated by adding place names, nicknames or official designations. *Cadet* is a familiar nickname for a younger son.

French-Canadians who settled in the New England states saw their surnames undergo weird transformations. Some were translated literally, as when *Boisvert* became *Greenwood* and *Lapierre, Stone*. Others, by reason of pronunciation, where strangely altered and *Lavoie* became *Lovewear*, and *Gauthier* changed into *Gochey*. After a generation or two the family began to spell its name as the town clerks did when making out the tax bills.

The Greek surnames were often quite lengthy and generally had to be shortened to fit American efficiency. Names like *Pappadakis, Pappachristides* and *Pappadimitracoupoulos* became *Pappas*. Others like *Constantinopoulos, Gerasimopoulos* and *Panagiotopoulos* were abbreviated to the terminal *Poulos*. Many other Greek names, not so difficult, receive slighter alterations in the land of the free.

The names of the minor nationalities such as the Hungarians, Armenians, Syrians, Lithuanians, Turks and Portuguese have modified their more difficult patronymics like the others. They have translated them, transliterated them, abbreviated them, and simplified the spelling, or have gritted their teeth and have stubbornly refused to part with or alter a single consonant.

While the Chinese in the United States have only a few different family names, the difficulty of phonetically representing them by English spelling produces many variants. The same name may be represented as *Heu, Hew* and *Hiu.* In this country the Chinese, while quick to adopt American given names, retain their family or clan names. Many, however, change the order of their names, putting their American forename ahead of their surname. Some Chinese Anglicize their surnames by a slight variation in spelling, as when *Yong* becomes *Young.*

The Japanese in America always place their surnames last. Because they are not too difficult to pronounce, the Jap is not tempted to change his name. Unlike European nationals, he cannot change his name and become an American—his yellow skin and oriental features keep him apart from Americans so nothing is gained by an American surname. Few Japs have therefore tried to English their names.

The Jap, who is so courteous and polite in little matters, recoils from the brutal use of nicknames. With his usual stress on formality and ceremony he would not consider using given names except in the intimacy of the family. American-born generations of Japanese seem to prefer American first names, but they seldom Americanize their family names.

Even English names have undergone a characteristic change in the United States and we have forms of English names not found in England. Many familiar English names are just Anglicized forms of Norman-French names. *Sidney* is a contraction of *St. Denis; Bridgewater* is a neat pronunciation of *Burgh de Walter.* Americans are apt to add *-s* to the short English surnames making them *Woods, Brooks, Johns* and the like. The territorial form of identification seen in *Charles Carroll of Carrollton* and *John Randolph of Roanoke* has not taken root in America.

Rare in America, but not uncommon in England, are surnames like *ffolliott* and *ffoulkes.* In the manuscripts of the preprinting era two small *f's* were sometimes used for a capital *F. Ffolliott* and *Ffoulkes* are commonly observed, but are incorrect.

There are undoubtedly almost as many different English names in the United States as in England (if not more) because the English emigrants were individualists and dissenters in nomenclature as in religion. It was not until after many were already here that the spelling of names became more fixed. Few settlers were of noble families so there was little prejudice against altering names. Every racial group that has come to this country has adopted English-sounding names.

Of all the immigrant peoples in the United States the Jews seem to be most willing to obtain what benefits they can by change of name. Whereas the usual foreigner attempts to eliminate the disadvantage of strangeness, the Jew, with one stroke, seeks to get rid of both foreignness and Jewishness. Again, Jews have less sentimental attachment for their surnames because they adopted them only at the end of the eighteenth, or at the beginning of the nineteenth century, and then sometimes only under compulsion.

In altering their names the Jews normally do not change their names outright but merely change them slightly both in spelling and sound to conceal the old Jewish names. This they regard as taking a "derivative" of the old Jewish surname. Thus *Asher* shades into *Archer* and *Ansell*. *David* becomes *Davis, Davison, Davies* or *Davidson*. *Isaac* metamorphoses into *Sachs, Saxe, Sace* or *Seckel*. *Jacob* easily turns into *Jackson* along with *Jonah* into *Jones*. *Levi* is touched up into *Lewis, Leopold* or *Low*. *Moses* transforms into *Moritz* or *Mortimer*. *Solomon* easily slides into *Salmon* or *Sloman*. Mr. *Cohen*, like Mr. *Smith*, has other reasons for his change and he converts into *Coen, Cohane, Cohn, Coles, Conn, Cowan, Coyne, Kahn, Kohn, Kohan* and many others, some going so far afield as to transmogrify into *Crane* and *Quinn*.

Members of the same family were not always careful to be uniform in the alteration of their surname. The old story is to the effect that the loving sons of Isadore Cohen erected a tombstone to his memory. They appended their names for all to read: Irving *Cahn*, John *Coles*, Sidney *Cowan*, Max *Kane*, and Samuel *Quesne*.

More Jews in America have German Jewish names than are warranted by the number of Jews who came from Germany. In the nineteenth century the German Jew was the aristocrat of Jewry, and consequently many newly arrived Jews from Russia, Poland, and the Slavic countries in general, took German names here. Immigrants of all nationalities, upon coming to democratic America, where everyone is the equal of everyone else, took surnames, because of a supposed aristocratic tinge, in an effort to lift themselves a step above their equals.

The Jews have adopted English forenames in great numbers and have dropped their Old Testament given names. There is in America a recognized custom of ancestral loyalty for Jews to take the first letter of a deceased parent's, or grandparent's name and give the child an English name beginning with the same letter. Thus there are numerous *Irvings* for *Isaac*, *Raes* for *Rebecca* and *Rachel; Moses* is represented in *Morris* and *Max*.

As some of these English forenames acquire a Jewish stamp by reason of excessive use, they are abandoned for more Anglo-Saxon-sounding names. Dr. A. A. Roback published a description of this practice entitled, "Sarah to Sylvia to Shirley."

Irving, Max, Milton, Stanley, Sidney and *Monroe*, were, for a generation, distinctly Jewish names. Masculine names like *Harry, Herman, Jack, Samuel,* and *Sol,* once so popular, are rare for babies today. *Beatrice, Dorothy, Florence, Helen, Lillian, Lucille, Ruth* and *Shirley* have lost much of their popularity among present-day Jewish babies. Taking the place of these names for boys are *Alan, Andrew, Bruce, James, Jay, Jeffrey, Kenneth, Mark, Michael, Richard, Robert* and *Stephen;* and for girls they are *Ann, Barbara, Beth, Carol, Ellen, Gail, Jane, Joan, Judith, Linda, Lynn, Nancy, Sue* and *Susan.* The new popular names in use by Jews today in America are not distinguishable from those of the rest of the population.

The Sephardic Jews preserved their Old Testament given names much more faithfully than the Ashkenazi. The latter would not think of doing the slightest thing to conceal their Jewishness, but do not hesitate to select thoroughly American forenames for their children. Many American Jews have selected first names without regard to their Christian meanings or traditions. Popular Jewish forenames are *Natalie* meaning "birthday (of Christ)" and *Dolores* meaning "sorrow (of the mother of Jesus)." *Noel* meaning "Christmas" is not unknown for Jewish boys. Names of Christian saints are common among our Jewish brethren. *Paul* and *Paula* are as frequently found among Jews as among Christians.

The Negroes, now thirteen million strong, are the largest group who have acquired their present names in this country. Although they have borrowed them from the white population, their names, taken as a group, have acquired a folk flavor that sets them apart in the eyes and ears of the attentive observer.

When Negro slaves were brought over from Africa they, of course, had names in their native tribes, but very few kept these names in America. The slaves were at first under the absolute control of the whites, who were not at all familiar with, or sympathetic to, the native culture of the black men. No effort was made to learn the names they used in Africa and names were assigned arbitrarily directly from the white man's civilization. To the early slave traders few were distinguished by individual names but were regarded simply as merchandise en masse in much the same way as the Western cattle raiser regards his herd. Thus, in 1675 a slave ship's journal might record that, "a neaggerman dep'ted this life whoe died suddenly," or a notice in New England might announce "a very likely negro man" for sale. Similarly, animals or birds in a pet shop seldom have names.

When one acquires a pet, or a grain farmer buys a cow, the first thought is to give the animal a name, and this is true even though only one pet is owned or the farmer keeps only one cow for milk production. The master who purchased a black man, particularly if the slave was to be used as a domestic, immediately gave him or her a name of his own choosing without inquiry as to the black's wishes. Thus few Negroes kept their African names. Where many slaves were purchased for use in the fields, the busy plantation owner or overseer did not bother to name them, and some of them kept their native names or else acquired new names among their fellow laborers.

Some of the African names persisted among the blacks in Jamaica. The native names that continued in use among the early slaves were not too difficult to recognize, although it is impossible to be certain in all cases because of their alteration and variation in this country, and due also to the fact that when they were written it was done either by a white man who had little or no knowledge of the African tongues, or by a very poorly educated black. Many odd appellations with the initials B, C, O or Q are probably of African origin, such as *Bamba, Bartee, Bayna, Bilah, Bohum, Cooba, Cubah, Cudjo, Cumba, Curiarah, Ocra, Ocraque, Ocrasan, Ocreka, Oessah, Quaco, Quamana, Quashe, Quomana* and *Quoney*.

When the white owner gave names to his slaves, he did it for a practical reason and not to bestow an element of personal importance. The name applied did not evidence a sense of dignity or equality, and did not show nearly so much care as is given in selecting a name for a racehorse. Quaint slave names, like *Bob Robert, Moses Carr the Prophet, Prophet Christian, Pirree Sylvanee Poke,* and *Apple White Scarlet,* betray, perhaps, the combined efforts of master and slave community. After emancipation they began to breathe a freedom of fancy and a grasping for plenty to alleviate quickly a remembered mental starvation; and such elegant and awe-inspiring names as *Marthine Nilline Feradine Hygine Corney White* and *Carter Avery John Wesley Mumford Jones* resulted.

Curious among the Negroes is the practice, occasionally found, of giving a story name. There was *George Solomon King Dick Lick A Loon Half At Log Cabin I Been Dar Ole Verginny Nigger Lie By De Fire Eat Parch Corn And Potatoes Ana Send De Dogs Ter De Simmon Tree And Have Guards After Dem Ter See Dat Dee Do Go*, the full name of an old Negro of Hale County, Alabama. Then there is *Frank Harrison President Of This United States Eats His 'Lasses Candy And Swings On Every Gate Williams*, of Martin County, North Carolina. In High Point, in the same state, lives *George Washington American Life Ready To Fight Come Brave Boys The British Are About To Land Taylor*. In Alabama a slave girl was named *Henry Ritter Ema Ritter Dema Ritter Sweet Potatoe Creamatarter Caroline Bostwick*, perhaps a desire to honor the whole Ritter family. Her surname was *Catten*.

Not exactly a story, but more a group of maxims and pious hopes, was the full name of the colored tenant farmer whose grandfather named him *Daniel's Wisdom May I Know, Stephen's Faith and Spirit Choose, John's Divine Communion Seal, Moses' Meekness, Joshua's Zeal, Win the Day and Conquer All Murphy*. He just called himself *Daniel Murphy* and lived quietly in Van Alstyne, Texas, until his death in 1949 at the age of sixty-six. When black Americans reach to select an unusual name, they are apt to become really fantastic.

In given names, particularly those of girls, the Negro reveals some of his primitive traits, such as his deeply religious nature, his love of ornamentation and ostentation, and his ear for the rhythmic and euphonious. A Negro girl was *Pism C*, named for the One-Hundredth Psalm. A collection of bizarre Negro given names includes *Commercial Appeal* (a Memphis newspaper), *Department of the Potomac, Oleomargarine, Pleasant Smiley, Prince of Wales, Superior Circulator* (father a porter in a shop dealing in stoves of that name), *De Word O'God* and *Sunday Morning*. In Athens, Georgia, when the census taker called in 1930 soon after the arrival of the stork, the child was christened *Census Tooken*. H. L. Mencken is of the opinion that most of the odd Negro names are invented by sportive whites and accepted to gain attention and favor. That some queer Negro names were so applied is not open to question. But it is unlikely that this is an explanation of a substantial number of them because, if it were true, Negro names would not fall into the pattern they do, as discussed here.

For Christian names the Negroes have chosen some of the oddest, gaudiest, most humorous, most picturesque, and sometimes most unaccountable, appellations. With their desire for pomp, they have appropriated all the gem names, as *Emerald, Garnet, Opal, Pearl, Ruby* and *Sapphire.*

Many of the men have received Scriptural names, but not the same style of common Bible names that are predominant among the whites. Bible characters have been commemorated by *King Solomon, Virgin Mary, Queen Esther, Angel Ann.* Biblical language has provided some names, as *Armor, Archangel, I Will Arise and Go Unto My Father, Pisalem Civ* (which, being interpreted, is Psalm CIV).

Negroes sometimes are attracted by the sound of medical terms. Mr. and Mrs. Emsy Jackson, of Pauls Valley, Oklahoma, named two sons *Tonsilitis* and *Meningitis,* and a daughter *Appendicitis.* Other forenames direct from the hospital, or selected with the aid of mischievous internes, are *Carcinoma, Iodine, Diphtheria* and even *Vagina.*

There is the story about the colored baby delivered in a hospital, who was brought home with a tag notation on its wrist, which the parents accepted as its fancy hospital name—*Positive Wassermann.* Patent medicines produce *Sal Hepatica* and *Peruna.* Other words have been used as *Vanilla, Elevator, Dill Pickle, Sausage* and *Million Dollar.* Vegetables have been employed, as *Butterbean, Tater, Turnip,* Liza *Cucumber* and *Goobey* (probably from goober). Institutions and societies have been used: *League of Nations, Methodist Conference South, Eastern Star, Blue Lodge, State Normal And Industrial College,* the latter called *Snic* for short. More than the whites the Negroes have used geographical names, and we find *America, Ohio, Florida* and *Mississippi.*

A present-day black in the South sports the appellation, *George Washington Lied.* Three children in a colored family were *Girlie, Little Brother* and *Baby,* which calls attention to parents just too lazy to think of a name to bestow. Sometimes a poor Negro family in the South may neglect entirely the giving of a name to a new-born infant, and some Negro boys thus grow to manhood with only the praenomen of *Son.*

Of course many humorous stories are told about fantastic Negro names. There is the one about colored children who were playing;

one was repeatedly called " 'Lectricity." Finally an onlooker asked if that were part of the game.

"No, suh, dat's mah name."

"How did you ever get a name like that?"

"Well, suh," was the answer, "my mammy's called Dinah and my pappy is Mose and dynamos sho make 'lectricity."

Our colored brethren have not hesitated to indicate the time or place of birth, as *Tiny New Year, January, Easter, Christmas* and *Sunday May.* A posthumous child named *Lucy Never Seen Joe* will not forget her father's name. Following the same idea, that their father never saw them, twins were named *Never* and *Seed 'Em.*

The Negroes received various odd names because the mother or some member of the family "seed it and thought hit a purty name." *Petty Larcény* (accent on the penult) was born while his father was doing time for that offense. *Mississippi Flood* and *Trouble* commemorate outside events. Sly sex humor account for such appellations as *Watermelon Patch* (where an illegitimate was begotten), *Haphazard, Loveless, Pleasant Time, Rascal, Evil, Lucky Blunder,* and *Lena Ginster.*

Names of famous people are especially favored by blacks, with the emphasis on Washington and Lincoln. The names of local dignitaries were often adopted in lively expectation of pecuniary appreciation. Colored people have been known to give their children many names, each after a different white person, in the hope of receiving a special gift from each person so honored. Twins in South Carolina were named *Mister Will* and *Mister John,* the baptismal *Mister* being used out of respect for their two white namesakes.

Followers of Father Divine, the Negro "god" of New York, took "heavenly" names such as *Morning Glory, Wonderful Meekness, Faithful, Newborn Lamb, Virgin Wise, Peaceful Smile* and *Sundial Love.* Although members of the cult brought suit, the New York court would not allow them to vote under their religious names. The Federal Government graciously allowed them to buy bonds in their heavenly names though.

Ignorant whites sometimes bestow outlandish names on their offspring, so that peculiar given names from the South do not always stamp one as having a dark skin. Free Negroes of today have a higher proportion of unusual or outstanding names than slaves did, and Professor Puckett, in an article in *The Journal of Negro History,* concludes that this tendency is increasing.

Among Negroes of this generation the most popular middle names are *Mae, Belle* and *Lee.* Also popular in the South as middle names are *Lou, Jo* and *Jean.* Sometimes feminine middle names are given to boys. Frank, blunt descriptive nicknames are often applied by blacks among themselves. A few examples are *Frog, Mush, Preacher, Cat-fish, Old Blue* and *Coon.*

It is, perhaps, not surprising to note that the two names, *Sambo* and *Rastus,* so popular in Negro minstrels to designate the typical black, are actually unknown as Negro Christian names today. *Dinah* and *Chloe* are comparatively rare among girls now. Among present day Negroes *Willie* is a popular Christian name for both sexes, being only slightly more common for boys than for girls. With colored girls the diminutive forms ending in *-ie* are very popular. Thus we find that names like *Annie, Carrie, Mattie, Bessie, Jessie, Minnie, Fannie, Lillie, Mamie* and *Maggie* are common for Negro girls.

While many odd names of Negroes have been cited, it must not be supposed that a substantial number of blacks in any given locality have unusual names. The given names that are most popular among Negroes are different from those among whites. Thus, according to research by Professor Newbell N. Puckett, the most common Negro male names are *James, William, John, Robert* and *Charles,* in that order. Among women the sequence is *Mary, Annie, Ruth, Helen* and *Dorothy.* Among Negro slaves the order for men was *John, Henry, George, Sam* and *Jim,* and for females, *Mary, Maria, Nancy, Lucy* and *Sarah.*

With slaves in this country a large proportion had short familiar names like *Jack, Tom, Joe, Bob, Dick, Ben, Ned* and the like. Many others had surnames like *Washington, Nelson, Anderson* and *Green* as given names. Biblical names were as common among slaves as among whites before the Civil War. Classical names such as *Caesar, Cato* and *Pompey* were frequently given to slaves, although probably not so often as many writers on plantation life would have us think. The important trend from the male slave appellations of yesteryear to the Negro names of today is a shift from the short pet, Biblical and classical names to the current popular English names. Louisiana Negroes are likely to have French or Spanish names. The most popular slave names of girls, even when they are common English names, are generally unusual as given names among Negro girls of our day.

This is also true of surnames. The most popular Negro surname is *Johnson,* with *Brown* next, followed by *Smith* and *Jones.* The popular

English surnames are much more common numerically among the Negroes than the incidence of such names in the South among the whites would lead one to expect. Washington occupies a much higher numerical position with Negroes than it does with whites. When one considers that the Negro community has had to acquire the greater proportion of its family names in a relatively few years, it is remarkable what a neat job has been done.

Slaves were often given additional names, particularly on the larger plantations, when it became necessary to distinguish one from another. When this happened, the addition of adjectives like *Big, Little, Old, Young* and *Granny* served the purpose. In divers cases other descriptive terms were applied exactly in the same manner as when our ancestors in England, having only one name, needed some descriptive term to identify them, which term eventually became a hereditary family name. During slave days the surname of the master was often applied to the slave. After the Civil War some continued with this surname so acquired, while others chose family names which evoked more pleasant memories.

Many Negroes, through ignorance or lack of need, neglected to acquire surnames after they were first freed. The family organization was not strong and the society tended to be matriarchal, that is, ruled by the women. Names were transmitted in the female line almost as much as in the male. Acquisition of family names proceeded slowly. During the First World War the demand for laborers was great and the Negroes moved North and went to work. A surname then became a necessity and the common ones were quickly adopted. They were easily spelled and if the worker could pronounce them, the time clerk did not have to inquire how they were spelled. Consequently Negro surnames have simple spellings; there is *Brooks* not *Brookes*, *Smith* not *Smythe* and *White* not *Whyte*, although they do often add a final *e* to names like *Greene, Clarke* and *Cooke*. New place-names or new occupations were not converted into appellations. Only long established surnames were used; the Christian name of the father was not converted into a surname.

The patronymical type of surname enjoyed the greatest favor with the laboring black man. *Johnson, Williams, Harris, Jackson, Jefferson, Jones, James, Thompson, Thomas, Davis, Robinson* are popular with them.

Next to the Negro, the largest group that has received names in the United States is the American Indian, although Indian names are still in a state of confusion. While each particular tribe or clan may have its own minor customs in respect to names, the Indians on this continent exhibit a striking uniformity in the meaning of their names and their use of them. All Indian personal names have definite meanings.

In many tribes the Indians often called their children by the following cardinal number names until circumstance or character suggested another name:

	Son	*Daughter*
First	Chaské	Wenonah
Second	Haparm	Harpen
Third	Ha-pe-dah	Harpstenah
Fourth	Chatun	Waska
Fifth	Harka	We-harka

Thus Longfellow writes of the mother of Hiawatha:

> Fair Nokomis bore a daughter
> And she called her name Wenonah,
> As the first-born of her daughters.
> —*Hiawatha*, iii, 23.

In some tribes the son is not so addressed if there was a daughter first, and the daughter is not so named if there was a son born first. For the first-born girl the form is sometimes *Winona*. The little girl may be called by that name for some months and then receive another name. The name *Winona* implies much of honor. If the maiden proves worthy, the name of the "First-born" may be resumed later.

When a child is born among the Shawnee Indians, two "name-givers," old and wise members of the tribe, pray and ponder all night on the name to be given, and then offer two names. With the Shawnees naming is a serious matter; the child should receive one that has never been used before. The parents finally select one of the two names suggested. Presents are generally given to the name-givers, but that it not obligatory.

Among other names the Indians have (a) totem, dream or mysterious names, (b) war or bravery names, and (c) names founded on man's past history, or past or present tribal customs.

In many tribes the Indian boy takes a new, adult name at puberty. He is sent to sleep in a secluded spot, to dream of an animal. In the morning, when he reports the visiting animal, he is named after it. Naturally the boy, expecting to dream of an animal does so. Unconsciously there is under the circumstances some selection; it would hardly do to dream of a mouse or a polecat. If the young Indian brave has thought seriously of the proper animals just before dozing off, he will likely see them in his slumber.

Names of Indians may be misunderstood even when correctly translated. For example *Stinking Saddle Blanket* might be regarded as an opprobrious name by white men who did not know that it was a subtle compliment to a chief who was on the warpath so much that he had no time to take off his saddle blanket. Incorrect translations are common. The fighter who bore the proud Indian name, *Young Man Whose Very Horses Are Feared*, through a bad translation, became *Young Man Afraid of His Horses*.

Most tribes of Indians allow their members to change their names at the critical epochs of life, such as puberty, first war expedition, first enemy killed, marriage; or after some notable feat, or even accident; elevation to the chieftainship; or upon retirement from active life. The latter event might mark the adoption of the name of the warrior's son. A new name might be given if the old one was unsuccessful, i.e., the bearer was sickly or otherwise unfortunate. In some groups the old name must be psychologically and symbolically discarded before the new name can be assumed.

Crazy Bull, the Sioux warrior, received his cognomen after a successful fight with a crazed buffalo bull. Afterward, being angry because his companions had not come to his aid, he brandished his gun and threatened them. They said that the spirit of the bull had passed into him. The girl known as *The-One-Who-Was-Left-Alone* owed her picturesque appellation to the fact that when she was only a few weeks old, an enemy tribe attacked her camp and killed both parents.

When two Navajo women quarreled at a spring over water, and the woman who owned the land refused to let the other take water, the affronted one hid near the water and when the owner appeared tossed a mangy dog into the pool. As a result of the fracas the one who threw the dog in became *Dog-In-The-Spring*, and the other, *Stingy-With-Water*. A Navajo boy became known as *Floury Flashlight*, after the flashlight he had stolen was found hidden in a sack of flour. The first daughter in a family to marry is honored by having her husband known to all the tribe as her father's son-in-law. When *Worthless-One-Eyed-Water* married the young Indian maiden, daughter of *Dirtywater*, he became *Worthless-Dirtywater's-Son-In-Law*. It is easy to see why there is very little duplication of names among Indians.

Most Indian names are symbolic. Thus *Tatiyopa* means "her door," and implies that the bearer's door was always open and she was hospitable. Names of the Red Man have been called picture names. There are really no set rules in respect to them. Indian names usually convey an idea of awe, grandeur, courage, swiftness or beauty.

Among the Cocopa Indians (of the southern section of the Colorado River delta) it was believed that originally the Creator bestowed upon each male ancestor a gens name. The women of a Cocopa tribe were given a single name by the Creator, it was thought, at the time the gens name is given.

It is among the Indians of the Pacific Northwest that the interest in names is most pronounced. Not only do their names possess great significance, as in other Indian tribes, but they also have social and financial implications. Many carry legendary and historical significance when they refer to a man's remote ancestor. When an heir inherits property of a relative, he provides several feasts, during one of which he assumes the hereditary name of the relative.

With the Kwakiutl Indians a boy is first given the name of the place where he is born as a personal name. When about a year old he receives a second name. At about the age of ten or twelve he obtains a third name. When he is about to take this name, he must borrow blankets which must be returned twice over after a year's time. If one has poor credit he may even pledge his name for a year, and during that period he must not use the name at all. For such a loan he may have to return three times as many blankets as he received if he wants to redeem his name.

In these tribes of the Northwest coast the people are divided into three classes: nobles, common people and slaves. The personal names borne by the nobles are their certificate of nobility and their property mark. For example, some of their names referring to property, when translated, are *Whose-Body-Is-All-Wealth, Too-Rich, About-Whose-Property-People-Talk, From Whom-Presents-Are-Expected* and *Throwing-Away-Property*. By their names they are able to flaunt their wealth before all, and can parade their property without fear of losing it.

The Kwakiutl Indians believe that if one of their number kills another, either in war or through just plain murder, he is entitled to the victim's name. In this manner names have spread from one tribe to another.

Some Indians had a custom of exchanging names as an expression of amity. In the early days of Pennsylvania, legend says that an Indian chief named *Win-go-hocking* greatly admired James Logan, Secretary to William Penn, and proposed that they exchange names. Not wishing to be known as Mr. *Wingohocking*, Logan was embarrassed. Then he had an inspiration, saying to the chief, "Thou mayst take my name, and I will give thy name to this beautiful stream running at our feet, which will flow on when I am dead, and cause thy name to be remembered forever." This may be pure romance because, while a creek in Germantown is still called Wingohocking, authorities translate the Indian word to mean, "favorite spot for planting."

Every list of Indian names presents a surprising European influence. An explanation of this is that some Indians were the offspring of early white adventurers who mated with Indian women. If the white man still tarried, the baby would be given a European forename. The mother might have something to say about the matter and the child might be given a combination, such as *Jenny Little Bear*.

While the white men gave their own names to the Indians, the practice was sometimes just reversed. They call the whites by some remarkable quality which they have observed in them. Upon learning the meaning of William Penn's surname, the Indians translated it into their own language by *Miquon*, which means a feather or quill. The Iroquois called him *Onas*, which, in their tongue, means the same thing. Navajo Indians were especially quick to apply names to the whites with whom they came in contact. Thus they dubbed the Indian Service personnel with such nicknames as *Yellow Fat Boy, Red Hairy Neck, Nose With Wart* and *Slow With Gas*, the latter being a paleface who was unusually careful in driving his car.

The acquisition of surnames by the American Indian arose from a steadily increasing contact with the white man's culture. New social and economic demands on the Indian forced him to adopt the white man's kind of surname. Some acquired them through intermarriage with the whites. Many took surnames when they went to work for the white man. When a brave commenced to work in a lumber camp, the company timekeeper demanded a first and last name for his records, and required that it be in English because of the difficulty of writing Indian names. If they could not produce English names, they were often arbitrarily assigned names on the spur of the moment.

That many translated their original Indian name to form their "white man's name" is evidenced by the common surnames of animals or birds, as *Crow, Frog, Wolf, Elk* and *Kingfisher,* which are borne by the Indians. To the surname thus formed was prefixed a common English forename. Some used the nickname by which they were known among the whites to form a surname. The Chippewa Indian, *Billy Boy* became "Billy Billyboy." More correct names were acquired at the Government boarding schools for Indians and at the local missions. A few acquired surnames as soldiers in the Civil War.

In the early years of the twentieth century President Theodore Roosevelt wished to help the Indians. Many lived in utter poverty on their reservations. Advisers told the President that their condition would be ameliorated if they were all assigned names, using our system of nomenclature, so that relationship could be traced and property and lands could be inherited in the family. It was suggested that no English name be arbitrarily given, but such as were well established might be retained if the bearer so desired.

Because the Indians were suspicious of the white man's motives and would have refused to accept names from the regular Indian Government agents, Mr. Roosevelt, in 1903, commissioned Dr. Charles Alexander Eastman, the full-blooded Sioux Indian who had married the poet, Elaine Goodale, to rename each individual on the reservations of the Sioux Nation. The Indian Service previously had been generally indifferent to the Indian name problem.

Dr. Eastman took his work seriously, and, over a period of several years, visited each branch agency or tribe. Upon arrival he caused the Indians to be called together and explained to them that the "Great Father" at Washington had decided to give them all new names and explained the reasons. Many were distrustful but he was able to relieve the anxiety of most of them and induce them to accept a name similar to the ones used by the white man. Elsewhere, Indians fought stubbornly against adoption of the white man's system of nomenclature.

The name-giver recognized the beauty of many of the Indian names and decided to keep as much of the Indian flavor as possible. When the Indian's name was not too long and could be consolidated into a single word capable of pleasing and ready pronunciation in English, he retained the original. For example, *Matoska* (White Bear) could be handled by the whites and consequently the name was retained in the original. Not so attractive in the Sioux tongue was High Eagle; so he gave that man the family name of *Higheagle*. It is readily perceived that the Sioux woman named *Tateyohnakewastewin* had an appellation that did not slip readily from the tongue of the average white man. The name meant "she who has a beautiful home," so she became *Goodhouse*. *Rotten Pumpkin*, not having any great amount of charm, was rechristened Robert *Pumpian*.

Elsewhere, Indians changed their names to the white man's system. *Bob-tailed Coyote*, with his tongue in his cheek, became the sleek Mr. *Robert T. Wolf*. Others received names through ignorance. Once when an Indian truant officer brought a small Indian boy to school, he was asked the boy's name. When he answered, "Des-to-dah" the boy was given the Christian name of Max and called Max *Destodah*. Later it turned out that *des-to-dah* was the Indian for "don't know," the officer having merely replied that he was ignorant of the boy's name.

Many Indians were given English forenames and then their children were named after them. The son of *Squally Jim* became *George James*. Others have poetical names of great beauty—*West Wind, Laughing Water, Little Moon, White Butterfly, Swift Bird, Fire Thunder, Cloud Chief* and *Lone Hill*.

Examination of large numbers of Indian names will disclose that generally they are intended to describe traits of character. These names contain the element of frankness rather than that of compliment. Tribal members are *Hard Heart, Bad Old Woman, Slow Woman, Full Stomach, Looks and Kills, Respects Nothing*. An old man was called *Foolish Woman*. Others are *Cherry Eye, Scabby Face* and *Crooked Leg*. Many contain names of animals as *Lone Dog, Fast Horse* and *Handsome Elk*. In general, the fiercer birds and beasts are preferred by the braves. One could go on for page after page, but these examples will suffice to illustrate the important characteristics of Indian personal nomenclature.

While we were engaged in World War II, the joke about Indian names was sometimes heard: Red Eagle, the Indian chieftain, introduced his family to his paleface visitor, "This is my son, Fighting Bird, and here," he added, "is my grandson, P-38." While this is a mere witticism, it well illustrates the evolution of names of Indians among the white man.

The Social Security officials start talking to themselves when they work on the records of various Indian employees. They find that the same man may use one name while with one employer and another upon changing jobs. But stabilization of names among the Indians may well have bizarre results. Private Amos *Two Babies* was in training at Fort Warren, Wyoming, when his wife, Mrs. Two Babies, arrived for a visit with three babies. They really had four, one having been left at home.

Then there was the Indian *No-Name* who caused an exchange of the following messages between Denver and Los Angeles in connection with an air reservation for him:

"Need reservation No-Name Los Angeles to San Francisco"—Denver.

"Reservation made No-Name Los Angeles to San Francisco"—Los Angeles.

"Re Your No-Name reservation, must have name for same"—Los Angeles.

"Re your message 'No-Name' is name. Passenger an Indian"—Denver.

Officials at the Denver induction center during the last war, inquiring as to a new recruit's name, told him to skip the fighting talk and confine himself to answering their questions. "But that is my name," insisted the recruit, "it's Charles Jonas Kills-The-Enemy." Mr. *Kills-The-Enemy* was a thirty-three-year-old Sioux Indian, a descendant of famous chieftains.

CHAPTER VII

Names in Other Countries

A name which you all know by sight very well,
But which no one can speak, and no one can spell.
—ROBERT SOUTHEY, *The March to Moscow,* Stanza 8

WHILE it is true that names seem to follow the same general principles in all countries, still each country has its own philological personality and history, and consequently its names developed differently. The various classes of surnames are found in most of the western countries. Each has some strange or curious modes or customs in connection with its personal names, so that it is well for the student of onomatology to inspect some of them; and that is the purpose of this chapter. Space is allotted to each country commensurate with the outstanding name customs which differ from the English, rather than the numerical or historical importance of the country.

Particularly is it true that surnames were derived from the father's name in the various countries throughout the world. As a very helpful means of identifying the names from different languages lies in a proper recognition of the patronymical affixes and suffixes, the following list is given:

Nationality	Patronymical Forms	Example	Meaning
Arabic	ibn-	ibn-Saud	son of Saud
Armenian	-ian	Boghossian	son of Boghos
Basque	-ana, -ena	Lorenzana	son of Lorenz
Chinese	-tse, -se	Kung-fut-se	Kung, the son of Fo
Czechoslovakian	-icz, -ov	Pavlov	son of Paul
Danish	-sen	Hansen	son of Hans
Dutch	-zon, -se, -sen	Cornelisse	son of Cornelis
English	-son	Robertson	son of Robert
Finnish	-nen	Heikkinen	son of Henry
French	de, D'	Depierre	of Pierre

Frisian	-kin, -s	Watkin	son of Walter
German	-sohn	Mendelssohn	Mandel's son
Greek (modern)	-pulos, -oula	Nicolopulos	son of Nicholas
Greek (old)	-idas, -ida, -ides		
	-id, -i, -at	Aristides	son of Ariston
Hebrew	Ben	Ben-Hur	son of Hur
Hindi	bin, walad	bin Timaji	son of Tima
Hindostanee	putra	Raja putra	son of Raja
Hungarian	-fi, -f	Petöfi	son of Peter
Icelandic	-son	Arnason	son of Arni
	-dottir	Stefandottir	daughter of Stefan
Irish	O', Mac	O'Brien	descendant of Brien
	Ni, Nic	NicHogan	daughter of Hogan
Italian	-i	Guidi	son of Guy
Lapp	-dotter	Larsdotter	son of Lars
Latin	-ilius, -idius	Hostilius	son of Hostis
Lithuanian	-aitis, -ait, -at	Adomaitis	son of Adam
	-ĕnas, -ónis,		
	-únas, -ùlis		
Norman	Fitz	Fitz-Gerald	son of Gerald
Norwegian	-sen, -datter	Larsen	son of Lars
		Sigurdsdatter	daughter of Sigurd
Polish	-ski	Petrowski	son of Peter
Roumanian	-escu, -esco, -vici	Bercovici	son of Berko
Russian	-itch, -ich, -vich,	Romanovitch	son of Romain
	-off, -ef, -if, -ev,	Iourief	grandson of Ioury
	-vna	Petrovna	daughter of Peter
Saxon	-ing	Ælfreding	son of Alfred
Scotch	Mac	McDonald	son of Donald
Spanish	-az, -ez (genitive	Alvarez	son of Alva
	ending)		
Swedish	-son	Pettersson	son of Petter
Syriac	Bar	Barzillai	son of Zillai
Welsh	Ap, Up, Ab	Upjohn	son of John

Next to the patronymical suffixes is the element in surnames from places meaning "of" or "of the," "the," "from," or "at." In English we have *Atwood* and *Bywater*, and, of course, many surnames, partly Englished, using foreign prefixes, such as *Delafield* (of the field). The most common of these place prefixes and suffixes should be recognized:

Dutch:	*-van, -vander, -ver, -von, De*
Flemish:	*De*
French:	*D', De, Dela, Des, Du, Le*
Italian:	*Da, De, Di*
Portuguese:	*Da*
Spanish:	*De, Del, De La, De Los*

Another important point is the ability to recognize the diminutive endings used by different nationalities. A difficulty here is that different languages sometimes have the same diminutive terminations, as will be seen from the following list:

Language	Diminutive endings
Dutch:	-je
English:	(See page 9)
French:	-eau, -el, -elle, -et, -ette, -ot, -otte, -on
French double diminutives:	-elin, -elet, -inet, -elot
(sometimes contracted to	-lin, -let, -net, -lot)
German:	
High	-el, -l, -le, -li, -lin, -len, -lein
Low	-ke, -k, -ich, -ig, -ken, -chen, -je
Old High	-izo, -licke, -kel, -zel, -zke
Gothic:	-ila, -ika
Irish:	
masc.	-ăn, -căn, -găn
fem.	-ĭn, -enn, -ne, -nat
Italian: (masc.)	-cello, -cino, -ello, -etto, -ino, -ucco
Russian:	-ja, -ka
Spanish: (masc.)	-cito, -ico, -illo, -itico, -ito

The totalitarian nations were quite sensitive to names and restricted people from giving their children forenames that did not reflect loyalty to the government. As early as 1926, Mussolini's cabinet decided that Italian babies must receive good, sound, Fascist names; in 1935 it became illegal for people to name their children *Hitler*. In 1938, in Italy, there was a campaign against entertainers using foreign-sounding names. The Nazis, in 1936, refused to allow a salesman to call his son *Lenin*. German musicians who had adopted foreign names were ordered by the Nazi Chamber of Music to resume their German names.

CHINA

The first nation to have hereditary family names was China, a nation which perpetuated the memory of the head of the family and carried filial respect almost to personal worship. This affection for one's forebears was undoubtedly the stimulus which led to the adoption of hereditary names to designate the family. From very ancient times the Chinese have had the most complete system of personal nomenclature found anywhere in the world.

About the year 2852 B.C. the Emperor Fushi decreed that family names must be used in China, although they did not become fixed until the time of Chan-Kueh (403-221 B.C.). All family names in China must be selected from a sacred poem, *Po-Chia-Hsing*, or Hundred Clan Names, which is attributed to the Emperor Yao; so the number is necessarily limited, especially as in the poem there are only 408 single and thirty double words, but no word is repeated. Native authors have carefully investigated these names, and have traced some of them back more than three thousand years. The names are arranged in rhythmical order, and the book is one of the first that a child learns by rote in school. Nearly a hundred million, or one-fourth of all the people in China, answer to the surnames of *Chang, Wang* or *Li*, which mean "draw-bow," "prince" and "plum," respectively.

About the beginning of the Han Dynasty (201 B.C.) the Chinese adopted a second name called *Pai-Ming* or generation name. Each family adopted a poem consisting of twenty or thirty characters, easy to remember, each character harmonizing with the rest but different from them. The first generation, after the adoption of the poem, then bears for a *Pai-Ming*, or middle name, the first character or word of this generation poem, the second generation takes the second character or word, and so on.

Thus each Chinese rightfully has three names: the first called *Shing* is the family or clan name; the second called *Pai-Ming* is the generation name; and the third, called the *Nai-Ming, Ju-Ming* or *Hsiao-Ming*, is the given, or "milk," name. About a month after a boy's birth he is given his milk name at a feast given for the purpose. It frequently consists of only one character and often has the prefix *Ah* put before it, so that a boy named *Ch'un Luk* will commonly be called *Ch'un Ah luk*, although *Ah* is really no part of his name. A favorite method of insulting an adult Chinese is to revile him in public by his milk name. A few families place the generation name at the end and the given name in the middle.

When a boy first goes to school he is sometimes given a "Book" name or *Shu-Ming*, consisting generally of two characters, to be used by those he meets in the progress of his education. After reaching maturity a Chinese is allowed a "social name," which he selects for himself and which is placed last. At marriage a Chinese receives a "great name," one form of which is used by relatives and another by acquaintances. If he enters official life, he takes an "official name." In addition he may have a "courtesy name," and writers often adopt a literary name, not similar to our pseudonym, but one used with other names. After death he may be given a posthumous name. All these names are not used in a meaningless way as we use John or William, but are mostly original with more or less appropriate significance. Each new name is not a change of name, but is an added name and all of them cling to a man throughout his lifetime.

A man may be best known in history by one name or by another. There is no uniformity. *K'ung Ch'iu* (the first being the surname and the second the milk name), who lived 551-478 B.C., adopted the literary name of *Chungni*, but became best known by the name of *K'ungfutse* (Master K'ung). The Latinized form of this latter name is Confucius, and he is so known in the Western world. Lin Yutang in his *The Importance of Living* gives a list of the various names of some important historical persons.

Finally, there is yet another name sometimes adopted, the *t'ong* name, which may be easily recognized by the word *t'ong* added to the name. A man of means who lives in the ancestral home is known by the name of the home, which is posted on a small board at his door. This name passes on to his descendants who continue to live in the home, and represents his family. Sometimes when the brothers separate and live in different houses, they continue this name, after adding words signifying "second family" or "third family" to designate the second or third sons. Some use this name in their business. Most business styles, however, are flowery combinations such as "Extensive Harmony" or "Heavenly Happiness."

Among the southern Chinese it is a very common thing for a descriptive nickname to be bestowed in addition to all the other names, and everyone calls him or her by it. The individual bears it complacently, knowing that he must accept the inevitable. When the nickname consists of only one syllable the *Ah* is used. These names are called "flowery names," although they mean *Dwarfy, Fatty, Flat-Nose, Small-pox-Marked* and the like.

No two persons in the same family association are allowed to have the same given, or milk, name; so the full name is a real means of identification and a distinct help to genealogists. Names of gods are never used as an element in personal names in China. The family name is derived from the paternal side and is transmitted both to male and female children. Chinese law does not permit a man to change his name except in the case of adoption into another family. One may not marry another with the same family name. Children or grandchildren must not speak or write the registered or given name of their fathers or grandfathers, it being considered unfilial and lacking in respect so to do. For the same reason, a wife does not use her husband's name and sometimes does not even know it.

Chinese emperors, upon attaining the throne, adopted a reign title which was used as the emperor's name. The former personal name of the ruler was sacred and was not to be used by the general public so long as that dynasty might last. It was death to the divulger of the secret name. Any character occurring in such a personal name was to be written, in ordinary usage, with some alteration or addition. A literary man, once having accidentally used the word *Ming*, which was the reigning monarch's secret personal name, was executed together with his sons, his wife and daughters banished, and his estates confiscated. The emperors were known after death by their dynastic title or "temple" name.

Girls are not so important and must be content with a milk name, marriage name and nicknames besides their surname which they retain after marriage, although by courtesy they are addressed by their husband's surname, as our Mrs. Brown may be called. In official documents both the maiden surname and the husband's surname are used. A Chinese lady will not give her name, and, in court will answer that she has no name, apparently from a feeling, partly of modesty and partly of fear, that a stranger might impertinently use it in addressing her. Wives of the lower classes do not exhibit this reticence in respect to their names and will disclose their names freely.

There is a custom of great antiquity among the Tibeto-Burman-speaking tribes of overlapping the names of father and son from generation to generation, called the genealogical patronymic linkage system. Under this practice the last one or two syllables of the father's name become the first one or two syllables of the son's name. Thus the son of *A-tsung-a-liang* might be *A-liang-a-hu*, his son *A-hu-a-lie* and the son of the next generation *A-lie-a-kia,* etc.

To avoid unnecessary confusion, many Chinese now are adopting the Western custom of putting their given name before their family name so that it is no longer possible to be sure just which is the given or milk name and which is the family name. In most cases when a name is hyphenated it is the forename, expressed with two vocables, although the family name is hyphenated in a few rare instances. There is no uniformity among Western writers as to whether certain elements of Chinese names are to begin with a capital letter; sometimes hyphens are used and sometimes each element is run together without the benefit of a hyphen.

ANCIENT ROME

Next in interest are the names of the ancient Romans. At first the Romans seem to have had but one name, or perhaps two, when used with the genitive case of the name of the one in whose possession, or under whose authority, the person belonged, as of the father in the case of a son or daughter, of the husband in the case of a wife, or of the owner in the case of a slave. But when they were divided into tribes or clans and families, they began commonly to have three, as *Gaius Valerius Catullus*. Patrician families were the first to use three names which distinguished them from the plebians. By the end of the republic, plebians also used three names.

These three names, known as the *prænomen, nomen* and *cognomen*, marked the different *gentes* and *familiæ* and distinguished the individuals of the same family. The *prænomen* was put first and marked the individual.

These were limited in number. Varro (116-27 B.C.) lists thirty-two *prænomina* of which the followir.g eighteen were the only ones generally in use: *Appius, Aulus, Decimus, Gaius, Gnaeus, Kaeso, Lucius, Mamercus, Marcus, Marius, Numerius, Publius, Quintus, Servius, Sextus, Spurius, Tiberius* and *Titus*. Some of these were confined to certain patrician families, as for instance, *Appius* to the *Claudii*. In other families tradition limited the choice; for example, the *Cornelii* used only *Gnaeus, Lucius, Publius* and *Servius*. If one of their number were in disgrace, a family might renounce the use of that *prænomen*.

The custom of using only certain *prænomina* became so strong that after a man had, say four sons, he would be obliged to use numerals for *prænomina*, and *Quintus* and *Sextus* were in frequent use. The comparative scarcity of the first four numerals suggested that most Romans had a free choice of at least four *prænomina*. Later the Romans forgot completely the meaning of their names. Cicero's only brother, for example, was called Quintus. When joined with the *nomen* and *cognomen*, the *prænomen* was regularly abbreviated.

The *nomen* followed the *prænomen* and designated the *gens*, and both the *nomen* and *prænomen* commonly ended in *-us* or *-ius*, as *Titus* and *Julius*. The *cognomen* was put last and marked the *familia*, as *Cicero* and *Caesar*. Thus *Publius Cornelius Scipio* points out Publius of the *gens* of Cornelius of the family of Scipio. In early Roman law when a man died without a will and without near kin, his property escheated to the entire body of Roman citizens bearing the same *nomen* as the deceased, because of the fiction that assumed all members of the same *gens* to be descended from a common ancestor.

Sometimes there was also a fourth name, another *cognomen*, called the *agnomen*, added to commemorate some illustrious action or remarkable event. Thus Scipio was named *Africanus*, from his conquest of Carthage and Africa. *Cunctator*, "the Delayer," was given to Q. Fabius Maximus because of his policy of delay in the war against Hannibal. In some cases the *agnomen* merely marked the *nomen* a man was obliged to renounce when he was adopted into another family. There might be several *agnomina*, and this was common practice in the second and third centuries A.D.

The *cognomen* was the one that was used, although in speaking to anyone the *prænomen* was generally used, as being peculiar to citizens since slaves had no *prænomen*. They were known by their owner's *prænomen* in the genitive case with the suffix *-por* (boy), as *Maripor* and *Lucipor*. Later they were given Greek names followed by their owner's *prænomen* in the genitive case.

When Roman slaves were liberated, they commonly took their former master's *nomen* and *prænomen*; sometimes they received the *prænomen* of another to whose patronage they considered their freedom due. Thus names which were once considered peculiar to the first families of Rome became common to all classes, even to the very dregs of society. Later, the former slave might even claim kinship to some noble or patrician family because of the similarity of name.

A daughter generally took her father's name with a feminine termination, as *Julia*, daughter of *Julius*. To distinguish her from her sisters and relatives she received a particular appellation, which, if used as a *prænomen*, was usually a feminine form of names common among men. Later these names for women went out of use and she was known only by the name of the *gens*. At the beginning of the empire they again took personal names but placed them after the name of the *gens* instead of before. Married women often used their own names followed by that of their husband in the genitive case.

About the time of Claudius (Agrippa), due to the irregular addition of names by persons wanting to be more than they were, family names became confused and finally entirely ceased to exist, so that by the time of the fall of the Roman Empire single names were once again customary. Hereditary and collective surnames became common again in Italy during the existence of the many Italian republics which arose upon the decline of the lower empire.

ITALY

The earliest family, or gentile, names in Europe arose among the Etruscans. When they first settled on Italian soil, they did not possess surnames. They were not great in number and did not need them for reasons of identification, but contrived to adopt second names to set themselves apart from the native Italians and as a stamp of nobility. By making them hereditary, they were able to call attention to their aristocratic status by pointing to their more or less illustrious ancestors.

As a gentile name marked the gentleman, and, indeed, even made the gentleman, it is not surprising to note that the Italians were not slow in adopting it.

Hereditary surnames were first used in Venice about the latter part of the tenth century but did not become common or fixed until about the twelfth and thirteenth centuries. From Venice they gradually spread throughout the republics now known as Italy. In the Middle Ages, as well as today, each Italian was legally known by his name coupled with that of his father. A married woman in Italy, as in Spain, never loses her maiden name. Surnames are less important than Christian names, which are used no matter what the age.

The feuds between powerful families in Italy gave impetus to the adoption of surnames. Men added names of the warring families to their own merely to show whose side they supported. We can recognize many of these names by the collective character which distinguishes them. They are peculiar, not to an individual or small family group, but to a party. Thus a man might be *Salvino degl-'Amati* or *Tibaldo de'Medici*, meaning "of the Amato" or "of the Medico," and he would not necessarily be related to these families. Force of example and desire to rise in the social scale were two things which influenced the spread of these collective names among the middle classes. Most Italian family names ending in *i* have sprung from the collective family name; a few, of course, have arisen from the known confusion of *i* with *o* or *a* among uneducated Italians. The prepositions *da, de,* or *di* have usually disappeared.

Local or territorial surnames are comparatively rare in Italy. Names of the smaller cities are borne as surnames chiefly by Jews, such as *Ferrara, Modena,* and *Pisa.* A parallel case in England is Scott's *Isaac of York.*

The most striking quality of Italian surnames is the large number of strange descriptive surnames to be encountered in that country.

Thus there is *Bentivoglio* (I love thee), *Frangipani* (break bread), *Asini* (donkeys), *Canacci* (bad dogs), *Boccaccio* (ugly mouth), *Ubbriachi* (drunkards), *Pochintesta* (little in head). Of course many have agreeable connotations as *Allegri* (the merry ones), *Bonamici* (good friends), *Bonfiglioli* (good children) and *Angiolotti* (little angels). Some even remind us of Puritan names, as *Graziadei* (thanks to God) and *Dito di Dio* (finger of God). Others are more carefree, as Signor *Lascialfare,* which would be translated to "Mr. Let-him-do-it."

As in other countries, there are various surnames derived from font-names such as *Uberti* (son of Hubert), *Guidi* (son of Guy) and *Lamberti* (son of Lambert). Trade names are common, and even now sometimes young people are called from the father's trade, as *Lorenzo del Sarto,* "the tailor's." The calm acceptance of these names is proof that the people do not resent being known by them—in fact, they seem rather proud of them.

GREECE

The Greeks, the most civilized and the most illustrious people of antiquity, did not produce surnames at an early time, although traces of the custom are to be found. Considering the history and location of Greece, this is surprising, especially in view of her pride in her past and her efforts to immortalize her heroes. But all their names were significant; every family exhibited a decided preference for certain names and they were transmitted from grandfather to grandson, from uncle to nephew. The Greeks, even with the example of the Romans to follow, were loath to alter their nomenclatural habits.

Children received either simple or compound names. Simple names are such as those of animals, as *Batrachos* (frog), *Leon* (lion), *Lycos* (wolf), and *Moschos* (calf); or after the color of the complexion, as *Argos* (white), *Melas* (black), *Pyrrhos* (red), and *Xanthos* (fair). Some other simple names were those of divinities, with slight inflections, as *Apollonios,* derived from Apollo; *Demetrios* derived from Demeter; and *Athenæus,* from Athene.

The compound names were more numerous. If parents believed that the birth of a son had been due to prayers to a god, the word *doron,* meaning "gift," might be added to the god's name, changed slightly, and we observe *Theodorus, Diodorus, Hypatodorus, Herodorus, Heliodorus, Cephisodorus* and many others. Some families pretended to be descended from the gods, and hence the names *Theogenes* (born of the gods) and *Diogenes* (born of Jupiter). By adding the word *-mache,* meaning "battle," which was meant to modify the name in an honorable manner, we have names like *Amphimachus, Promachus* and *Telemachus.* Other common elements are *agenor* (he who directs it), *damao* (I tame), and *thoos* (swift). Scarcely any degrading names are found in Homer, although they are not now so uncommon in Greece.

With the early Greeks, polysyllabic names were considered more noble than short ones, which were deemed fit only for the poorer classes and slaves. Many of the names which appear to be simple are really merely short forms of compound names.

SPAIN

The first family names in Spain originated in the warning cries used by the Christians during the Moorish invasions (which began about 711 A.D.), and served as shouts for help and encouragement as well as exultant cries of victory. The head of the family became known by his cry. Family names were developed in the latter part of the twelfth century. Towards the end of the thirteenth century they became hereditary.

Family pride and party spirit were thus important influences in the establishment of permanency in Spanish names. The hatreds between the families and their ambitious aims were hereditary; and the appellations became rallying words or banners under which friends and relations ranged themselves, actuated by the same desires, the same resentments and the same hopes as their predecessors.

Before this time the Spaniards had surnames but they were not hereditary. The son of Gonzalez, a warrior who is looked upon as the founder of the kingdom of Castile, was named Fernand Gonzalez; his son was known as Garcia Fernandez. Later these names became hereditary in much the same way as patronymics did in England. Nicknames and place-names also developed into surnames as they did in England.

A large proportion of the female names in Spain are derived from the Virgin or her attributes, such as *Concepcion* (conception or beginning), *Mercedes* (mercy), *Consuelo* (consolation), or from some belief or legend about her.

Due to the desire to retain the names of the families, children take as surnames both of the parents' names connected by *y*, as *Juan Blanco y Alvarez.* If Juan married Consuelo Diaz y Gonzalez, the surname of their children would be *Blanco y Diaz.* The Portuguese connect the paternal and maternal surnames with *de* instead of *y.* Where the two families are very prominent, the surname may consist of all four of the grandparents' names, as *Blanco Alvarez y Diaz Gonzalez*. In addition, one or more estate or place names may be added, as *de la Madrid* and *de Haro*.

In some cases the *y* may be dropped out, particularly if the mother's name contains a particle, and we might have *Arcineaga de la Torre*. In modern times a hyphen may be found sometimes instead of the *y*. The mother's surname, in usage, may be represented by the initial only, as *Rivera G*. The letter would not be used in conversation but would be an important part of the owner's signature. Wives may keep their own names, adopt their husband's, or drop part and keep part. The particle *de* is placed before the husband's surname when used by the wife. Generally when a daughter marries, she drops her mother's surname and substitutes that of her husband preceded by *de*.

Children may receive two or more forenames. When *María* is used, because it is so common, an added identification is sometimes appended, as *María de los Dolores* (Mary of the sorrows). The second element in the Christian name may resemble a surname in form and thus be confusing. There may be two forenames with one surname and the same name may appear both in the given name and in the surname.

From the preceding, it will be seen that an ordinary person in Spain may have a long complicated name, as *Diego Maria Concepcion Juan Nepomuceno Estanislao de la Rivera y Barrientos de Acosta y Rodriguez,* who would be known in short as *Diego Rivera*. Members of the nobility, descending from famous families with many estates and desiring to represent a number of ancestors, can, with their titles added (now legally abolished, but retained in social usage), produce a really fancy appellation. Law has followed custom and many sections of the Spanish Civil Code are devoted to the principles of the name as a form of property, the right to use it, penalties for misuse by unauthorized persons, number of Christian names that may be registered, formalities for changing names, use by illegitimate children, and so forth.

The leading surnames in Spain are (in this order) *Garcia, Fernandez, Lopez, Gonzalez* and *Rodriguez*. In general, Mexican names follow closely the principles of Spanish names.

HUNGARY

Among the Hungarians the surname is placed first, the same as the Chinese, although, like the Chinese, the English-speaking peoples often change the order of names of Hungarians. Those not familiar with Magyar names are sometimes deceived.

Surnames of the nobility in Hungary commonly end in *-y*, which has the same significance as the English *of*, the French *de* and the German *von*. There are *Endrássy* (from Endrās), *Body* (from Bod) and *Kanizsay* (from Kanizsa). As in most other countries, the nobles were the first to take surnames and generally adopted place-names. Adding a terminal *-h* was also a sign of nobility, as in *Kossuth*.

But not all names terminating with *-y* were noble, as *Arany* (gold), *Hegy* (hill) and *Nagy* (big). Hungarian surnames may, like others, be divided into the usual four classes. There are the patronymics like *Petöfi* and *Janosfi*, that is, sons of Peter and John. We find the usual color nicknames such as *Fekete* (black) and *Vöros* (red), and other descriptive terms like *Kopasz* (bald), *Sánta* (creeper), *Kemény* (hard) and *Szemes* (good eyes). There are local names such as *Zöld* (green) and *Madá* (bird), the last of which may also be a nickname. The most popular surnames are those designating an occupation, such as *Kovacs* (smith)—the most popular surname in Hungary—*Varga* (shoemaker), *Asztalos* (carpenter), *Molnar* (miller) and *Szabó* (tailor). Diminutives are very rarely used by the Magyars.

FRANCE

French names follow, or rather set, the pattern for English names. Of course the language varies from English more than German does, but allowing for this different language group, one can see that the origin and derivation of inherited family names among the French is similar to the English in its overall aspects. All the common French surnames, with only minor variations, are found in England because the English were bilingual at the time surnames arose and French was the language of the court.

The chief points of difference between English and French surnames are three: (1) the more common retention of prepositions and the article, (2) the more common use of diminutive suffixes, and (3) the aphesis, or decapitation, of baptismal names.

In English, names like Atterbury, Atwater, Bythesea and Underwood, while not at all unknown, are not particularly common. Prepositions and articles were often used when the surname was not hereditary but only a descriptive phrase. As the surname became fixed the prepositions and articles were dropped in England. But not so among the French. They have *Lacroix* and *Delacroix* (cross), and *Lasalle* and *Delasalle* (hall). Names of towns commencing with a vowel generally had *de* prefixed, e.g., *Dorsey* (Orsay) and *Davranche*. Surnames commencing *Du* (of the) point to their French origin, and we often see

Dupont (bridge), *Dumas* (homestead) and *Dupuy* (hill). Occupative names also retained prepositions and articles, e.g., *Dufaure* (smith), *Augagneur* (worker) and *Lequeux* (cook). The French even retain the preposition and article with the patronymic and nickname type of surnames. With the former there are *Lasimonne* (Simon), *Demichel* and *Dubertrand*, and with the latter, *Lebœuf* (bull) and *Larousse* (red). The common use of prepositions and articles suggests a possible French origin for all unusual surnames commencing with *D* or *L*.

While the English use the common diminutive suffixes with the various pet forms of baptismal names, the French proceed with much greater freedom, often using double diminutives. For example, with the French form of William we find diminutive forms such as *Guillaumet, Guillaumin, Guillaumot, Guillaumy, Guille, Guillemain, Guillemard, Guillemat, Guillemaud, Guillemeau, Guillemenot, Guillemin, Guillemineau, Guillemot, Guillermin, Guillet, Guillin, Guillot, Guillotin, Guillon* and several dozen more. Also we find, surprisingly enough, that the diminutive suffix is freely used with the occupative surnames. Thus along with *Berger* (shepherd) we find *Bergeret, Bergeron, Bergerot* and others. Every occupative name may be found with one of the many diminutive suffixes attached.

The tendency of the French to stress the last syllable has produced an aphesis, or decapitation, of many given names. For example, there is *Colas* from *Nicolas, Bastien* from *Sebastien, Jamin* from *Benjamin,* and *Strophe* from *Christophe.* Sometimes the fragment is very hard to trace. Thus, we get *Mas* from *Thomas*; diminutive suffixes may be added to make *Masset* or *Massenet* or *Massillon,* and then from another decapitation we may obtain *Sillon.* Tracing this back to the original Biblical name is difficult indeed.

The French qualify their patronymics with an adjective much more than they do across the channel. In English there are a few compounds with John, as *Littlejohn, Meiklejohn* and *Prettyjohn,* with perhaps one or two with Peter and an occasional *Goodwillie*; but in France most of the popular Christian names are so used. Thus we find *Grandclement, Bonbernat* (Bernard), *Grandcolas* (Nicolas), *Petitperrin* (Pierre) and *Grosclaude. Bon* is used with many forenames and also with other words.

The common Christian names in France have produced more variant forms of surnames than in England. Pierre has produced about two hundred derivative family names, while Jean and Etienne have accounted for more than a hundred each. Surnames, derived from female names, are found more frequently among the French. This does not indicate illegitimacy, but rather points to the importance of the mother in the French family. The most used Christian names at the time surnames were being adopted were the Biblical names; and in modern times the emphasis is more on the Biblical and the Greek and Latin font-names than on the Teutonic names.

The most popular surnames in France are *Martin, Lefevre, Petit, Durand* and *Dubois*. But the common surnames in France are not nearly so ubiquitous as in other countries, and so the problem of identification is much simpler. When a mistake is made by reason of the resemblance of names, an old proverb is often recited: *"Il y a plus d'un âne à la foire qui s'appelle Martin* (There's more than one donkey at the fair named Martin)."

GERMANY

German surnames follow very closely the pattern of English surnames. Like English names, the surnames most frequently found are those derived from occupation. Also like English family names, the most numerous are those derived from place-names. German names differ from English names in having a larger proportion composed of compounds; but in a language where elements are often combined into long words, we would expect this characteristic.

Diminutives are very common in German names. In the earlier part of this chapter German diminutive suffixes are given. It needs only to be noted here that the essential element of such diminutives are the *k* in the north and the *l* in the south. Also the Germans use the endings *z* and *sch*, both of which are sometimes found combined in the same name.

When the full Christian name becomes a surname in Germany, it generally does so without change or addition of patronymical affix or suffix. Patronymic forms like *Mendelssohn* are not common. When forenames were cut down, particularly those that came in with Christianity, the last part was just as likely to survive as the first. This tendency is similar to that among the French, and the Germans use *Hans* from *Johannes* and *Klaus* from *Nicolaus* and the like. Also, like the French, adjectives compounded with given names are common, and we find *Aldejohann* and *Jungjohann* for the old and young Johns, *Grossjohann* and *Kleinhans* for the large and small, and many other similar compounds. Old or large John represented the father while young or small John was the son; these names are true patronymics.

Many German surnames of local origin can be easily recognized by the endings, such as *-au* (wet meadow-land) as in *Gneisenau*; *-horst* (wood), as in *Scharnhorst*; and many others such as *-berg* (mountain), *-brück* (bridge), *-burg* (castle), *-dorf* (village), *-hain* (hedge), and *-reut* (clearing).

Occupative surnames are more numerous in Germany than in England because of the German trait of meticulous differentiation. The English use commonly a dozen or more compounds with *-smith*, but the Germans have several hundred not uncommon surnames with *-schmidt*. Again the Germans use *-macher* much more than we use *-maker*. Indeed, many of our names ending with *-smith* or *-maker* are translations from the German. But the most common compound among the Germans is *-meyer* (farmer). There are more than a thousand different German surnames in which the element *meyer*, in one or another of its spellings, is a part of the name.

The German *von* simply means "of." In most cases it dropped out of surnames when they became hereditary, like the *de* formerly in many English names. Later, by usage, it came to indicate nobility, and was then added to family names of all kinds including occupational surnames. It is correct to use the *von* only when the full title is used, but not when the surname only is mentioned.

Like the French, the Germans have been slower in discarding their grotesque nicknames than the English. One reason, perhaps, is that the Germans, on the whole, were slower in freezing their surnames into a hereditary status. The animal nicknames are common, although many of them, as in England, came from the signs found in front of houses and business establishments.

The five most common German family names, in the order of their popularity, which includes variant spellings, are *Schmidt, Müller, Meyer, Schulz* and *Hoffmann*. German names containing any of the letters *ä, ö, ü* admit of variant spellings using *æ, œ* and *ue* respectively, and vice versa. Diminutive forms, as in English, are quite common.

While both French and German names loom large in this country, very little can be written showing their divergence from English surnames because French, German and English family names are almost exactly alike in principle, the chief variation being the difference in language. Much can be learned about odd English surnames by comparing them with their counterparts in French and German. The work of Weekley is greatly strengthened by his use of this comparative method in connection with the interpretation of surnames.

In the early part of the twentieth century, the most popular fore-
names for boys in Germany were found to be *Wilhelm, Paul, Friedrich,
Johannes* (Hans) and *Karl,* and for girls, *Margarete* (Gretchen),
Martha, Frida, Anna, and *Elsa.*

HOLLAND

Many Dutch surnames are from place names and have the prefix
Van or *Vander,* meaning "of" or "of the," as *Vanderveer* (of the ferry),
Vanderbilt (of the mound), *Vanderburg* (of the hill) and *Vanderbeck*
(of the brook). *Ver* is a contraction of *Vander.* Some have the prefix
Ten meaning "at the" as *Ten Eyck* (at the oak) or *Tenbroeck* (at the
marsh). Many are farm names. Other prefixes are *Voor* (before or in
front of), as *Voorhees* (in front of Hess, a town in Guelderland) and
Onder (below), as *Onderdonk* (below Donk, which is in Brabant).

Then there are also the prepositions *op* and *on,* the former of which
in names is sometimes altered to *up,* as in *Updyke.* Farm names, especially, carried *op* rather than *van.*

At the time of the emigration to the United States, the custom of
Latinizing the Dutch names of university graduates was common.
Thus the names of all the early ministers were so altered. *Jan Meckelen-
burg* became *Johannes Megapolensis,* and *Evert Bogaert* became *Ed-
wardus Bogardus.*

There are many names of local origin which end with the element
-man, as *Geldersman* (man from Guelders). Other local surnames
have a preposition attached, as *Van Loon* (of county of Loon, Belgium)
and *Van Rijn* (of Rhine).

The patronymic form of the surname is common in Holland. The
ending is usually *-se,* an abbreviation of *-sen.* Sometimes it is further
abbreviated to *-z* or *-s.* We have *Martense* (son of Marten), *Lefferts*
(son of Leffert), *Denyse* (son of Denis) and *Janse* (son of Jan). For
centuries each son took the given name of his father, with *-zoon* or *-sen*
added, as a surname, which thus changed with each generation. When
this practice ceased in the eighteenth century, some adopted occupational surnames such as *Brouwer* (brewer) and *Bleecker* (bleacher).
These are not ancient family names.

To the Christian names of girls, the diminutive *-je* is usually added.
A Dutch writer says that this is because the female sex is looked upon
as inferior to the male, but probably the real reason is that this diminutive is regarded more as an expression of endearment.

The eldest son is generally given the name of his father or one of his grandparents; thus certain given names are frequently repeated in certain families.

Many odd Dutch surnames, when translated, do not seem so queer. Thus we have *Stuyvesant* (quicksand), *Bogaert* (orchard), *Wyckoff* (parish court) and *Dorland* (arid land).

NORWAY

In Norway most of the people lived on small farms. Their full names consisted of the given or first name, with the given name of the father with *-sen* or *-datter* added thereto plus the name of the farm on which the person lived. A brother and sister might be named *Ole Halvorson Berge* and *Anne Halvorsdatter Berge*, respectively. If the girl went to live on another farm called *Lillesand*, her name would become *Anne Halvorsdatter Lillesand*. As they lived in small communities, the given name was generally considered to be of sufficient identification in itself.

The Norwegians had a custom of handing down Christian names in a certain fixed order, not unlike that in many other countries. The first son was named after the father's father, the first daughter after the father's mother; the second son and daughter were named after the mother's parents. Subsequent children were named after other relatives. Each family had its characteristic names, and the first name alone was generally sufficient to identify the family to which a child belonged. The genealogy of the oldest son could easily be identified because his name and his father's alternated for generation after generation. Thus *Lars*, the son of *Ole*, was the grandson of *Lars* and his father, *Ole*, the grandson of *Ole*, and so on.

The farm names were descriptive. When a large farm was broken up into smaller ones, each new farm often received its name from its original part of the large farm. Thus there might be the *Hov* (a pagan temple) from the time when each patriarchal family had its public temple, the religious center for the whole tribe; *vin* (the meadowland) might produce new names ending *-vin*; farms having names compounded with *-set* or *-sœtr* (a dwelling place), referred to that part of the large farm where the dwelling stood. Instead of a building with several rooms, the early farm community consisted of various buildings around a courtyard, each a single room. Compounds with *-land* (a cultivated field) also show how the new farm was started from one of the fields of the old one. *Liland*, for example, is the field where flax was grown. Names terminating in *-stad* (place), usually compounded with a personal name, designate the new individual's place, partitioned from the rest. Other important Norse farm terminations are *-boer* (large farmstead), *-borg* (castle), *-by* (homestead), *-dal* (valley), *-gaard* (large family farm), *-heimr* (dwelling and the cultivated fields around it) and *-rud* (clearing).

Residents of Norwegian cities have borne hereditary surnames from about the fifteenth century. The aristocracy and high military officers first took surnames in imitation of the German nobility. Clergymen followed suit by about 1700. As the inhabitants of cities took names, most chose the farm names. Since every Norwegian looked upon himself as being principally a farmer, few adopted occupational surnames. Thus, the large majority of Norwegians have either patronymical surnames or local surnames, that is, farm names. If a newly married couple went to live on the wife's farm, the name of that farm would be used and the farm name of the husband would be dropped. In Norway the farm name was permanent rather than the personal name.

DENMARK

In Denmark around the turn of the century about sixty per cent of the people had surnames ending in *-sen*. This was caused chiefly by the law of May 30, 1828, which ordained that thereafter children at their baptism should be given not only a baptismal name but also a family name. Whether the people were silently opposed to the reform or the priests were sadly lacking in imagination or both, it is hard to say. Before this time, the registers displayed in one column the name of the child and in the next the names of the parents. After the act became law, the name of the father was entered after the name of the child with *-sen* or *-datter* added, as *Hans Petersen* or *Marie Petersdatter*. Now if Petersen had become the family name it would not have been so bad. But Hans Petersen's sons received *Hansen* as their surnames. To get away from this, another act had to be passed in the latter 1860's, providing that a child must be given the surname of the father. The effect of this law was to multiply the *-sen* names unreasonably. In 1904 Denmark passed a law to encourage people to choose other kinds of surnames, but the effect was to encourage hyphenated names, as many people clung to their *-sen* names, but added another name, derived mostly from names of places or occupations. If an adequate law had been adopted in the early part of the nineteenth century, much confusion would have been avoided.

Until about a hundred years ago, each landowner in Sweden was obliged to support a man in the militia of the province, and to keep him in readiness at all times. To maintain the soldier, the proprietor set apart a small portion of the land for his use. The soldier worked his plot of land and also customarily did some work for the lord. Often the soldier took the name of the place as a surname, either adding it to his former surname, as *Johnson-Tor*, or dropping the Johnson and using only the soldier name. Sometimes he was called by an attribute, as *Tapper* (brave). If he was moved to another district, he received, as a rule, another name, and the next soldier who took his place took his surname. One might thus have several soldier surnames in succession.

Also when a man enlisted in the standing army or provincial militia, he adopted a "soldier name," with the approval of the authorities. The reason for the encouragement by the government was to avoid the confusion caused by the many common patronymical names, like *Andersson* and *Petersson*. Soldier names became popular during the first quarter of the nineteenth century while the country was engaged in war with Russia. The custom continued until about 1875. These names adopted upon entering the armed forces were known as soldier names and carried a certain distinction. They were usually of one syllable, as *Varg* (wolf). Normally the children of a soldier would not use the soldier name, but the grandchildren often adopted the soldier name as a family name, particularly when their own family name was too common.

Advocation of a new surname by the government was not confined to soldiers. The government circulated suggestions for new family names, listing various name elements and suggesting combinations. As surnames were not fixed in Sweden until near the end of the nineteeth century, people felt free to adopt a new name. Formerly the son of *Anders Petersson* might be *Nils Andersson*, while his son might be *Karl Nilsson*, etc. Even today this patronymic kind of surname is the most common type. Occupational names are rare.

The Swedish people have always been fond of nature—they like the trees, flowers and fields. Summer is brief, but it is used to the limit for walks and hikes through the woods and countryside. When name elements were to be promoted, it was only natural for this nature-loving people to think of words referring to nature. Thus the following name elements are common: *berg* (mountain), *blad* (leaf), *blom* (flower), *bom* (dam), *dal* or *dahl* (valley), *felt* (field), *fors* (rapids), *gren* (branch, of a tree), *holm* (islet), *hult* (grove), *kvist* and *qvist* (twig), *löf* (leaf), *lund* (copse), *mark* (ground), *ros* (rose), *strand* (shore), *strom* (stream) and *vall* (pasture). Names of trees, as *alm* (elm), *asp* (aspen), *ek* (oak), *lind* (linden), and *seder* (cedar), were common. *Nord* and *söder* for north and south are often seen. There are some other name elements which are popular, such as *-ander* (man), as in *Melander* and *Polander*; and *-sköld* (shield), the latter being a nobility name element indicating a noble family.

Some of these name elements are found principally at the end of a name, others usually only at the beginning, while others are seen as first or last element indifferently. Two name elements were combined to form a family name with no thought that the meanings would fit together, as *Björkdal* (birch, valley) or *Stenfelt* (stone, field); there was no intention that *Björkdal* would represent a birch tree in the valley or *Stenfelt* a stony field.

The Swedes consciously adopted these surnames and gave their attention to the phonetic combination of the two words, with little or no stress on the meanings. Thus there are no Swedish diminutives. Other peoples have not taken surnames in this determined manner, except the Jews in Eastern Europe, and they have combined elements in exactly this same way.

FINLAND

A majority of Finnish surnames contain the diminutive termination *-nen*, which with Christian names gives the patronymic type of name. Thus *Mikkonen* and *Mattinen* refer to the son of Mikko and the son of Matti, respectively. Names like *Mikkonen* really obtain their meaning of son of another by development from the meaning of "little Mikko." This arose from the Finnish custom of giving the male baby the name of the father and then distinguishing him from his parent by the use of the pet, diminutive ending.

Not only does this diminutive termination serve in Finland for a patronymic, but it is used with all classes of surnames, and is thus a sort of surname termination which can be employed with practically every surname with propriety. There are names like *Seppinen* (smith), *Peuranen* (deer) and *Mustonen* (black), and *Jokinen, Jarvinen* and the like, which refer to river and lake. Besides, the termination *-nen* is also much used with ordinary words in the language to convey the connotation of smallness, either actual or as a pet phrase; it is also employed as an adjective ending, as *puinen* (woody) from *pun* (tree). Physical features of the country have provided the people with many of their most popular surnames, either alone or in combination with other words. We meet *Aalto* (wave), *Jarvi* (lake), *Joki* (river), *Kallio* (ledge), *Laakso* (valley), *Maki* (hill), *Niemi* (peninsula), *Puro* (brook), *Saari* (island) and *Wuori* (mountain). Some of them are more specific, as *Jarvenpaa* (head of the lake) and *Joensuu* (river's mouth).

Another important termination is *-la*, an abbreviation for *kyla*, meaning town or village, as *Koskela* (the town near the falls or rapids) and *Saarela* (the island town). Such names designate the person who came from such places. Some families have adopted typically Finnish surnames from their great epic poem, the *Kalevala*, such as *Kullervo, Lemmikki* and *Väinämöinen*.

Modern Finnish Christian names are much like those used by English-speaking peoples, in meaning, if not in form. Many have been taken from the Bible. Others have been taken from nature, as *Ilta* (evening) and *Aamu* (morning) or from abstract qualities, as *Varma* (certain), and *Tyyne* (calm), or from words like *Toivo* (hope) and *Rauha* (peace).

Since Finland gained her independence in 1918, many with foreign-sounding names, particularly those with Swedish names, began to adopt new ones which carried distinctively Finnish connotations.

SCOTLAND

Surnames were introduced into Scotland in the reign of King Malcolm III in the latter half of the eleventh century. "He rewarded his nobles with great lands and offices and commanded that the lands and offices should be called after their names," according to the *Chronicles of Scotland*.

Scotch names may be divided into the Lowland Scotch and the Highland Scotch. The Lowlanders dispossessed the Gaelic-speaking Highlanders of much of their richest territory and consequently earned their implacable hatred.

It is from the Highlanders and their clans, famous in song and romance, that we get many of the Highland surnames like *Bruce, Cameron, Campbell, Douglas, MacDuff, MacPherson* and *Stewart*. The Highlanders acquired the habit of taking to themselves the surname of the chief of their clan. It was thus that they could flaunt their membership in a powerful clan. A powerful and feared name was protection.

In a Scotch Highland clan members use as a surname the name of the reputed ancestor, or the chief of the clan, originally prefixed generally by *Mac*, as *MacKinlay*, *MacEwen* and *MacCallum*. The feminine equivalent of the masculine *mac* is *nic* (daughter of), and in Gaelic *mac* surnames take *nic* when used as a female personal name. To distinguish one person from another, a characteristic name was often added to the Christian name, as *Boyd* (yellow-haired), *Duff* and *Dow* (black) and *Bain* (white), all from the color of the hair. The name of the father might be added in other cases.

The chief, or laird, was known by his name and the name of his property added, which was often the same, and he would be styled *MacTavish of MacTavish*, or *MacTavish of that ilk*. Nowadays to emphasize chieftainship the surname is duplicated, as *Macleod of Macleod*. In the Middle Ages, in Scotland, many things were done "to please the lairds," and taking his surname was one of those things. When a chief traveled he was attended by many officers and servants, among them the *Henchman, Bard, Piper's Gilly* (one who carried the pipe), *Peadier* (the spokesman) and *Gillimore* (the broadsword-bearer), all of whom are represented in modern surnames.

When the clan became too large, it might split up into septs, perhaps when a chief with several sons died. Each son would gather around himself devoted followers and raid a neighbor's lands. The clan Alpine had seven subclans: *MacGregors, Grants, MacIntosh, MacNabs, MacPhies, MacGarries* and *MacAulays*. The ancient clan Chattan had as many as sixteen septs. Because of this subdivision among clans, most of them cannot trace back to remote antiquity. For protection, an individual who had been excluded from his own clan for some offense found it advisable to join another clan and adopt the clan surname; thus not all the members of a clan were really related, although an inner ring was so composed.

Many families had two surnames. One was common to the whole clan, as *MacDonald* and *Buchanan*; the other was the genealogical surname used to distinguish a branch of the clan. This latter name was taken either from the Christian name, territorial designation or some personal characteristic of the first man of the branch who separated from the original family.

Not all of the Highland names are of Gaelic origin. Many Normans settled in Scotland and produced what we now regard as typically Scotch names, *Frazer, Lindsay, Bruce, Leslie* and, possibly, *Ross*.

Most of the Norman-Scotch names are territorial in origin. The Norse also brought some of their names to the Scotch. We recognize them in such names as *Macaulay, Macdougall, Macleod, Macmanus* and *Macsorley.*

The Scottish *Macs* may be classified according to the nature of the element to which the prefix is attached. Of course the majority represent personal names, as *MacEwen* or *MacIan.* Others are of an occupational nature, as *MacTaggart* (son of the priest) and *MacPherson* (son of the parson). Still others are of a descriptive nature, as in *MacMillan* (son of the bald servant), *MacDougall* (the dark stranger), and *MacCulloch* (son of the boar). About fifteen per cent of Scotch surnames have *Mac* as an affix.

There are few important differences between Lowland Scotch personal names and English names. The common practice of sons taking their fathers' names as surnames produced many with patronymical surnames, as *Robertson* and *Donaldson.* Pet forms produced names like *Robson* and *Wilson.* Sometimes the termination -*son* was dropped and the family surname became *Andrew, Edgar, Henry* or *Hendry, Thom* and the like. Local surnames were probably not so popular as in England but they were abundant. In the larger towns, the burgesses called themselves after the street in which they lived. Although *Smith* is the most popular Scottish surname, trade surnames are not encountered quite so often as in England.

In many of the small Scotch fishing towns and hamlets the fisherfolk did not move from place to place, and consequently all were descended from a few common ancestors. It is not uncommon to find only two or three surnames in a town. To distinguish one from another, nicknames, or tee-names, were in common use. Grocers, for instance, invariably inserted a tee-name, or other description, afer the name in their accounts. *Buckie, Beauty, Biggelugs, the King, Rochie, Snipe,* and *Toothie* are examples of these nicknames, and the bearers were so addressed. Few nicknames of this type ever became hereditary family surnames.

Until the nineteenth century wives did not take their husbands' surnames, and the custom is still not legally essential. In most old Scots entails, a man was required to take his wife's name upon marriage.

IRELAND

Curiously enough, surnames were adopted in Ireland more than a hundred years before they appeared in England. Ireland was the first country, after the fall of the Roman Empire, to adopt hereditary surnames. Keating and others have stated that surnames became fixed in the reign of Brian Boru (1002-1014), who, it is claimed, urged all to adopt surnames. But neither Brian nor his sons adopted hereditary surnames, although later descendants adopted the name *O'Brien*. While the process of surname forming was probably in existence before Brian's reign, and was not complete for almost two centuries after his death, it is improbable that he stimulated hereditary surnames by law. Surnames have been found in Ireland as early as the beginning of the tenth century. Many Irish patronymics became fixed during the eleventh and twelfth centuries. Between the eleventh and sixteenth centuries surnames were more universally used in Ireland than in other countries.

The head of a tribe frequently gave his name to his descendants and followers, who called themselves by the chief's name preceded by *hua* or *hy* (grandson), which has been Anglicized into *O'*. The following couplet is oftentimes heard:

> By Mac and O, you'll always know
> True Irishmen, they say;
> But if they lack both O and Mac,
> No Irishmen are they.

In many parts of Ireland it was popularly believed that the prefix *O* was a kind of title among the Irish while *Mac* was a mark of no distinction. However, *O* is no more aristocratic than *Mac*. A few early Irish names have *mac* at the end, as *Blathmac* (son of the flower), *Fionnmac* (fair youth) and *Felmac* (poet's son).

Mac surnames are, generally speaking, of later date than *O* surnames. The *O* was formerly used much more than *Mac* (about seven to one), but this involved no distinction of rank. In general, all Irish surnames are of the patronymic type, that is, formed by adding *O* or *Mac* to the ancestor's name. If the father's name was chosen, *Mac* was used; but if a grandfather or more remote ancestor's name was used, the prefix *O*, meaning "descendant of," was used. Sometimes *Mac* was prefixed to the father's occupation, and we have *Macgowan* (smith's son) and *MacIntyre* (carpenter's son). *O* is seldom found prefixed to occupational names. Nicknames and place-names as surnames in Ireland are rare but not entirely unknown.

Some foreigners adopted *O* and *Mac* so that now and then we find these names designating others than the Irish. There are said to be today fully 1,600 distinct *Mac* surnames in Ireland and over 1,550 *O* surnames. Before a vowel or a liquid, *Mac*, in Irish, tends to become *Mag*, e.g., *Magee* (MacKay), *Magrath* (MacRae) and *Maginnis* (Mac-Innes).

Previous to the Anglo-Norman invasion, personal names in Ireland were purely Celtic, as the Irish were hesitant about adopting the Latin and Greek names of saints, Hebrew names, or the Teutonic names of the Anglo-Normans. After the Conquest, unlike the English, the Irish were very slow in leaving off their ancient Hibernian nomenclature, and, until the reign of Elizabeth, the large bulk of the names were Celtic. The English became impatient, and, in 1465, enacted the statute of 5 Edward IV, set out in Chapter X, ordering the adoption of English surnames. While this law was not generally enforced, some Irish families did English their names. After the defeat of the Irish at Kinsale, they were persuaded that they should have English surnames, and there was a widespread rejection of the *O* and *Mac*.

The centuries of English domination were hostile to the old Celtic names, and because of the opposition of the English ruling and landlord class the great majority dropped the prefix. The mutilated modern forms, however, still have a Celtic air about them. Of this class are *Hearne, Hynes, Rooke, Owens, Reynolds, Conway* from Ahearne, O'Heyne, O'Rourke, O'Howen, MacRannal, and O'Conwy. The Murphys, the greatest in number of any name in Ireland today, descend from *MacMurrough*, the royal family of Leinster. Other Murphys were originally *O'Murchadoo*, an offshoot of the MacMurroughs.

The change of language, from Irish to English in the nineteenth century, had an important influence in tending to Anglicize Irish names. The *O* and the *Mac* were resumed by some as late as about 1800.

Many large clans were divided into branches, and these branches did not have the prefix. The *MacCarthys* of South Munster were divided into the *Moore, Reagh* and *Muskerry* clans; the Connaught *O'Connors* consisted of the *Don, Roe* and *Sligo* branches. These subdivisions are often place-names, and when used as family names thus did not admit the prefix, as is also true of sub-clans which received epithets like *Don* (brown) and *Roe* (yellow).

In adopting the names of saints, the Irish put the words *giolla*, or *maol*, meaning "servant," before the saint's name and then sometimes prefixed the *Mac*. Thus, typically Irish names are *Gilpatrick, Gilchrist* and *Mulconry*. *Mac* before *Gill* sometimes changed into *Kil* and we thus recognize *Kilkenny* and *Kilpatrick*.

WALES

The poverty of the Welsh surnames is known by all who have observed the prominence of *Jones*. Hereditary surnames were not universal among the poorer Welsh classes until the beginning of the present century; the Christian name of the father continued to be the surname of the son.

Cognate with the Scotch and Irish *Mac* is the Welsh *Map* shortened into *Ap* or *Ab*.

Most modern Welsh surnames have been formed in a simple manner by taking the forename of the father in the genitive case, that is, with the addition of the *s*, as in the common Welsh names of *Edwards, Evans, Hughes* and *Williams,* the latter of which is the commonest Welsh surname, followed closely by the ubiquitous *Jones*. Many other Welsh surnames consist of the father's name coalesced with the patronymic *ab* or *ap* as *Bellis* (ab Ellis), *Bevan* (ab Evan) and *Price* (ap Rice). In the same manner *Hugh* became *Pugh* and *Howell* became *Powell*, and thus were formed most all of the Welsh surnames beginning with the initials *B* or *P*.

JAPAN

With the Japanese the personal names consist usually of a family name and a single prename. Most of the surnames are only the names of localities in which the families bearing them resided, as *Yama-moto* (foot of the mountain), *Ta-naka* (among the rice fields), *Shim-bashi* (new bridge) and *Matsu-mura* (pine tree village).

The prename of one person is seldom used by another. For boys the name often terminates in *-taro* for the eldest son, *-jiro* for the second son, *-saburo* for a third and so on down to *-juro* for a tenth son, as *Gentaro* and *Tsunejiro*. Sometimes these terminations are used without any prefix. They mean "big male," "second male," "third male," etc.

Personal names of the upper classes have two or more syllables. Women's names are usually taken from the name of some flower or other graceful natural object, and are preceded by the honorific *O* and followed by the title *San*, as *O-Matsu San,* meaning "the Honorable Miss Pine Tree." Some districts have their own peculiar prefix or suffix which is used in place of the usual one. Both prefix and title may be dropped if the name has many syllables or under certain conditions of intimacy. Among the higher classes, ladies add to their names the honorific *-ko*, which has the value of a caressing diminutive.

In addition to forename and family name there are special names added by writers and artists. Many of these arise by virtue of the artist or writer giving a fanciful name to his residence, such as *Bashō-an* (banana hermitage), and *Suzunoya-no-Aruji* (master of the house with a bell), and then calling himself after his residence. These names are taken and dropped at will. Actors and professional entertainers also select an "artistic name," which among such families of entertainers becomes a hereditary name.

Scholars affect appellations similar to our nicknames, which are not considered vulgar but, on the contrary, highly elegant. Geisha girls adopt professional appellations, most of which can be easily recognized as such by a prefix or suffix relating to longevity, wealth, pleasure, youth or luck.

An interesting feature of Japanese names is the frequent use of the honorific—an additional syllable before or after the name which we translate as the slightly ridiculous "honorable." For example, there is the terminal *san*, as in *Suzuki-san*, which adds a note of respect and we translate, "Honorable Mr. Suzuki." There are various degrees of the honorific, such as *dono*, seen in official correspondence, *kakka*, used among important officials, and *kun*, used among boys. One reason, perhaps, for the frequent use of the honorific is the lack of personal pronouns, and the use of the honorific is often about the only way of indicating the third person. The honorific is also used in reference to common objects, and a Jap customarily speaks of his "honorable coat" or his "honorable pen."

Another singular group of Japanese prenames are those which include a numerical category used in a literal or figurative sense. Thus *Ni-shin* (two relatives) was used to refer to both father and mother; *Shi-ku* (four troubles) referred to birth, old age, sickness and death; *Go-shiki* (five colors) meant usually red, blue, yellow, black and white. Other numbers were used, in combination with other words, with reference to certain things, as 12 (signs of the zodiac), 13 (lunar months of the year), 36 (list of poets), 47 (famous loyal knights of Ako), 69 (stations on the highway from Yedo to Kyoto), and one thousand (poetical phrase for Japan). Many numbers both large and small have a significance only in the mind of the giver of the name. An example more easily understood by us is *Ik-ken shi-eki* (one humility, four advantages), which is a mathematical way of saying that "he that humbleth himself shall be exalted."

Modern emperors have no family name, and, after their death, are usually known by an era or reign name selected by them upon their accession; thus Mutsuhito's reign (1867-1912) is referred to as the *Meiji* Era. When the present emperor, Hirohito, dies, he will be known in Japanese history as *Sowa*. The suffix *-hito* is reserved for emperors and princes of the blood and means "benevolence." Since the tenth century it has been used with every imperial name. Buddhist priests choose for each believer immediately after death a posthumous appellation which is inscribed on the funeral tablet. Also other exalted personages have posthumous, honorific appellations conferred.

In ancient times there were two kinds of hereditary family names in Japan, the *kabane* and *uji*. Both were granted by the sovereign only to a few. There are today a limited number of *kabane* and they are really class or caste distinctions. *Uji* was bestowed by the emperor in recognition of some special merit or as a reward for service. Only families of high rank thus had surnames. The common people had to be content with personal names alone, until the beginning of the Meiji Era, when the government ordered everyone to take family names and made change of names unlawful. While millions of families at this time took family names, whole villages took the same name, often the name of the locality; and today there are said to be only about ten thousand different surnames in Japan.

RUSSIA

Russians commonly have three personal names, a Christian name, a patronymic derived from the father's given name, and a surname, in that order. Thus *Valeri Pavlovich Chkalov* is Valeri, the son of Pavlov, of the family of Chkalov. Names inflect according to gender. Masculine surnames end generally in *-in, -ov, -ev* or *-sky*. Feminine surnames are usually inflected forms of masculine surnames. The wife or daughter of Tolstoi, for example, would be surnamed *Tolstaya*, although in English the same form for both is often used. The present Family Code of the Soviets allows a wife to keep her name after marriage.

Male patronymics usually end in *-ich* or *-vich* meaning "son of" while feminine patronymics end in *-vna*, meaning "daughter of." All the sons of Ivan would bear the patronymic, *Ivanovich*, as a middle name, while all the daughters would use *Ivanovna*.

Russia never has had an aristocracy like that in Western Europe, although there have been efforts to imitate it. Russian family appellations have never followed the estates. Perhaps the principal reason is that many of the petty princes were merely migratory rulers and might, by election or conquest, be called upon to reign over other principalities. None of the more ancient Russian nobles were named after their estates. In 1785 the right to add the names of estates to family names was granted to the nobility by official act, but few bothered to do so.

Among the common people it is a mark of respect to address a man by his family name even without the addition of the given name. Persons of little consequence, in times past, used the humiliating diminutive -*ka*, as *Vaska, Alyoshka,* and *Feodka.* Later, even persons of distinction signed their names using the diminutive of humiliation. The ancient termination -*vitch* was converted into a special reward, and in the latter part of the eighteenth century the Czar himself designated the persons who were to be allowed to bear it. Others naturally adopted the form without official permission, and today it is extremely common.

Many workers and peasants in Russia, after the Revolution, changed their names, seeking to eliminate the offensive nicknames given their ancestors by masters and landowners in the time of serfdom. And thus when *Krasnoshtanov* (red pants) wished to be known as *Orlov* (eagle), *Polovinkin* (half a man) as *Korolev* (king), *Durakov* (fool) as *Umnov* (wise), the government encouraged the changes. It also liked to see them abandon names with a religious meaning, as when *Dakonovy* (deacon) changed to *Voliny* (liberty), and *Bogoiavlenskaya* (appearance of God) switched to *Komsomolova* (young communist).

To make sure there was no criminal intent, one who desired a new name was compelled to wait three months after registering his desire while a careful check was made. When too many began to change from mere caprice, the government, in 1933, increased the fee from three rubles to sixty-one rubles.

Some of the present day Communist leaders have names with unusual meanings, probably dutifully imitating Stalin (steel). There is Gromyko (thunder) and Molotov (hammer). Others do not have names suggesting force. Zhukov (beetle) and Bukharin (from Bokhara) are more prosaic. But Vishinsky derives from *vyshnya* (cherry), and Skorobogaty is from *skoro* (quick) and *bogati* (rich).

Because scholars are not agreed as to the transliteration of the Russian alphabet, Russian names are spelled in various ways in English by different people. A writer using one system might even spell a proper name under another system because of the personal preference of the bearer. The spelling of Russian names is further jumbled by the fact that spelling varied in each district in Russia. This is why there are so many different spellings of the patronymical endings.

POLAND

During the latter part of the fifteenth century and the beginning of the sixteenth century, the greater nobles in Poland, quickly followed by the lesser nobles, adopted hereditary family names. With scarcely an exception they took the name of their manor, almost always with the *-ski* or *-cki* termination. A nobleman living in the village of Jarek might be called *Lord Jarecki*, meaning the "lord of Jarek." In time, the title "lord" was omitted and Jarecki became a family name.

The middle classes, kept down by the triumphant successes of the patricians, did not adopt family names until a late period, when they began to imitate the nobles and the foreigners who were attracted to Poland by commercial enterprise. Many of the tillers of the soil did not acquire hereditary surnames until late in the eighteenth century. The expansion of Poland into Lithuania and Ruthenia influenced names there, and, by 1600, a great many of them ended in *-ski*.

Polish surnames may be divided into four classes just like those of most other countries. There are the patronymics, *Michalski* (Michaelson) and *Piotrowski* (Peterson); the place names, *Warszawski* (from Warsaw), *Krakowski* (from Cracow) and *Górecki* (mountain); the nicknames, *Bialy* (white), *Dobry* (good) and *Niewiadowski* (ignorant); and occupational and official names, *Cieśla* (carpenter), *Król* (king) and *Szewc* (cobbler). Particularly numerous are animal and bird names, as *Koń* (horse), *Koza* (goat), *Krowa* (cow), *Lis* (fox), *Ptak* (bird) and *Sowa* (owl). Many others refer to an inanimate object, as *Kamien* (stone), *Kleszcz* (tongs), *Pudło* (box), *Róg* (horn) and *Ruda* (ore).

Everyone is familiar with the *-ski* termination in Polish names. This ending has three important uses. With local names it means "of" or "from," as *Lwowski* (from Lwow). The Duke of Wellington is thus denominated *Wellingtonski*. It is also seen in some other names, as *Dobrowolski* (of good will). With patronymics it means "son of," as *Jankowski* (son of Jan). And sovereigns have used it as a minor designation or title of honor when they have granted subjects the right to add *-ski* to their family names. Probably about thirty per cent of the surnames in Poland terminate in *-ski*, with about ten per cent in *-wicz*. With the upper classes the *-ski* ending predominates.

The terminations *-czyk*, *-iez*, *-czak*, *-wiak* and *-wicz* also mean "son of," and are added to names derived from father's or ancestor's first name, as the "son of Jan" might be called *Janczyk, Janowiez, Janczak, Janowiak* or *Janowicz*. These endings originally had a connotation of "small." The ending *-czyk* is often added to occupative names, as *Piekarczyk* (baker) and *Rybarczyk* (fisher). The patronymic terminations are also added to other names, as *Bogdlanowicz* (offspring, God-given).

The same kind of name may take many forms as when *Kowal* (smith) may be found in the short form or as *Kowalski* or *Kowalczyk*.

For the sake of euphony the Poles do not hesitate to alter the spelling of their names. Thus *-ski* becomes *-cki* in *Górecki* (from the mountain) and *-czak* becomes *-czyk* in *Szewczyk* (shoemaker). Vowels and consonants are inserted or deleted freely to give a more harmonious sound.

All surnames of women end in *-a*. Before her marriage Madame Curie was Manya *Sklodovska*, the daughter of Vladislav *Sklodovski*. The wife of Wladysław *Orzechowski* might be Katarzyna *Orzechowska*; or *Pan Kowal's* wife might be *Pani Kowalowa* (Mrs. Smith). The daughter would be *Panna Kowalówna*.

Typical and common Polish first names are *Bolesław, Kazimierz, Stanisław* and *Wladysław* for boys, the names of early hero-kings. Another common boy's name is *Wojciech,* the name of the Czech bishop who converted Poland to Christianity. These same names do for many girls by the addition of the feminine *a*, as *Kazimiera, Stanisława* and *Wladysława*. Other common girls' names are *Halina* and *Wanda*. When Poland became Christianized about the tenth century, the saints' names of the Catholic Church were introduced and tended to crowd out many of the old Slavish first names.

In talking with Polish children, the Poles frequently used diminutives to modify expression in much the same way as we would employ a difference in tone. Thus suppose a child is named *Marja* (Mary) and we wish to speak to her with the expression of "dear Mary," we would say *Mania*, or *Maniusia* for "very dear Mary." If in anger or exasperation, we would use the humiliating augmentative *-sko* and say *Mańczysko*. Further, when we wish to speak endearingly of *Bolesław* we would say *Boleś*, but to belittle him, we would refer to him as *Bolek*. Nicknames and diminutives are well-nigh the only wear for children.

TURKEY

In 1933, to avoid confusion, there being so few given names in use, the Turkish Government decided to introduce a bill providing for the compulsory use of family names, and the law became effective January 1, 1935. Families were then at liberty to choose names of their own liking, referring either to a person, occupation or place, or to a historical event. In the latter case, they would have to prove some link or connection with the affair. Names which could not be reconciled with national tradition or custom were not accepted. Those who did not suggest a name were assessed fines, and had their names assigned by the authorities. Many heads of families selected names in striking contrast to their physical appearance or station in life.

Before this time the Turks did not use surnames. At birth each Turk had two names given to him, and these were registered together with his father's names. He was then known either by his own names or by one of them coupled with one of his father's names. Certain pairs of names naturally arose from association, as *Mehmet* and *Ali, Ismail* and *Hakki, Mustafa* and *Kemal, Osman* and *Nuri*.

At the time surnames were enforced by law, the titles *Aga, Effendi,* and *Pasha* were abolished. The title *Bey,* which is roughly equivalent to English *Mr.,* is used, and is inserted between the given name and the surname. Generals who had previously used the title *Pasha* are now to be known by their military rank.

ARABIA

Many Arabians are named after their son, a custom known as "technonymy," and the prefix *abu-,* meaning "father," is used, as *abu-Bakr* (the father of Bakr); and this kind of name, after the child is born, becomes the principal name and takes precedence over their numerous other names. (Recall Leigh Hunt's famous, *Abou Ben Adhém.*)

Other names commence with *ibn-,* as *ibn-Ahmad,* meaning "son of Ahmad," sometimes written without the hyphen. This patronymic form is used not only with forenames, but with descriptive terms. The third common prefix in Arabian names is *Abd-,* meaning "servant."

Proper names abound in Arabia compounded of the name of *Allah,* similar to the Hebrew use of *Jah* or *Jehovah.* "If you have a hundred sons, call them all Muhammad," is a saying of the pious. Thus, the most popular of all names are those of the Prophet. The name *Muhammad* was in common use before the birth of its greatest bearer, and its meaning appears to be "highest praise." The Prophet's daughter, Fatimah, who survived him, has had many namesakes among the women in Arabia.

Mohammedan custom forbids anyone to use in his name the word *abd* (servant) before any name except the name of God. Thus there is the well-known *Abdallah* or *Abdullah,* "servant of God," equivalent to the German *Gottschalk,* or the Irish *Gilchrist,* "servant of Christ." For the sake of variety the name *Abdallah* may be modified by substituting one of God's standard titles of which there are many among Moslems. Thus one man may be *Abd-el-Rahman,* "servant of the Merciful," another *Abd-el-Aziz,* "servant of the Mighty," or *Abd-el-Hamid,* "servant of the Praised," or *Abd-el-Krim,* "servant of the Bountiful." Other vowels are used in place of the *e* in the article *el* to indicate the case. Some authorities assert that no fixed standard of hyphenation is necessary.

In Arabia's ancient days, poets and others were often called after the name of their mother when she was a member of a prominent family. Other times it was a term of abuse pointing toward an unhappy event. Later the metronymic was used without any unpleasant implication. Sometimes poets have been named after one characteristic word used in some of their poems. This practice is so common that special treatises have been written about it.

Nicknames were in use among the ancient Arabians, as well as the more modern ones, and we notice *ibn-Faswa* (son of the midget). When honorific titles came into use in Arabia, they exhibited a disposition to displace the original name; thus the title *Saladin* took the place of the original name, *Yūsuf b. Ayyūb.* Arabians have various kinds of names, but they bear no relation to each other as our forenames and surnames do.

Change of name is easy and frequent among the Arabians. The Prophet, like the Hebrew God, changed the name of many of his followers. There is a propensity to attach importance to the meanings of names and to suppose that they have some effect on the fortunes of the bearers. Slaves change their names on manumission. Converts to Islam habitually change their name, usually selecting one which belongs to an Islamic saint.

INDIA

In India the high caste Hindu believes that the more often the name of a deity passes his lips the more merit he stores up for the future life. Consequently he deliberately names his children after the gods. The Hindu pantheon is crowded so the choice is not unduly restricted. Both Shiva and Vishnu each have a thousand names, and any of them may be slightly modified when naming the child. The names of the dreaded spirits are not used for fear of inviting harm. If some of them bear human names, it is because they were probably originally human beings.

These names of the gods are sonorous and picturesque. *Shiva* means "happy," *Vishnu*, "a pervader," *Krishna*, "black," *Rama*, "one who delights," and *Lakshmana* means "lucky." Forenames generally end in a vowel to which is added a syllable which designates the caste or position. Women often take the name of a goddess to which is added the syllable *-bai*, meaning lady. A Brahman is endowed with a sacred name which he mentions only when prayer is offered.

In the ancient code of Manu, women's names receive particular attention. As translated by Georg Bühler, the writer says, "The names of women should be easy to pronounce, not imply anything dreadful, possess a plain meaning, be pleasing and auspicious, and in long vowels, and contain a word of benediction." The high-caste Brahman is warned not to "marry a maiden . . . named after a constellation, a tree, or a river, nor one bearing the name of a low caste, or of a mountain, nor one named after a bird, a snake, or a slave, nor one whose name inspires terror." In the next verse is the admonition: "Let him wed a female free from bodily defects, who has an agreeable name."

When a person rises in importance, he adds to his personal name a family or caste name. Certain suffixes are added by certain castes; thus *-gupta* might be added to the name of one of the Vaishyas caste and *-dasa* to that of the Shudra caste.

Family names often denote a profession or trade, and in some instances were first conferred by the old rulers. Family names are also formed by adding the suffix *-kar* or *-wallah* to the name of the place of origin of the family, as the *Chiplunkars* and *Svratwallahs*. Synonymy is sometimes found, that is, the practice of varying one's name by substituting a synonym for one of the component parts, as when *Dhanurgraha* (bow-grasping) becomes *Dhanurdhara* (bow-holding).

Hindu names have become so divergent in their spelling that in late years spelling reforms have been undertaken. Calcutta University standardizes the spelling of its students' names.

Honorific prefixes or suffixes are common. The most popular honorific is the suffix *-ji* or *-jee*, as in *Ramji* or *Jamshedjee*. The suffix *-devi* is a feminine honorific. Many honorific titles are prefixed to names, and sometimes appear to be part of the name, such as *Babu, Baba, Lala, Sobhi, Pandit, Raja* and *Maung*.

In Western India it is a common practice to insert the father's name between the forename and the family name, as in Russia, but elsewhere in India the practice is rare. To the father's name is added the patronymic form *-bin* or *-walad*, meaning "son of," although these suffixes are sometimes omitted. Thus *Vasudev Pandurang Chiplunkar* would be a Hindu whose personal name was Vasudev, his father's name, Pandurang, and his family name, Chiplunkar, testifies that he came from the village of Chiplun. In Southern India the village name precedes the personal name. A woman's name is followed by that of her husband and his surname.

Names of Moslems are derived not from the gods but from their religious and secular history. When a Mussulman is admitted to the faith, he commonly receives a name expressing, generally, his devotion to Allah.

GYPSY

Gypsies have a double system of nomenclature, each tribe or family having a public and a private name. By their public name they are known to the Gentiles and by the other name to themselves alone. The public names are English; the private ones come from their own Romany language. For example, a family known as *Smith* to the public would have *Petulengro* as the private name, which might be translated as horseshoe-maker (or possibly tin-worker). There are only two occupational names commonly used by the Gypsies—*Cooper* and *Smith*.

The rest of the Gypsy family names are English surnames of a highly aristocratic character, as *Hearne, Lovel* and *Stanley*. The explanation lies probably in the fact that the various tribes sought the protection of certain powerful families, and were permitted by them to locate on their estates; in appreciation they eventually adopted the surnames of their patrons. Their Romany, or private, names then became very crude translations of the English surname. For example, Boswell was translated *Chumomisto*, that is "Kisswell," when they confounded *bos* with the vulgar *buss*, "to kiss." This superficial translation of surnames is particularly noticeable among the Spanish gypsies.

CZECHOSLOVAKIA

Among the Czechoslovaks there is the feminine grammatical ending of "ova" to indicate a woman. Thus *Zeman* (gentleman) is a masculine name while the feminine form is *Zemanová*. Sometimes, if the name ends in a vowel, *a* is added. Mr. *Černý's* wife is Mrs. *Černá* (black). In surnames the suffix *-ak* is frequently noted and means "like" or "as." For example, there are the names *Cermak* (like a robin) and *Chudak* (*Chudý*, poor).

The patronymic ending -*sky* has a wider signification than most patronymics as it also means "of" or "of the." The singular, masculine genitive -*ov* is often used for the patronymic, as *Pavlov* and *Petrov* for sons of Paul and Peter respectively. Diminutive forms are common, as *Masaryk* (little butcher). Double or even triple diminutive endings are not unknown.

Diminutive forms are frequently found in given names, the most common diminutive being -*ka*. There are various pet forms of given names which indicate degrees of affection. For example, commencing with the least degree of affection and proceeding to the most affectionate form, for John we would have *Jan, Jano, Janko, Janík* and *Janiček,* and for *Mary, Maria, Mara, Marka, Mariška, Marěnka and Marulienka,* the latter being more Slovak.

HAWAII

Hawaiian names have a characteristic swing to them. In almost all cases they consist of alternating consonants and vowels. Since Hawaiian has such an exiguous alphabet, consisting of only the five vowels and *h, k, l, m, n, p* and *w,* many of their names may be recognized by their limitation to these letters.

In writing, the name must be followed by the letter *k* for *kane* (man) or *w* for *wahine* (woman), which takes the place of our *Mr., Mrs.* or *Miss.* The Hawaiians make no distinction of sex in their names. Names meaning "The Moon upon the Sea" or "The Pink Flush of Dawn" are just as likely to designate a rough, burly man as a dainty maiden. A ravishing beauty may have a name meaning "Long Crooked Back" or "Door Yard Rubbish."

When a baby is named in Hawaii, the parents are not limited by the fund of existing names. In fact they are not in anywise limited to the names in existence, and few font-names are consciously repeated on the islands. With a choice so free the mother can choose from earth, sea or sky, and she does. Some incident of birth or occurrence happening at that time is likely to suggest a name. When a queen was confined in a dark room because of eye trouble about the time of the birth of her son, he was named *Hale-Pouli* (darkened house). When a servant offered unclean water and it was thrown in his face with the cry *wai-lepo-lepo* (dirty water), the name bestowed on the servant's child, born about that time, was *Wai-lepo-lepo.*

The action need not be connected with the birth of the baby. Historic events or public acts have their influence. Kings conferred names as a favor or distinction. A royal party made a tour in bright red sweaters. Upon taking leave of their hosts, the king conferred the name *Ka-Huakai-Ula* (the tour in red) as a special gift for the next child and it was so named. As an incident might be set out fully, a name could run to a great length.

Chiefs, particularly, bestowed long names. For example, there is *Kauike-a-Ouli Kalei-o-Papa Kumau-o-Lani Mahina-Lani Kalani-Nui-Waiakua Keawe-Awe-loa-o-ka-Lani,* which should be enough for one person. The *Lani* in the above name is a title of honor, equivalent to *Highness* or *Excellency* and so is properly used only in princely names. But just because it does denote royalty, some common people use it.

In late years the Hawaiians are tending to change the style of their names to agree more with ours.

JEWS

The German Jews possess artificial names of great beauty. Jews were late in adopting surnames and did not take them until compelled to. By edicts, in 1809, in Frankfort on the Main, in 1812, in Prussia, and in 1813, in Bavaria, the Jews were forced to adopt surnames. As this was long past the normal surname period, few selected occupational or patronymic family names. They did choose compounds which sounded well, as *Blumberg* (flower mountain), *Goldstein* (gold stone), *Rosenthal* (rose valley) and *Blumenthal* (valley of flowers). Names compounded with *Rose, Gold, Fein* (fine) and *Blum* (flower) were quite popular.

Those Jews who resisted the law were assigned surnames not so complimentary by intolerant officials. Some were even ridiculous or contemptuous, and a few Jews were impelled to pay a bribe to petty German officials to tone down the surnames assigned to them. In Austria, commencing in 1785, the Jews were compelled to register their new surnames, and government officials exacted various sums in return for granting names with a pleasant sound since names used by Christians were forbidden. Names derived from flowers and gems were assessed at the highest amounts. Names like *Stahl* and *Eisen* could be obtained for smaller sums, while penniless Jews received ludicrous or opprobrious names, as *Eselskopf* (donkey's head), *Wohlgeruch* (good smell) and *Küssemich* (kiss me).

Bohemia, in 1787, forced the Jews to adopt surnames. Until 1836,

in Bohemia they were restricted to Biblical names. Thus, Jewish names
of Biblical origin are numerous, as *Aaron, Cohen* and *Levy*. Also
Napoleon, in France, in 1808, required the Jews to use family names
and limited their free choice, forbidding them to take names of
localities or of famous families. Poland required Jews to adopt family
names as early as 1821, while Russia obliged them to take family names
after 1844. Jews of Spain, Portugal and Italy adopted surnames without compulsion, usually taking place names.

Cohen is the most popular Jewish name, and one of the earliest
family names in history. It indicates descent from the *kohanim*, the
priestly families The *kohanim* were given special distinction in religious ceremonies, and thus a member of the family would attach
to his ordinary name the title to acquaint others with his status in the
community. *Levy,* another common Jewish surname, signified priests
of an inferior order. This Hebrew word *Lewi* gave rise to a host of
surnomial forms, most of them beginning *Lev-*.

In the Yiddish spelling of *Cohen* the first letter may be transliterated
either as *c* or *k*, the second as *a* or *o*, the third as *h*, and the last as *n*,
whence come many of the variant spellings, *Cahn, Cohn, Kahn, Kohn*
and the like. Since the vowels are not always supplied, the *e* can be
left out or changed. Russian-speaking Jews used *Kahane, Kagan,
Kogan,* and *Cohon*. The Irish *Cohan* is not related to the Hebrew
name.

The patronymic type of surname is popular among Jews by reason
of their practice of identifying themselves by naming their father, as
Moses ben ("son of," often abbreviated to b.) *Isaac*. In Arabic-speaking
countries they used the Arabic *ibn*. Indeed, they used the common
patronymical forms in all countries, as well as the diminutive forms.
Mendel is the diminutive of *Menahem*.

Vocational surnames are less common among the Sephardim than
among Ashkenazim, where they were often used as descriptive terms
in official registers. Functions in the synagogue provide names such
as *Cantor*. Combinations with *Rabbi* are found, as *Rabbinowitsch* and
Rabbinersohn.

Mention has already been made of the use of place-names by the
Sephardic Jews. Among the German and East European Jews the
name of the city from which they had emigrated, or from which they
had been exiled, was added to their forenames. This accounts for such
surnames as *Berliner, Breslau, Danziger, Auerbach, Lipschitz, Brody,
Laski,* and *Mannheimer. Horowitz, Hurwitz, Hurwich, Howitt* and

Russian *Gurevitch* came from the Bohemian city of Horovice. *Ginzberg* and *Ginsberg* came from Ginsberg, in Bavaria.

Some Jewish surnames developed from family escutcheons, especially in southwestern Germany. The famous banking family of *Rothschild*, for example, originated from the red shield identifying their house, No. 148, in Judengasse of Frankfort-on-the-Main. Curiously, it originally bore the sign of a green shield. Another important Jewish name is *Schwarzschild*, or black shield. Animal names are common among the Jews, such as *Wolf, Fuchs* (fox), *Adler* (eagle), *Ochs* (ox), *Löwe* and *Lyon* (lion), and *Hirsch* (stag). *Katz*, however, does not refer to "cats," but is an abbreviation of *kohen tzedek,* "priest of righteousness," a form of the surname, *Cohen.*

The tendency of the Jew is to assimilate his name to those of the non-Jewish majority of any country in which he lives. The willingness of Jews to change their names to those popular in their locality is probably partially accounted for by their recent adoption. Since surnames have been used by them for such a short period of time, and then often by force of law, they do not arouse treasured associations and family pride. But the reverse of this process has revealed itself in modern Israel. There in Palestine, the Jew takes the most Hebrew form he can find; in many cases, the system of patronymics has been revived, the Jews substituting for their foreign surname, the first name of their fathers, preceded by the Hebrew *ben*.

In antiquity, many Jews had two names, one for use in Jewry, and the other, a Greek or Latin one, for use among the Gentiles. This custom is widely prevalent and has continued up to the present day. The secular name is used and registered in the usual way. The "Hebrew name" is a religious name used in the church, although in the ghettos it was sometimes used in ordinary business. It is given to boys when they are circumcised, and to girls when the father visits the synagogue, usually the first Sabbath after birth. Converts receive it on the occasion of the ritual baptism. The Hebrew name is used in marriage certificates and inscribed on the tombstone. Almost always it is the name of a close relative who has passed away. Usually it is a Biblical name, but there is no rule on the subject. Sometimes the secular name is a translation of the Jewish name or connected with it in some way. Perhaps this use of the Hebrew name is a further reason why Jews in all countries are so free to take secular names of the countries in which they live and change them so easily.

The Nazi declared names like *John* and *Elizabeth* Jewish names and therefore taboo for all loyal party members. First Storm Troopers and then "Aryan" Germans were advised that they must not use Jewish names. In their persecution of the Jews, in 1938, the fanatic followers of Hitler set aside some 185 male names and 91 female names as Jewish, and required Jews bearing other names to add *Israel* or *Sarah* to their names to identify them as Jews. This restriction was not lifted until September, 1947. The Nazi courts said that the question of the names to be given German children belonged to the sphere of public law, and refused to countenance the application of Jewish and most Bible names to "Aryan" children. Stimulated by the Nazis, France, in March, 1942, forbade Jews to change their family names. In July of the same year, Norway stopped Jews from bearing Norwegian-sounding names.

CHAPTER VIII

Personal Names in the Bible

A good name is better than precious ointment.
—ECCLESIASTES, vii, 1

THE Bible is an important document in connection with the study of personal names as it has had a prodigious influence on our surnames and Christian names. It has been estimated that more than half the people of the civilized world have names originating from the Bible. A curious fact is that while about 3,037 men are referred to by name in the Bible, only 181 women are so mentioned.

It is appropriate that we take a chapter to discuss the names of persons and of God in that holy work. Because the Bible contains writings of great antiquity, it will also have to be referred to hereafter in the chapter on primitive names.

The word "name" itself is used many times in the Bible. Strong's *Concordance* lists it about 1,085 times. The "Name of God" is used as a short phrase to mean the revealed character of God, for all that is known about Him. In the same way, "Name of Jesus" is employed by Christians.

To understand the personal names in the Bible it is first necessary to know the names applied to God in the Old Testament. Proper names for God were more important then when the existence of one God only was not so firmly established. We worship God today with no thought of His name as we cannot conceive of there being other gods.

Dionysius the Areopagite, an early Christian mystic, compiled a treatise on the names of God in the fifth century, A.D. He contended that no name fits God because he stands above all things that have names, and, since he is the creator of all things, all names of all things could be applied to Him.

The three most important names for God in the Hebrew Old Testament are *Elohim,* meaning "one who is worshipped or adored"; *El,*
"strength or power"; and *Jehovah* or *Yahveh,* in appearance the third
person singular imperfect of the verb, "to be." Among the Jews there
were said to be seven names for God which were so sacred that they
required special care, and a scribe, when writing them, must not stop
after once beginning the name until completion. If an error is made
when writing one of these names, it may not be erased. Besides the
above three names, the other four were *Adonai,* meaning "Lord";
Ehyeh-Asher-Ehyeh, "I am that I am"; *Shaddai,* "almighty, or all
sufficient"; and *Zeba'ot,* "armies or hosts of men."

We will discuss in some detail only these three outstanding names
for God in the Bible, *Elohim, El* and *Yahveh.* They all reach back
into such remote antiquity that there is wide disagreement among
men of learning as to their exact origin and meaning. We shall here
concern ourselves chiefly with the derivations most widely accepted
by the best authorities.

The first name for God in the Old Testament is *Elohim.* It occurs
in the first chapter of *Genesis* and generally throughout that book.
It is found 2,570 times in the Bible.

Elohim is a plural form, *Eloah,* the singular. *Eloah,* however, is
found only a few times in the Old Testament and then chiefly in the
poetical and later books. To one knowing the Hebrew striving
for the worship of one God this use of the name in the plural may
seem somewhat irregular. Some have explained it by saying that it
signified the Trinity in the Godhead—Father, Son and Holy Spirit—
but most Bible scholars are of the opinion that the plural is most often
used for reasons of emphasis, to express greatness, dignity, excellence
or intensity of some kind and thus designate the one true and only
God. They base this opinion on usage in connection with other Hebrew
words and on the fact that generally the verbs used with *Elohim* are
not in the plural.

As Eloah, derived from the verb, *alah,* "worshipped or adored,"
Elohim might be understood to express "the most worshipful," the
Being to whom worship, reverence and adoration are supremely due.

Next the name, *El,* appears early in the Bible, but is found only 217
times, and then chiefly in poetry. At first sight this may be thought to
be either a shortened form, or root word, for Elohim, but most authorities ascribe an independent origin to the term. Its plural form is
Elim. Lexicographers pretty generally agree that it signifies "strength,

might or power." In its use as a common noun it is analogous to our
Anglo-Saxon, *God*, although it doesn't agree with it in meaning—*God*
probably means "one who is invoked, or to whom sacrifice is offered."
Although used often as a common noun, it is also a name for God
because God Himself used it in His manifestations to Abraham and
Jacob.

And now we come to the most important name of all—*Yahveh*, or
Jehovah, as it is printed in our Bibles. This is strictly and absolutely
the "proper Name" of God, not being given, as the other names sometimes have been, to heathen gods. Yahveh is the word in the Hebrew
text whenever in the authorized and revised English versions of the
Bible we find the word LORD printed all in capitals, and it occurs
6,823 times in the Old Testament, and not once in the New Testament.
In the New Testament the word for God in the Greek, Hebrew and
Aramaic manuscripts is always translated "Lord." The Revised Standard Version, being prepared by the American Standard Bible Committee, will substitute *Lord* for *Jehovah* because the Committee
considers that "Jehovah is not a functioning religious term."

This name was first disclosed by God from the burning bush to
Moses in response to Moses' plea that He tell him His name so that
the children of Israel would know that Moses was truly sent to them
by God, to lead them out of bondage. It is set out in *Exodus* iii, 13-15,
where God replied,

I AM THAT I AM: Thus shalt thou say unto the children of Israel, I
AM hath sent me unto you. Thus shalt thou say unto the children of Israel,
The LORD [Jehovah] God of your fathers, the God of Abraham, the God
of Isaac, and the God of Jacob hath sent me unto you: this is my name for
ever, and this is my memorial unto all generations.

It has been suggested that God here gave His proper name to Moses
not merely so he could tell it to his people, but to bind his promise.
The pronunciation by God of His name may thus be similar to the
setting of our signature to a document. If another write my name, it
has no binding force on me; but when I sign it to a document I thereby
signify my assent to the contents.

The original Hebrew for "I AM THAT I AM" is *Ehyeh-Asher-
Ehyeh*. When God speaks His name He used the first person, but
when another utters the Name, he uses the third person, *Yahveh*, "He
is," rather than "I am." However in other and later pronouncements
by God, He used the third person, as in *Exodus* vi, 2 and *Isaiah* xlii, 8.

Elsewhere in the Bible God disclosed His name, as in *Exodus* vi, 2-3, where He said, "I am the LORD [Jehovah]: And I appeared unto Abraham, unto Isaac, and unto Jacob, by the name of God Almighty [El Shaddai]: but by my name JEHOVAH was I not known to them." In *Exodus* xxxiv, 5, He proclaimed: "the name of the LORD." In *Isaiah* xlii, 8, He said, "I am the LORD: that is my name."

The meaning of the most sacred name of God is therefore to be derived from the Hebrew verb, *hayah*, "to be," and the name of God therefore signifies self-existence. There is considerable diversity of opinion among Hebrew scholars as to the exact primary meaning of the name, whether it comes from the past, present or future tense of the verb, some denying that the Hebrew language has a true future tense. John repeatedly speaks of God as the Being "which is, and which was, and which is to come" (*Revelation* i, 4, 8; xi, 17). In general, scholars have assigned to the sacred name of God the meanings, "He who is, He who was, and He who will be," or eternal self-existence. Of course there are investigators who have professed to find the origin of *Yahveh* in the Egyptian, Chinese or Chaldean languages, but the most conclusive arguments favor the Hebrew.

Naturally, as the name *Yahveh* was revealed by God Himself, the Jews have always regarded it with extraordinary reverence from very ancient times. Because of this sacredness they have refrained from pronouncing it, the reader in the synagogue substituting the word *Adonai*, "Lord," when it occurs by itself. If *Adonai* is found with it in the text, *Elohim* is read in place of it. If the Jews thought thus to keep the Name from the pagans, they were unsuccessful, because this secrecy they gave the Name, originating in reverence, merely heightened its power in pagan eyes and it became by far the most important magical name, as described in the chapter on "Primitive Names." Later the Jews even substituted incorrect spellings for *Elohim* and *Adonai*.

In the Hebrew the name is spelled יהוה (YHVH, in English), pronounced, "Yod He Vav He," and is often called the Tetragrammaton, or four-lettered name. The Tetragrammaton in its pronounced form is the *Shem-ha-meforsh*, "the Name as clearly pronounced," which in course of time came to be used in the sense of "the Ineffable Name." The *Shem-ha-meforsh* also is used to designate an amulet or phylactery with the Tetragrammaton on it. In its written form the Tetragrammaton is called the *Azkarah*. Other substitutions for *Yahveh* by the Jews are "Lord," "the Name," "the Name of four letters," "the great and terrible Name," "the unutterable Name," "the ineffable

Name," "the incommunicable Name," "the Holy Name" and "the distinguished Name."

Traditionally, after the captivity, the Jews pronounced the Name only once a year. This was by the High Priest in the Temple on Yom Kippur or Day of Atonement, and then in an indistinct manner while invoking the blessing (*Numbers* vi, 24-26) during the chant of the priests, so that the people listening could not hear it. On this occasion the people would prostrate themselves and recite "Praised be the name of His glorious kingdom forever and ever." In the *Mishnah* it is stated, "In the Temple they pronounced the Name as it is written, but in the provinces by a substituted word" (Sotah 7.6 and Tamid 7.2). After the destruction of the Temple the Name was never pronounced at all.

Josephus, among many other Jewish writers, adheres closely to this interdiction. In Book II, Chapter XII, Section 4, after saying that Moses, before the burning bush, requested God to reveal His name, Josephus writes, "Whereupon God declared to him his holy name, which had never been discovered to men before; concerning which it is not lawful for me to say any more." In the Rabbinical writings *Yahveh* is distinguished by various euphemistic expressions, as "the Name," "the Name of four letters," "the great and terrible Name," "the peculiar Name," "the separate Name," and many others. Maimonides refrains as much as possible from writing not only the Tetragrammaton but also the name, *Adonai,* substituted for it. Even today the great majority of the Jews never write the Tetragrammaton in full nor do they pronounce it. They note it in writing generally by some abbreviation, often by from one to four Yods, or sometimes the Yods combined with some other sign.

So that even the suggestion of writing the Most Holy Name may be avoided, when some other word is intended, the Jews have a special way of writing the number fifteen. It would naturally be *Yod-He* (ten and five); but *Yod-He* spells *Yah,* a short form of the Ineffable Name. So for fifteen the Jews write, in Hebrew, *Teth-Wau* (nine and six). Then for sixteen and succeeding numbers they go back to *Yod-Wau,* etc., for the Name is no longer in danger.

The true pronunciation of the Name has been forever lost and today no scholar can be sure of the exact sound, particularly of the second syllable. Without going into the various theories and arguments for the different pronunciations, it may be said that the majority of the leading Hebrew theologians agree that the correct English transliteration is probably *Yahveh* or *Yahve.* Among German scholars the name is given as *Jahweh, Jahveh, Jahve* or *Yahweh*, but they use *J* for English Y and *w* for *v*. Practically all agree that *Jehovah* is not a correct rendering of the Name, but it is now so familiar to the people that Bible translators refuse to substitute a strange form.

The Hebrew alphabet is composed almost entirely of consonants and the vowels have to be filled in when the words are pronounced. Now, in the Hebrew, vowel points are added to indicate what vowels are to be used, but this practice has been in vogue only for the last thirteen or fourteen hundred years.

Jehovah is formed from the Tetragrammaton, giving it the vowels of *Edonai* or *Adonai*, and is strictly a Christian form, never having been employed by the Jews. It was first used in 1270. The whole matter has been well illustrated by Wilbur Fletcher Steele in *The Independent* (November 17, 1898) by supposing that English was written with consonants only. Suppose "JHVH S M SHPHRD, I SHLL NT WNT" was written. Now giving JHVH the vowels of "Edonai" (Lord) it would be written "JeHoVaH iS My SHePHeRD, I SHaLL NoT WaNT."

Now, suppose that our language was written a hundred years ago without vowels. Then there might be the following inscription: "WSHNGTN WS TH FTHR F HS CNTR." Then suppose Washington became so sacred that it would be blasphemy to utter his name, and, whenever it appeared, "My Master" was used. Then suppose that the vowels are inserted, but the sacred name was given the vowels of "My Master." The inscription would then be read, "WySHaNGTeN WaS THe FaTHeR oF HiS CouNTRy." Next imagine that the Koreans became interested in our literature and history in a religious manner. They would innocently think and speak of the great *Wyshangten* as the great American saint. Similarly with *Jehovah*.

The Jewish prohibition on pronunciation of the Name is founded on *Leviticus* xxiv, 16:

"And he that blasphemeth the name of the LORD, he shall surely be put to death, and all the congregation shall certainly stone him: as well the stranger, as he that is born in the land, when he blasphemeth the name of the LORD, shall be put to death."

Compare the attempted stoning of Jesus in *John* viii, 58-59, when the Jews heard him pronounce the sacred Name. One of the martyrs of Hadrian's time, Hananiah b. Teradion, was burned at the stake because he uttered the Name.

To the Jews, blasphemy was not what we call swearing or cursing, but consisted only in utterance of the sacred Name. The third commandment says (*Exodus* xx, 7), "Thou shall not take the name of the LORD thy God in vain."

When in early times one Jew thought that another Jew had unlawfully uttered the sacred Name he must rend his clothes, that being a symbol of rejection and also the common sign of mourning. The custom was based on *II Kings* xviii, 37. The rents were not sewed up again, indicating deepest mourning. But if a heathen or unbeliever blasphemed, Jewish hearers were not required to rend their garments. Also when testifying to the matter in the Jewish court witnesses were not expected to tear their clothes a second time, if they had rent them upon first hearing the sacred Name pronounced.

In the *Mishnah* (Sanhedrin 7.5) it is stated:

The blasphemer is not culpable unless he pronounces the Name itself. R. Joshua b. Karha says: On every day (of the trial) they examined the witnesses with a substituted name (such as) "May Jose smite Jose." When sentence was to be given they did not declare him guilty of death (on the grounds of evidence given) with the substituted name, but they sent out all the people and asked the chief among the witnesses and said to him, "Say expressly what thou heardest," and he says it; and the judges stand up on their feet and rend their garments, and they may not mend them again. And the second witness says, "I also heard the like," and the third says, "I also heard the like."

One modern, gentile writer felt so strongly about using the sacred name, *Yahveh*, that he rushed into print with a pamphlet entitled, *Away with God and Christianity*, later softened, in a second edition, to *God is Not the Name*. In it, with copious quotations from the Bible, he attempted to show that God was only a title for Yahveh, which should be used and that His worship should be designated *Yahwism*. *Christianity* and *God* were terms, he contended, which were provided by the Devil to divert to himself the worship which should be given to Yahveh. Passages in the Bible which do not support his thesis were explained as "errors in translation."

Modern Biblical criticism has laid great stress on the names used for God in the Bible. The documentary theory of the Pentateuch commenced almost two hundred years ago with the observation of the use of *Elohim* and *Yahveh* in the first five books of the Bible. That portion using the name, *Elohim* was designated the *E* document, and the writer who called God *Yahveh* (or Jehovah) is thought to be the author of the *J* document.

Yah, as a name for God, occurs a few times in the Hebrew Bible, independently of any other name. Some have thought this to be the original form of the Divine Name, but it is now generally held to be a shortened or abbreviated form. This form seems to be free of the prohibitions attached to the Tetragrammaton, and has been freely used in many personal names among the Biblical Jews, as we shall soon see.

Names given by the Hebrews to their children were often formed by reason of some peculiarity in the person of the new-born infant or to some event that had recently happened to the family or nation. Other names were given in a spirit of prayer because they expressed some moral or religious truth or some hope, expectation or desire on behalf of the child. Names like *Samuel* or *Shemaiah*, meaning "God hath heard," may have been given to mark the fact that sons were born in answer to prayer. Scriptural names were not arbitrarily chosen, but were selected with the idea of expressing some important religious truth relating the bearer to God.

The most important name in the New Testament was given by God, for we read in *Matthew* i, 21, where the angel of the Lord said to Joseph concerning Mary, "And she shall bring forth a son, and thou shalt call his name JESUS: for he shall save his people from their sins." The name had also previously been revealed to Mary (*Luke* i, 31).

Jesus thus means "Yahveh saves." Jesus is the Latin form of the Greek word for the Hebrew, *Jehoshua*, contracted to *Joshua*. Isaiah prophesied that they shall call His name *Immanuel*, meaning "God with us" (*Isaiah* vii, 14). Jesus was not called Immanuel and Bible scholars have not yet succeeded in presenting a convincing explanation of the seeming discrepancy. Some have contended that Immanuel was never really intended as a name, but only as a symbol to the faithful that God would be with His people in the time of crisis. Others have pointed to the obvious fact that if Jesus had adopted the name of Immanuel, the Jews would have attempted to kill him before he had embarked on his ministry. But perhaps a more rational explanation is found in the similarity of meaning between the name *Jesus* and the name *Immanuel*, and the fact that significance rather than sound made a Hebrew's name.

At first the words, "the Christ," were applied to Jesus as a title which meant "the Anointed One." After the Resurrection it gradually became a proper name, being applied by Christians only to Jesus of Nazareth.

The Holy Name Society of the Catholics is an ancient association formed to promote veneration of the Holy Name of Jesus. It also crusades against profanity among Catholic men.

Many other names have been applied to Jesus and there are many books on the names and titles of Jesus (mostly of a devotional character); upon close inspection many of them will be found to have been used only to call attention to His attributes or character. In the same way the Mohammedans put a great deal of emphasis on the ninety-nine "beautiful names" of Allah.

That personal names are important in the Bible is revealed by the names given or changed by the direct intervention of God. In the New Testament, besides designating the name of Jesus, He also directed Zacharias to name his son, *John* (*Luke* i, 13).

The Old Testament recites that God directed *Abram* to change his name to *Abraham* and the name of his wife from *Sarai* to *Sarah* (*Genesis* xvii, 5, 15). He explained, "for a father of many nations have I made thee." Abram means "exalted father," while Abraham means "father of a multitude." Sarai (not explained in the Bible) means "contentious" or "quarrelsome," whereas Sarah denotes a "princess." In a similar manner He changed *Jacob's* name to Israel (*Genesis* xxxii, 28). He directed Abraham to call his son *Isaac* (*Genesis* xvii, 19); Hagar to call her son *Ishmael* (*Genesis* xvi, 11); and David to call his son *Solomon* (*I Chronicles* xxii, 9).

The names of various other persons in the Bible were also appointed by God. Surely names must be important or God would not select so many of them. Moses changed the name of *Oshea*, the son of Nun, to *Jehoshua* (*Numbers* xiii, 16).

Names among the Biblical Hebrews were deemed to be important and were always given with an acute consciousness of their meaning. Witness the Bible recording the meanings of such names as *Reuben*, meaning "see, a son"; *Simeon*, "bearing"; *Levi*, "my joining"; *Judah*, "praise"; *Dan*, "He judged"; *Gad*, "a troop"; *Asher*, "blessed"; *Issachar*, "hire"; *Zebulun*, "dwelling"; and *Joseph*, "He adds" (*Genesis* xxix, 32 to xxx, 24). New Testament names were also given with reference to some trait in the child, hope, or commemorative of some event occurring at that time. A careful study of all parts of the Scriptures will reveal the fact that the Bible fairly teems with allusions to the meanings of personal names.

Basing his opinion on name meanings, Dr. Nathaniel J. Reich, of

Dropsie College, has advanced the theory that *Laban* (in the Bible, *Genesis*, xxix) was an albino and his daughter, *Leah*, also was an albino, and that is why Jacob loved Rachel more than Leah. He points out that *Laban* means "white" and *Leah* means "weary," which would fit in with the description of an albino. The name of *Laban* would not refer to his hair or beard because, presumably, the name was given early in life. In *Genesis* xxix, 17, it says: "Leah was tender eyed; but Rachel was beautiful and well favoured."

According to Hebrew modes of thought and expression in regard to proper names, the significance rather than the precise form of a word made it a person's name. Within certain limits the form might be changed if the meaning remained unchanged, or only slightly changed. Thus persons are mentioned in the Bible at different times under different forms which mean the same; however, our Bible versions generally use the same form in order to be consistent. But see *Numbers* x, 29, where Moses' father-in-law is called *Raguel,* while in *Exodus* ii, 18, he is mentioned as *Reuel*. Both forms mean "friend of God." In the New Testament the apostle, *Thomas,* was also called *Didymus,* and both mean "twin," the former in Aramaic and the latter in Greek. *Peter* and *Cephas* are two names for the same person and both mean "rock," the first being Greek and the second, Aramaic.

It is characteristic among ancient peoples to form their personal names from the names of their gods. This is particularly true with our Hebrew names in the Bible; the names of God enter freely into their composition. Proper names compounded with *El* occur very early in the sacred record. The first is *Mehujael,* the great grandson of Cain, meaning "stricken or smitten by God." These very early names are probably not the names actually borne since Hebrew is not the earliest language, but are probably translations of those names into the Hebrew tongue.

An examination of the ordinary proper names of persons in the Bible will disclose the fact that the majority include one or another of the shorter forms of the Divine name. *El*, at the beginning, as *Eliakim,* or at the end, as *Israel,* is of very frequent occurrence. *Jah* is found more often, although it is not always so apparent in our mode of representing the Hebrew names. The names which end in *-jah* and most of those which begin with *Jeh* or end with *-iah* have the Divine name *Jah* or *Yahveh* as a syllable in their composition. Also many of the names which terminate in *-i* or *-ai* contain a fragment or mutilated form of *Jah*. Many more names contain *Jah* at the end than at the beginning, probably in accordance with Jewish habits of reverence to assign the Divine name the less rather than the more prominent position.

At the same time there are names which apparently contain the Divine name but do not actually do so. *El* is not God in *Eli* or *Abel* or *Rachel*; *Jah* is not the name, *Jah* or *Yahveh*, in *Jahleel* or *Jahaziah*, nor is *Jeh* in *Jehiel* or *Jehu* nor *iah* in *Beriah* and *Aphiah*.

As an example, take the verb, *Nathan*, in itself the name of several persons, which means "He hath given," referring, of course, to God. *El* can be added to it, either at the beginning or end and we have *Elnathan* and *Nathaniel*. In the same way *Yahveh* can be used and we have *Jonathan* and *Nethaniah*. The verb for "hath graciously given," *Hanan*, a name, can be used and we have *Elhanan*, *Hanniel*, *Johanan* (can be shortened into John) and *Hananiah*. All of these Hebrew names are found in the Old Testament.

There are many names in the Bible which appear very different but are actually different only because *El* or *Jah* is used. *Ezekiel* and *Hezekiah* are the same and mean "God, or Yahveh, shall strengthen." *Eliakim* and *Jehoiakim* mean "God, or Yahveh, establishes." *Elisha* and *Isaiah* mean "God, or Yahveh, [is] salvation."

Sometimes the same person may be intended when *El* is at the beginning of the name as at the end. A son of Simeon was called *Jemuel*, "God circumcises [him]," and elsewhere is called *Nemuel*. This name is an obvious reference to the Jewish custom of giving the name on the day of circumcision, the eighth day after birth.

Two well-known, but curious, names are *Elijah* and *Joel*, which contain both names for God. They establish that "God is Yahveh" or "Yahveh is God," and may be rendered, "My God is Yahveh" or "Yahveh is God." The probability is that Elijah and Joel are identical and both are meant to have exactly the same meaning.

Composite names in Hebrew are usually made up either of two names or a noun and a verb. When the Divine Name forms a part, it is the noun, and then some action is ascribed to God or predicated with respect to Him, and the name is thus a complete sentence. For example, there is *Zebadiah*, "Yahveh has given," and *Jehoshaphat* "Yahveh judges." Some characteristic of God or relation in which He stands to men is stated, as *Elidad*, "love of God," *Maaziah*, "consolation of Yahveh."

In all the heathen nations of antiquity, personal names occur compounded of the names of their gods. Some of these are mentioned in the Bible, the most conspicuous of which are *Baal* and *Nebo,* such as *Baalhanan* and *Nebuchadnezzar. Baal,* however, has been applied to the Hebrew God. In its meaning of "Lord," in the sense of master or owner, it has been freely employed in Old Testament writings.

Many Hebrew personal names contain the word *Ab,* "father," as *Abimelech,* meaning "[whose] father is king." Other such names are *Abiathar,* "[whose] father remains," *Abinadab,* "noble father," *Abner,* "[whose] father [is] Ner," *Abigail,* "[whose] father rejoiceth." *Ab* is also combined with *Jah,* as in *Abiah* or*Avijah,* meaning "[whose] father [is] Yahveh." The frequency of the use of *Father* in the Bible, referring both to a parent and a quality, prepares us to expect to find the word in proper names. Other names in the Old Testament have the elements *ben,* "son," *ah,* "brother," *melech,* "king," and *amm,* "kinsmen or people." Some authorities are of the opinion that in this type of name we find secondary references to God.

Some Hebrew personal names are names of animals, as *Rachel,* meaning a "ewe," *Caleb,* "dog," *Debora,* "bee," *Tabitha,* "gazelle," *Hamon,* "ass," *Johab,* "dove," and *Nahash,* "serpent." The use of animal names as personal names was most common in the earliest Hebrew periods, the tendency to use names with a religious significance not being so marked as it afterward became.

Names compounded with *El* were in use from the earliest to the latest times. Compounds with *Yahveh* or *Jah* were rare before David's time but became common after that. The semidivine compounds, that is those formed with *ab, adon, ah, am, baal, dad, did,* and *melech,* had ceased to be formed by the time of the Exile. The names compounded with *El, Elohim* and *Yahveh* gradually became the favorite class of names, being very popular in the later periods.

Although the word *surname* is found in the Bible it is not used in the sense of a family name. The closest thing to a family name found in Holy Writ is a designation of some persons as Rechabites, Korahites, etc., from the name of a common ancestor.

However, in the Bible we have the beginnings of surnames, a descriptive word used when it was necessary to distinguish between individuals with the same name, and it was based on the same kind of elements as compose surnames today. Thus we find *Simon Barjonas,* i.e., "the son of Jonas." The local element is found in *Simon of Cyrene,* and the nickname or descriptive element in *Simon the Zealot.* Similarly we find *Judas Barsabas, Judas of Galilee* and *Judas Iscariot,* the first a patronymic and the last two referring to the place from whence they came. It is doubtful, however, whether these descriptive surnames were ever used in the lifetime of these individuals, and it is probable that they arose only in writings about them long after their death. We find expressions like "Lebbaeus whose surname was Thaddaeus" (*Matthew* x, 3), "and Simon He surnamed Peter" (*Mark* iii, 16), and "Simon, whose surname is Peter" (*Acts* x, 5), but these are alternate names rather than surnames.

Unlike the English language, names with the initial *Z* were quite popular in Biblical times. There are ninety-six names in the Bible commencing with the letter *Z*. The most popular name, in that more characters in the Bible bear it than any other name, is *Azariah*: twenty-eight different persons mentioned in the Bible bear this name. Next to *Azariah* is *Zechariah* which is the name of twenty-seven characters; then comes Shemaiah, the name of twenty-five different persons; *Meshullam* names twenty-one, while *Maaseiah* follows with twenty.

Most of the famous names in the Old Testament designate only one person, such as *David, Solomon, Abraham, Samson, Isaac, Jacob, Noah, Rachel, Samuel* and *Sarah*. In the New Testament there is just one *Thomas*, but nine bear the name of *Simon*, seven, *Joseph, Judas* and *Mary*, five bear *Simeon* and *Alexander*, while *Gaius, James, John* and *Philip* have four each.

Names in the New Testament have influenced our nomenclature today more than those of the Old Testament, probably because they are there often found in their Latin and Greek forms, which are more immediately related to our language than the older Hebrew words. Another reason is the attitude of the Catholic Church in favoring the names of the disciples of Jesus and His apostles. Many of our most popular Christian names and surnames are traceable directly to the New Testament.

The influence of names in the Bible is evident. A large proportion of the people, not only in this country, but the whole world over, bear Bible names. A hundred years ago names from the Old Testament were prominent. Today the most common name for boys is the Biblical *John*, and for girls, the Biblical *Mary*.

CHAPTER IX

Primitive Names

As his name is, so is he.
—I Samuel, xxv, 25

IT IS indeed a primitive group that does not name its individuals. Very few tribes have been discovered that exist without some sort of personal appellation, although certain aborigines in Australia have been found to be without personal names; Herodotus and Pliny record that the Astantes in Africa did not have proper names. When you consider it, you will see that men without names can be little higher than animals when they can live together without feeling the imperative need to designate each other in some exact way by the spoken word.

Among the most primitive people the first sounds with meanings were probably proper names. The earliest names invented by primitive man may even have been songs. The early talkers were probably lively men and women babbling or singing merrily on for the mere pleasure, like a child, of producing sounds. It has been suggested that a string of syllables sung to some rude kind of melody may have been so characteristic of a certain individual that it came to be repeated by others to signalize his approach, thus evolving into a name for him.

Perhaps names were first formally bestowed at some important religious ceremony, because the crude and sometimes ludicrous name by which a man might be addressed would be out of place there and not suitable for solemn intonation. Among people on a low level of culture names became a most important and vital part of themselves, with an influence and a force all their own.

Even surnames or family names have been discovered among primitive peoples. The peoples of some South African tribes use the name of the earliest known ancestor as a surname. This is called the *Shibongo,* or laudatory name, and is used when one wishes to flatter another or be especially respectful to him. Consequently, adults prefer being called by this byname.

Although early Anglo-Saxon and Germanic families did not have family names, they did make some attempt to identify the offspring with the family through certain well-defined principles. According to Henry Bosley Woolf in *The Old Germanic Principles of Name-Giving*, the chief principles were alliteration, variation and repetition. The first may be illustrated by the pedigree of the early Danes mentioned in *Beowulf*, which contains the following names with *h* as the initial letter: *Healfdene* had sons, *Heorogar*, *Hrothgar* and *Halga*; the first son bore *Heoroweard*, the second *Hrethric* and *Hrothmund* and the third, *Hrothulf*.

Variation is the practice of forming a new name by the change of a name-theme, as *Ælfred* and *Æthelred*, *Wiglaf* and *Wigmund*, or the addition of an element to an uncompounded name, as *Gode* and *Godgifu*, or the transposition of name-themes, as *Wulfbeorht* and *Beorhtwulf*. Many old Germanic peoples practiced this principle in bestowing names in a family. Both girls and boys were given names that varied with that of their parents. Sometimes the name of a child is composed of two elements, one from the father's name and one from the mother's—a double variation—*Wulfstan,* the famous Bishop of Worcester, was the son of *Ethelstan* and *Wulfgifu*. This explains why the meaning of Teutonic names can usually be obtained only by translating the two name elements and recognizing that they usually have little or no relationship to each other. This principle is also found among the ancient Hindus, Persians, Greeks, Slavs and Celts.

The third principle, that of repetition, is the one with which we are so familiar. It consists of repeating the exact name of the father for the son. Many kings' names bear witness to this practice. A study of the genealogies of the West Saxon kings as given in the *Anglo-Saxon Chronicle* will disclose copious examples of all of these principles, alliteration, variation and repetition.

In framing names on the principle of the double list, certain elements are generally found first and certain others generally last, while a few are found in either position, with little regard for their meanings. In Anglo-Saxon names the most usual first elements were words meaning royal, noble, fortunate, beloved. The list of endings contains words signifying ruler, guardian, spear, sword, wolf, bright, helmet. Examples are: *Ethelbert* and *Albert* (noble, bright), and *Edgar* (fortunate, spear).

The animals that served chiefly as models of perfection to our early forbears were the bear, wolf, boar, eagle, swan, raven and serpent. Elements of religion were mixed with them. The bear was the chief of the beasts in the North and was worshipped by the people. Another sacred animal was the boar. The wolf and the raven were regarded as of good omen. The swan and the serpent were generally confined to feminine names.

The tenacious adherence of superstition in our times has branded many names as unlucky in certain situations. Both *John* and *Jane* are held to be unlucky names, particularly among royalty, and long lists of unlucky monarchs can be cited in support of the proposition. *Davis, Davies, Thomas* and *John* were regarded as unlucky for sailors and fishermen in Wales, while *Jones, Yorath, Howe, Lloyd* and *Leyahon* were regarded as fortunate.

On the other hand, some names in the past have been thought to be favorable. Cicero tells us that the rolls of Roman levies were sure to begin with favorable names like *Victor, Felix, Faustus, Secundus* or *Salvius Valerius.*

It is remarkable that, by coincidence, men of the same name have begun and ended great states and empires. *Cyrus,* the Great, son of Cambyses, founded the Persian empire; *Cyrus,* the son of Darius, ruined it; *Darius,* the son of Hystaspes, restored it again, but *Darius,* the son of Arsamis, utterly overthrew it. *Philip,* the son of Amyntas, greatly extended the kingdom of Macedon; *Philip,* the son of Antigonus, completely lost it. *Augustus* was the first emperor of Rome; *Augustus* was the name of the last Roman emperor of the West. *Constantine* the Great founded the city of Constantinople (now Istanbul); *Constantine* XI, the last, surrendered it to the Turks more than eleven centuries later. *Leopold* I was the first king of modern Belgium; is *Leopold* III the last? *Peter* I was the first king of Yugoslavia; *Peter* II appears to be the last.

In early times in America the name *Doctor* was sometimes imposed on a seventh son in allusion to the belief that seventh sons possessed an intuitive knowledge of the use of herbs. In parts of England and among the Negroes in America there is a superstition that one will become wealthy if the initials of his name spell a word.

Some races give a provisional name at birth merely for practical purposes and then bestow a real name, such as that of an honored ancestor, or the so-called totemic or theophoric name, with a prescribed ceremony when the child reaches a certain age, as shown by some visible sign, such as the first tooth, end of suckling, puberty, etc. A few tribes give set names according to order of birth. Sometimes the true name is not given until the child, if a boy, has killed an enemy, or, with both boys and girls, at the time of the initiation ceremonies. Complicated systems of name-changing among primitive peoples sometimes arise by ethnic fusions. In some West African tribes a child is named after the day of the week on which it was born.

The Ibo, of Nigeria, give a child two names at birth. One is given by the father's family and the other by the mother's family. In later life only one name is used, that selected by the more prominent family. When there is controversy as to which this shall be, each family may use the name chosen by it. Young couples in our day often do not resolve their difficulties so neatly.

The Shawnee myth of *Yellow Sky* is an illustration of the use of names and their supposed power. Yellow Sky was a daughter of the tribe who dreamed that she had been brought into this world to perform an important, mystic mission. None could understand the meaning of her evening songs. On one definite condition she consented to become a wife and that was that her husband should never mention her name. If he did, a terrible thing would befall him. When she sickened and died her last request was that he would never breathe her name. For five years he lived in solitude, but one day while beside her grave an Indian asked him whose it was and, without thinking, in reply he spoke her name. The next morning a large buck was quietly feeding near Yellow Sky's grave—it was the unhappy husband.

Swedish folk-lore recites how a bridegroom and his friends were riding through the woods when they were transformed into wolves by the evil spirits. After many years had passed, the still mournful bride passed through the same forest and thought of her husband, and thinking, shrieked out his name. Immediately her lost lover appeared before her and took her in his arms. The sound of his name had broken the power of the evil spirits.

Another curious illustration of the belief of early man in the magical power of names is the *Tom Tit Tot* type of folk-tale which is well-nigh universal. There are many versions, but they all center around the power which comes from learning the elf's name. Following is a short synopsis of the story:

Once upon a time there was a woman who told the king that her daughter could spin the extraordinary quantity of five skeins a day. The king said that he would marry the daughter and give her everything she wanted for eleven months out of the year, but that during the last month she would have to spin five skeins every day or he would kill her. The girl could not spin at all, but she and her mother thought that the king would forget his whim. So they were married and for eleven months the girl had everything she wanted. At the end of that time the king put her into a room, bare but for a spinning wheel and a stool, and gave her some food and some flax and said she would have to produce five skeins each day, and away he went. While the girl was crying she heard a knock at the window and a small black thing with a tail hopped in and offered to take the flax each morning and bring it spun at night. As pay he would give her three guesses each day as to his name and if she failed to guess it before the month was up, she would be his. She agreed as she thought she would surely guess it before the month was up. He kept his part of the bargain, and each day she failed to guess his name. The evening before the last day the king came to visit her and dined with her. He said that he had been out hunting that day and, hearing a humming in an old chalk pit, he went over quietly and peeked in and saw a funny little black thing spinning its spinning wheel rapidly, singing—

> "Nimmy nimmy not,
> My name's Tom Tit Tot."

The girl jumped with joy but did not say a word. The next day when the thing came back with the skeins the girl, pretending to be afraid, made two wrong guesses and then said, pointing her finger at it—

> "Nimmy nimmy not,
> Your name's Tom Tit Tot."

Upon hearing his name, the thing shrieked in rage and flew into the dark, and she never saw it again.

This story in its German form is known to many under the title, *Rumpelstiltskin*, due to the work of the brothers, Jacob and Wilhelm Grimm. Both stories express the utter defeat of the dwarfs when their names are known.

At the time of the Spanish conquest the most important Indian people in Guatemala were the Quichés. With them, legend has it that after the Creator had made the birds and animals, He observed that they could not utter His name. He therefore made man and reduced the animals on the face of the earth to be eaten or killed.

Among some savage peoples the rather widespread custom exists (called teknonymy) of naming the parents after the children, particularly the first born, as "the father of Obong" and "the mother of Obong." When a child grows up, the parent is sometimes renamed after a younger child. When all the children reach adulthood, the parents may be named after their grandchildren. This change of name practice is called, "making oneself young." Sir James George Frazer tells of a man who, having lost four children, named himself grandfather of the fifth to deceive the evil spirits into believing that he had no children. Some Eskimos take new names when they are old in an effort to get a new lease on life.

Among some of the Indians of South America after a ceremonial killing of a captured enemy, the executioner rushes wildly for his hut to escape the spirit of the victim. At the same time his sisters and female cousins hurry through the village shouting, "This is my brother's new name," and proclaiming the new name by which he must thereafter be known. Others who have participated in the ritual also must change their names to escape the dead man's spirit.

One characteristic of names, found widely among numerous tribes and peoples scattered throughout the earth, is the possession by each individual of a secret name which others do not know. The belief was that if others knew it, they would attain power over the owner of the name. It is universally supposed that when one sneezes his name has been pronounced by an enemy or some malignant spirit; hence the evil influence is, in every part of the world, counteracted by some protective formula, such as "God bless you" or "Zur Gesundheit." The primitive man regarded his name as a vital portion of himself, endowed it with the properties of an *alter ego*, and took care of it accordingly.

In some tribes this concealed name was known by the older men but not by the women; in others only the parents of a child knew it, and it was not communicated to the child until the latter was able to guard its secrecy. Women in some tribes never knew their secret names—perhaps the tribe had discovered that women could not keep secrets. Among some peoples each person had both a secret name and a public name. For instance, the Indian princess, Pocahontas, who saved John Smith, bore *Matokes* as a secret name. Private names are never mentioned except on the most solemn occasions, and then in a whisper and never in the presence of other than the initiated members of the group.

The care which savage peoples took of their names is shown by their extreme reluctance to tell them to a stranger. This has caused some explorers to think that certain tribes either had no names or had forgotten their names, when there was only present a fear that the stranger would, upon learning their names, exercise an evil power over them.

In some tribes this taboo extends only to disclosure by the individual of his own name. When an Ojibway Indian is asked his name, he will look at some bystander and ask him to answer, and will, in turn, answer for the bystander. The Ojibways think that if they repeat their own names, their growth will be stunted and they will be small in stature.

Numerous peoples have thought that their breath and their name have a vital connection. American Indians, when asked their names by the whites, have either refused point-blank or have professed not to understand what is wanted of them. This reluctance, through superstition, to divulge their names is widespread throughout the world. The gypsies are averse to disclosing their names to strangers.

Among some tribes this taboo on personal names occurs only at certain times or under certain circumstances. Various African tribes refrain from speaking a man's name when he is hunting or fishing as they think the woods and waters are full of spirits who, if they know the hunter's or fisherman's real name, will so work against him that he will kill or catch little or nothing. If a distant one is mentioned inadvertently by name by a child, the mother will rebuke it saying, "Don't talk of the birds who are in the heavens," or "Silence! Don't speak bad words." The early inhabitants of Britain believed that if a warrior's name was mentioned while he was fighting, he would be killed.

When a savage's real name must be kept secret, it is customary to call him by a nickname or by a secondary name. These are not a part of the man himself and may be divulged without endangering his safety. Sometimes they are called after the names of their children, as the father or mother, or even uncle, of so and so (naming a child). Childless couples may be called "the childless one."

Another superstitious naming custom, found in various primitive groups throughout the world, is the taboo on pronouncing the name of a relative, particularly one by marriage. One might expect that there would be no taboos with regard to the names of persons among close relations, but this is often where the restrictions are the strongest.

Husbands and wives, especially the latter, are forbidden to speak the names of their spouses. In India a woman can annoy another most intensely and bitterly by charging her with having mentioned her husband's name. It is a crime not easily forgiven. Among the Warramunga a woman may not speak a man's ordinary name, which she knows, while he has in addition a secret name which she does not even know. Wives are often forbidden to utter publicly the names of their husbands' relatives, and sometimes may not even use the interdicted word in its ordinary sense. In some tribes the taboo extends only between certain persons, as between a man and his mother-in-law.

Among the Nufoors of Dutch New Guinea, if a person inadvertently utters a forbidden name, he must at once throw himself on the floor and say, "I have mentioned a wrong name. I throw it through the chinks of the floor in order that I may eat well." In other savage tribes the person would hang his head in shame, which would not be relieved until he had given a present in compensation to the person whose name had been used in vain. Often the names of persons tabooed are also the names of common things, such as moon, bridge, cat, etc., so that these words cannot pass the lips of the relative and he must use a description when speaking of that thing. In some places the restriction is so strong that a word merely resembling the sound of the name cannot be used.

A brother-in-law or sister-in-law might be called the husband or wife or brother or sister of someone whose name it was lawful to speak. Among the natives of parts of New Britain, to speak the name of a brother-in-law is the grossest insult that can be offered to him, and is recognized as a crime punishable with death.

This reluctance to tell one's name is discerned in our present-day childhood rhymes, the first originating in North Wales:

> "What is your name?"
> "Puddin' and tame."
> If you ask me again,
> I'll tell you the same."

and

> "What is your name?"
> "Puddin' and town.
> If you ask me again,
> I'll knock you down."

That speaking the name will call a spirit to our presence is recognized in the old proverb that says, "Talk of the devil and his imp appears," now often humorously repeated when mention of an acquaintance is followed by that person's immediate appearance. The survival among us of the words, "a name to conjure with" and similar phrases, indicates that we are not long emerged from that phase of culture in which the names of gods and men were thought to be mysteriously bound up in their personalities.

To many savage races the name was as real and intimate a part of one as his soul. The custom of giving a child the name of his father, or other more remote ancestor, originated in the belief that the father or other ancestor, thereby passed his soul, or a part of it, to the child. Among the ancient Egyptians the *Ran* or *Ren,* the name-soul without which no being could exist, was the last to leave the body at the time of death. To keep this soul alive, or to "make the name live," the Egyptian inscribed it on some stone, and then hid it to protect it from the exorcism of an enemy.

We today have such an elaborate knowledge of the names of the early kings of Egypt because of their practice of making their names live by seeing that they were inscribed on monuments. Some of the rulers' names are not known to us because their enemies were successful in obliterating them, thinking that thereby they fully eliminated the kings.

The importance of personal names in the Egyptian civilization is exhibited by their extraordinary precautions to preserve them and their prayers that the name may "grow" and endure as long as the names of the gods. Nothing could exist without a name. Indeed the preservation or remembrance of the name is one of the principal objects of the Egyptian *Book of the Dead*, that strange set of instructions the purpose of which was to enable the deceased to make his way in the underworld without restraint or hindrance, and to overcome his enemies, largely through the knowledge of their names.

For example, a chapter (XXV in the English translation of Dr. E. A. Wallis Budge) professed to give the deceased the faculty of remembering his own name. Dr. Budge translates it as follows:

(1) The CHAPTER OF MAKING A MAN TO POSSESS MEMORY IN THE UNDERWORLD. The overseer of the house of the overseer of the seal, Nu, triumphant, the son of the overseer of the house of the overseer of the seal, Amen-hetep, saith:—

(2) "May my name be given to me in the Great House, and may I remember my name in the House of Fire on the night (3) of counting the years and of telling the number of the months. I am with the Divine One, [and I sit on the eastern side of heaven]. If any god whatsoever should advance unto me (4), let me be able to proclaim his name forthwith."

Many other portions of the *Book of the Dead* concern themselves with names and illustrate the great importance attached by the Egyptians to the knowledge of the names of men, gods, supernatural beings, etc., and the deceased who was ignorant of these names must have fared very badly in the underworld. Thus, in an early chapter, it is said that the deceased knoweth Osiris and his names (with whom he is given absolute identity, being actually called by the name of the god); in another chapter the deceased is obliged to tell the names of every part of the boat wherein he wishes to cross the great underworld river; in another chapter Anubis makes him declare the names of the two leaves of the door of the Hall of Osiris before he will let him in; and even the bolts, bolt-sockets, lintels and planks will not allow him to enter until the deceased has proved to them that he knows their names.

Entrance into the seven Ārits, or mansions, could not be gained without a knowledge of the names of the several doorkeepers, watchers and heralds. Similarly, the pylons and domains of Osiris could not be passed through by the deceased without a declaration by him of the names of each. The idea underlying all such directions to the dead is that the person who knows the name of a god can invoke and obtain help from him by calling upon him by his name, and that the hostility of a fiend or demon could be opposed successfully by repeating his name. The knowledge of the names of demons constituted the chief power of the magicians of olden times. The many amulets of the Gnostics, which were inscribed with various names of beings with supernatural powers, are the practical expression of the belief in the efficacy of the knowledge of names which existed in Egypt from time immemorial and are so well illustrated in their *Book of the Dead*.

Stepping back further along the chain of cultural development, we find that savages will often change the name of a sickly child to mislead the evil spirits who have been tormenting it. In India, after a young one died the parents bestowed a repulsive name on the next child, such as *Ugly* or *Useless*, to deceive the spirits, who would conclude that it was not worth their while to torment one who was so little regarded in its family.

Among the superstitious Jews in the Middle Ages two families with a common name would not reside in the same dwelling. The spirits would not know which was to be their victim and might choose either. A person would avoid visiting a sick person who bore his name. If one with the same name were present in the sick room at the moment assigned for the death to take place, the well person might be attacked.

In the more backward parts of Japan when several children die, the next one is carried to some lonely spot in the fields and left there. The baby is then picked up by a peasant, hired for the occasion, who pretends to have found it and carries it back and presents it to the parents who receive it as a foundling and name it *Suté* (the foundling). Thus the evil spirits are tricked into believing that it is not the child of the parents.

When a primitive man has had what he regards as a run of ill luck, he will likely change his name, feeling that thereby his destiny can be changed. Whenever a person is ill or has a bad accident and recovers, many aboriginal customs decree a new name. The idea in regard to such change of name is the principle of rebirth. When a boy becomes a man, or a tribesman becomes a chief, or a man becomes a medicine man, he is born again and so must be renamed, just as the infant must be named when it is born.

The pronunciation of the names of the dead is particularly taboo among many savage peoples. One cause of war between tribes was "naming the dead," that is, pronouncing their names. The Australian aborigines are very careful to abstain from all use of the name of one who has departed this life. Among the Todas a man changes his name when another with the same or a similar name dies. The chief reason for this reticence among primitive peoples seems to be a fear of the ghosts of the dead, and a desire to shut them out by thus consigning them to oblivion. Among the Victorian tribes, and also among some American Indian tribes, all the near relatives change their names from a fear that the sound of the familiar names will lure the wandering spirit back to its old haunts. Persons with similar names are likely to change their names promptly upon the death of another because the ghost may hear their names spoken and be confused into thinking it has heard its own name.

Further, when the name of a deceased happens to be that of a common object, the word for that object is dropped out of the language and a new word is coined, causing constant flux in the language. Thus, among the Australian aborigines, when a man named *Karla*, which meant "fire," died, a new word for fire had to be introduced. In some tribes this change of language was only temporary; in others it was permanent. This extraordinary, but rather widespread, custom adds an element of instability to the language and renders the record of past events precarious if not impossible. This taboo against mentioning a deceased individual by name suppresses all historical knowledge within a people. History cannot be written or even carried forward from generation to generation without names! A few races solve the problem by choosing a new name for the deceased leader immediately after death.

The natives of many primitive tribes, if compelled to refer to a departed one, speak the name in a whisper so the spirit cannot hear; others refer to "the lost one," or "the poor fellow who is no more" or some such periphrasis. In some tribes the members select names by which they are to be known after their death. Some tribes observe this taboo only during the period of mourning; others relax it only after several years have elapsed when the mourners have forgotten their grief. If the ghost, while out walking, hears them bandy his name about, he will conclude that his kinfolk are hardhearted and are not mourning him properly, and he will come and trouble the people in their dreams.

Chief *See-yat*, a big, rough leader in the Suquamish tribe, was feared and disliked by many. Later he settled down and let a Catholic missionary baptize him. He then got along with the whites so well that, in 1853, when they founded a town in what is now the state of Washington, they named it after him using the spelling, *Seattle*. In spite of his conversion to Christianity, this recognition worried him a great deal. His former belief was too strong to be shaken easily—if anybody mentioned his name after he was dead, his spirit would be troubled. But perhaps the pronunciation of Seattle by the white settlers is so far removed from the original that his spirit does not recognize it.

Among the Goajiros of Colombia to mention the name of the dead before his kinfolk is a terrible offense which is punishable by death; the relatives will kill the offender then and there. If they cannot catch him, the penalty shrinks into a fine, usually of oxen. In 1655 Metacomet, later called by the English, King Philip, having heard that another Indian had spoken the name of a deceased relative of his, came to the island of Nantucket to kill him and was restrained only by the active intervention of the English. A. G. Morice, who lived for some time as a missionary with the Carrier Indians of British Columbia, tells of attending a white man's funeral and being shocked to hear the deceased's name mentioned. In primitive society individuals are seldom designated as the son of their father. New personal names must continually be invented because the old ones can never be used again.

On the other hand, some primitive tribes believe that when a child is born, it is merely one of their dead who has returned to live with them again, and they hasten to give the baby the name of one of its deceased ancestors. The choice is made either by some law or custom of the social group, or by divination, such as by dreams, or by reading a list of the names of the ancestors to the child and taking the one chosen by the child, as signified by his sneezing or crying.

The primitive Lapps worshipped their dead relatives. They regarded the name as a kind of soul, and, in order to possess the character of a dead kinsman, one must take his name. Dead men, they thought, would aid only those of the living who bore their names. When a woman was pregnant, she was informed in a dream what name to bestow on her baby—what man would live again in the child. If she did not learn this in a dream, the father, or other relatives, must obtain the information by consulting the *shaman* or by divination. If the child cries more than it should, or falls ill, a new name may be given after the first has been washed away. The early Norwegians believed that, after death, the soul went with the name and the individual was restored to new life when the name was given to a new-born child.

In discussing the various taboos concerning names among primitive peoples, many specific examples have been omitted to avoid tiring the reader. But it is curious to note that these taboos and customs concerning names among savage races exist, in varying degrees, among widely separated tribes throughout the world, although anthropologists are unable to trace any definite connection between their cultures. The same or similar name superstitions are found among American Indian tribes, black African peoples, aborigines of Australia, peoples of India and the early Ainu of Japan. We can only conclude that taboos in the use of personal names go so far back in dim antiquity that they must have arisen shortly after the earliest origin of names.

Since the names of ordinary persons are held so sacred, it is not surprising to learn that the names of chiefs, kings and priests are guarded with the utmost care. Many peoples prevent the utterance of the birth name of the sovereign by visiting the death penalty upon violators. Only the highest mandarins in Siam have the privilege of speaking the king's name.

To numismatists, a king who ruled in India, circa A.D. 65, was known as the *Nameless King*. His coins are found throughout the whole extent of the Kushan dominions south of the Himalayas and the Hindu Kush from Kabul to Mathurā. They give his titles and even his head appears on some of them, but not his name. This is probably because of the taboo against using the name of the potentate.

Words which resemble the name of the chief in sound are changed. The Zulus, for instance, will not speak the name of their chief, or of any of his predecessors whose names they can remember, nor will they use words similar in sound to these names. Thus because of intermixture among the various Zulu tribes many words will have several synonyms. One tribe may be able to use one word while it is taboo to a neighboring tribe.

The names of the priests, and other officials in ancient Greece who assisted in the performance of the Eleusinian mysteries, might not be spoken during their lifetime. After their consecration they acquired new and sacred titles. Their old names were apparently inscribed on tablets of bronze or lead and then thrown into the sea. How could a secret be more profoundly kept than by consigning it to the depths of the sea? This is a clear illustration of the confusion between names and corporeal things.

Just as the furtive savage keeps his name secret, so does he think that his gods, to keep their power, must keep their names secret. If he can learn to pronounce their names, he can free himself from their power and even obtain the means to force them to do his bidding.

This is well illustrated by the story of the Egyptian Isis, who wormed the name of the god *Ra* from him and thus became the great goddess.

Isis, so the story goes, was a woman, mighty in words, who became tired of the world of men and wished to enter the world of the gods. She meditated in her heart, saying, "Cannot I by virtue of the great name of Ra make myself a goddess and reign like him in heaven and earth?" For Ra had many names, but the great name which gave him power over gods and men was known to no one but himself.

Now Ra was by this time grown old and he slobbered at the mouth and his spittle fell upon the ground. So Isis gathered up some of the spittle and earth with it and kneaded thereof a serpent and laid it on the path where the great god traveled every day to his kingdom. And when he came forth, according to his wont, accompanied by all his company of gods the sacred serpent bit him, and the god opened his mouth and cried and his cry went up to heaven. And the gods with him cried, "What aileth thee?"

But the great god could not answer, and his jaws rattled, his limbs shook and the poison ran through his flesh. When the great god had quieted his heart, he cried to his followers, "Come to me, O my children, offspring of my body. Never have I felt such pain, neither can sickness cause more woe than this. I am a prince, the son of a prince; my father and my mother uttered my name and it remained hidden in my body by him that begat me that no magician might have dominion over me. I went out to behold that which I have made, I walked in the two lands which I have created, and lo! something stung me. What it was I know not. Was it fire? Was it water? My heart is on fire, my flesh trembleth, all my limbs do quake. Bring me the children of the gods with healing words and understanding lips, whose power reacheth to heaven."

Then came the children of the gods and they were sorrowful. And Isis came with her healing words, and she said, "What is it, divine Father? What is it?"

The holy god spake and said, "I went upon my way, I walked after my heart's desire in the two regions which I have made to behold that which I have created, and lo! a serpent that I saw not stung me. Is it fire? Is it water? I am colder than water, I am hotter than fire, all my limbs sweat, I tremble, mine eye is not steadfast, I behold not the sky, the moisture bedeweth my face as in summer-time."

Then spake Isis, "Tell me thy name, holy Father, for whomsoever shall be delivered by thy name shall live."

Then answered Ra, "I made the heavens and the earth, I ordered the mountains, I made the water, I stretched out the two horizons like a curtain. I am he who openeth his eyes and it is light and who shutteth them and it is dark. I make the fire of life. At my command the Nile riseth, but the gods know not my name. I am Khepera in the morning, I am Ra at noon, I am Imu at eve." But the poison was not taken away from him and the great god could no longer walk.

Then said Isis to him, "That was not thy name that thou spakest unto me. Oh tell it unto me, that the poison may depart, for he shall live whose name is revealed."

Now the poison burned like fire and became hotter. The god said "I consent that Isis shall search into me and that my name shall pass from my breast unto hers." Then the great god hid himself from the gods and his place in the ship of eternity was empty.

Thus the name of the great god was taken from him by Isis, and she then spake, "Depart, poison, go forth from Ra. It is I, even I, who overcome the poison and cast it to the earth, for the name of the great god hath been taken away from him. Let Ra live and let the poison die." Thus spake great Isis, the queen of the gods, she who knows Ra and his true and great name.

The pious Germanic Jews would not believe that knowledge of the name could give one power over God. Trying to reconcile religion with the superstition around them, they asserted that there was a separate power in the name as well as a power in God. They believed that invocation of God's name would not oblige God to do the will of the invoker, but that the Name itself has the power to fulfill the wish of the man who properly utters it.

Among ancient peoples the belief is widespread that their gods created themselves in the beginning by uttering their own names. An Egyptian story of the creation says that the great god *Neb-er-tcher* (in another version, *Khepera*) made his mouth, and then created himself by uttering his own name as a word of power. Utterance of names, not only of beings but of inanimate things, was regarded as an act of creation. The Egyptians thought that any abuse of a man's name injured him personally and obliteration of it spelled disaster.

A sect in California contends that the true name of the God back of Jehovah is *Aum*, revealed to them by Jehovah and Jesus, and claims that it is many times referred to in the Bible when "Word" or "Amen" is used. These people believe that Jesus knew and used *Aum* as a name of power and that the chanting of *Aum* lifts them into a spiritual vibration with *Aum*.

Each Roman city had its tutelary deity who protected it, and his name was jealously guarded from other peoples who might learn it and thus attain power over the god to receive his blessings. The policy of Rome was to offer the god of a city it was attacking an equal or greater place in Rome's pantheon to induce the god to remove his protection from Rome's enemy. Cities also had secret and sacred names. The secret name of Rome was Valentia.

To the Mohammedans, Allah is only an epithet in place of the Most Great Name, *El-Izm-el-Aazam*. Allah is an Arabian form of the Hebrew *Eloah* or *Elohim*. The three great gods of the Hindu pantheon have as their symbol the mystic *Om* or *Aum*, the repetition of which is believed to be all-efficacious in imparting knowledge of the Supreme.

The many failures in practice in using sacred names of gods were easily explained by the rule that the pronunciation must be accurate and the cadence, tonality, rhythm and accent of the syllables must be just right. A single mistake destroyed the whole evocation. A single apparent success, in a thousand unsuccessful attempts, was recognized as decisive proof.

Many legends are told of Jesus' use of the incommunicable Name. Two of them are found in the spurious thirteenth century pseudo-life of Jesus, called the *Toledoth Jeschu*, telling how Jesus acquired his great power through exact use of the unspeakable Name. One recites how this great name of God (the Tetragrammaton) was engraved on the cornerstone of the Temple. For when King David (so reads this account) dug the foundations, he found a stone on which the sacred Name was graven and he placed it in the Holy of Holies. But as the wise men thought that some inquisitive youth might learn the name and thus be able to destroy the world, they caused to be made, by magic, two brazen lions which they set, one on each side of the entrance to the Holy of Holies. Now, if anyone learned the sacred name, the lions would begin to roar so loudly that as he came out he would be frightened and bewildered and would lose his presence of mind and forget the Name.

Now Jeschu, so one story goes, went secretly to Jerusalem and proceeded to the Temple and there learned the holy Name. After writing it on parchment, he uttered the Name with intent that he would feel no pain and then cut into his flesh and hid the parchment therein. Then Jeschu, again uttering the Name, the wound healed immediately. When he left the Temple the lions roared and consequently he forgot the Name. He hastened outside the town, cut into his flesh and studied the writing so that he retained the Name thereafter in his memory.

The other legend relates how Jeschu and Judas had a combat in the air before Queen Helena, whoever she might be. When Jeschu had spoken the incommunicable Name there came a wind and raised him between heaven and earth, and everyone marveled. Then Judas spoke the same Name and the wind raised him also, and he seized Jeschu and tried to cast him down. But Jeschu again spoke the Name and they flew around in the air and strove one with the other. Finally Judas prevailed and cast Jeschu to the ground; the elders thereupon seized him and his power left him. But his disciples rescued him, he washed in the Jordan, and with the Name his power returned and again he wrought miracles.

Indeed the name *Yahveh* has been used so much and so many miracles have been ascribed to its use by Jewish, Christian and pagan peoples that it has been the outstanding magical name used by the ancients. In the Rabbinical writings known as the Talmud, wonderful results are ascribed to the use of the Tetragrammaton correctly written or pronounced. This power has thought to be the secret of success used by Hebrew leaders, such as Moses and Solomon.

Further, pronunciation of the Tetragrammaton was awe-inspiring because many believed that incorrect utterance was likely to bring down the wrath of God on the head of the person invoking God by His Name. The magic practitioner was repeatedly warned to prepare himself correctly, by fasting and abstaining from unclean things, and to purify himself in body and soul with ritualistic cleansings. In addition, the people, in compliance with the command contained in *Leviticus* xxiv, 16, would be likely to kill one who pronounced the Name. The term *Tetragrammaton* itself became a magic Name of God.

Besides the Tetragrammaton other "Names" of God were formed. The Jews had 12- and 42- and 72-letter names which, during Talmudic times, were taught only to a select group of the most worthy. They probably varied at different times. Other names were discovered with a varying number of letters, but the above were considered to be the most potent.

Many of these Names of God were merely groups of letters assembled from certain verses in the Bible. For example, the very potent and awe-inspiring 72-letter name was probably 72 syllables, not letters, based on the three verses of *Exodus* xiv, 19-21, each of which contains, in the Hebrew, 72 letters. The name was made up of 72 triads by joining the first letter of the nineteenth verse, the last letter of the twentieth and the first of the twenty-first to form the first three-letter term. The next consisted of the second letter of verse nineteen, the next to the last of 20 and the second of 21. The rest of the three-letter terms were formed in this order from these verses. Tradition had it that this was the name that Moses learned at the burning bush (*Exodus*, Ch. iii).

Magical names for God and the angels were formed by both Jews and Gentiles, in all sorts of ways by juggling the letters of religious texts. In magic the name itself is important and its meaning is beside the point. The Jews took over magic names from other religions the same as pagans borrowed the Jewish names. The very fact that a name was strange and meaningless gave it an efficacy not found in familiar names. The sorcerer did not have to understand the meaning of the name.

By the proper use of names the Jews in the Middle Ages thought that one could produce a *golem*, or image, and give it a certain life which would enable it to serve the sorcerer who created it. Such a being, however, was never equal to a human; it was always defective in some particular, such as lacking the power of speech. Many legends concerning these *golem* were current in Germany. The Frankenstein monster is an example.

Although the Names of God were effective in bringing forth His power, they were sometimes supplemented through the use of names of specific angels. There are an infinite number of angels and the more that could be set to work the better the task was done. The most frequently used angel names were those of the three archangels, *Michael, Gabriel* and *Raphael*. There were said to be seventy names of angels which were good for protection against all kinds of perils. Names of God and of angels are often lumped together in grand profusion the better to accomplish the magic task.

A typical example of a conjuration used by the superstitious Hebrews, set out in the mystical *Sixth and Seventh Books of Moses*, is the following:

I, N. N., a servant of God, desire, call upon the OCH, and conjure thee through water † fire, air and earth, and everything that lives and moves therein, and by the most holy names of God, Agios, Tehirios, Perailitus, Alpha et Omega, Beginning and End, God and Man-Sabaoth, Adanai, Agla, Tetragramaton, Emanuel, Abua, Ceus, Elioa, Torna, Deus, Salvator, Aramma, Messias, Clerob, Michael, Abreil, Achleof, Gachenas et Peraim, Eei Patris et Peraim Eei filii, et Peraim Dei spiritus Teti, and the words by which Solomon and Manasses, Cripinus and Agrippa conjured the spirits, and by whatever else thou mayest be conquered, that you will yield obedience to me, N. N. the same as Isaac did to Abraham, and appear before me, N. N. this instant, in the beautiful, mild, human form of a youth, and bring what I desire. (This the conjuror must name.)

Throughout the years up to modern times the title, *Baal Shem* (Master of The Name), was applied to Jewish magic-workers, or healers, who were thought to have the power to call God to their aid by invoking the Ineffable Name. The best known was a kindly shepherd of Poland (1700-1760), who was called *Baal Shem Tov,* "the Kind Master of God's Name."

CHAPTER X

The Law of Names and Change of Names

An ill wound is cured, not an ill name.
—George Herbert, *Outlandish Proverbs*, 1640

THE legal name of a person is the name by which he is generally known in the community, and any act by such a name is legally binding. A name is really a matter of fact rather than a matter of law. It would appear that a man might have two legal names if he were known as much by the one name as by the other. A legal name has been defined as the word or combination of words by which a person is distinguished from other individuals, and also as the label or appellation which he bears for the convenience of the world at large in addressing him, or in speaking of or dealing with him. A few courts have, from time to time, misled by their fixation on other elements of a case, acted contrary to the statement commencing this paragraph but these cases have been in the decided minority. The lawyer, after long experience, has grown to expect courts now and then to fail to decide technical points correctly due to the unfamiliarity of the judge in that field.

An example of this occasional misstep of justice is found in a recent decision of the Illinois courts. Whereas the courts in that state have many times reaffirmed their decision that a person's real name is the one by which he is known, yet in 1945 in the case of *People vs. Lipsky*, Antonia E. Rago, a woman lawyer who continued to be known by her maiden surname after her marriage, insisted on voting under that name. Upon the refusal of the election officials to let her vote, she brought suit against them. Decision was given in her favor by the trial court, but it was reversed by the Illinois Appellate Court on the grounds that when the registration act provided for registration under the new name when one's name was changed by marriage or otherwise, compliance with the statute was mandatory.

That the Illinois Supreme Court might also have fallen into the same error is shown by its action on March 19, 1946, in adopting a rule refusing to allow lawyers (other than married women) to change their names upon the roll of attorneys. Previously the court had, upon proof of formal change of name, ordered the clerk to change the lawyer's name upon the roll of attorneys. Since this rule of the court does not prevent a lawyer from changing his name, there seems to be no sufficient reason for carrying a different name on the official attorneys' roll.

Perhaps the Illinois court had in mind the case of Joseph F. Mall, an attorney, who in 1930 legally changed his name to Joseph F. Haas, the family name of several politicians highly successful at the polls, a popular Joseph F. Haas having died a few years before, and a John F. Haas being then a well-known judge. For two years he used Mall and Haas indiscriminately in his practice. Then in 1932 he ran for the Republican nomination for judge of the municipal court. Whereas in his previous political races he had consistently lost, in a field of fifty-seven seeking twelve positions on the ballot he now managed to finish twelfth; but was snowed under in the election when the newspapers gave him so much unfavorable publicity. The bar association sought to disbar him and offered to produce both lawyers and laymen to testify that they had voted for him under the impression that he was either one of the well-known government officials bearing the surname *Haas*, or of their family. The Supreme Court refused to oust him from the practice of law on the grounds that there was no proof that he had changed his name with intent to deceive the voters, and irrelevantly pointed to several others among the candidates who had surnames which were the same as sitting judges in the county. Many persons with inadequate conceptions of ethical principles have changed their names for election purposes.

Generally in law the name of a person consists of one given name and one surname. When there is more than one given name the courts are divided, some holding that all the given names together constitute one Christian name, while the rest hold that the first one is the true Christian name. In the absence of specific evidence on the point the given name is the one bestowed by the parents and the surname is the one borne by both parents. There is a presumption of law that one's name is that by which he was christened and his father's surname. Illegitimates bear the surname they have acquired by reputation.

In England and America a child's surname is assumed to be that of its parents. Scotland is different. There a father confers a surname as well as a Christian name on his children. Usually he gives them his own surname, but he has sometimes, for various reasons, been induced to give his children other surnames. When there has been a marriage to an heiress and the groom has assumed her surname, together with his own, he will often bestow the wife's surname, only, on the first-born son. A Scots birth certificate recognizes this right to confer a surname on the child by specifically requiring that the baby's surname be recorded and not left to inference as in England. The Scots system is convenient as it obviates the inconvenience of a change of name later in life when the son is destined to succeed his mother.

Formerly the Christian name was the more important of the two. Sir Edward Coke, that learned exponent of the English common law, wrote in 1628: "Special heed is to be taken of the name of baptism, as a man cannot have two, though he may have divers surnames." (Co. Litt. 3a (m).)

In the early law reports, greater importance was attached to the Christian name because it was the designation conferred by the religious rite of baptism, while the surname was frequently a chance appellation. As late as the fifteenth century the Christian name was frequently the sole name used in legal proceedings. Surnames were at first added merely as descriptive of the individual to distinguish him from others of the same Christian name and were not meant to be permanent. They grew into general use with few laws requiring their adoption or regulating their use.

Tied up with the early English common law about names, or rather lack of common law about names, is the rather surprising insistence upon the most meticulous accuracy in the spelling of names and descriptions in legal actions. Misnomer, as it was called, was fatal to success in a lawsuit. Let the name of the defendant be set out incorrectly, even by the clerk, and the medieval lawyer rushed in with a plea in abatement. In 1307 a woman went to court contending that Adam de Staundoun "disseized her of her freehold," or as we would say, ousted her from her land. Adam merely called attention to the fact that he was called "Adam de Staunton" and not "Adam de Staundoun" and the jurors gave a verdict in his favor. This was by no means an isolated or unusual case. In a day when few persons could spell their own names and those who could varied the orthography from time to time, this concern of the law courts for extreme nicety was more than just a trifle ridiculous.

The law now regards the sound of a name as more important than the spelling. Because of the variant spelling of names, resulting from ignorance and the arbitrary orthography adopted by some, the courts have formulated the doctrine of *idem sonans*. Under this sensible rule the use of a name is merely to designate a person and that object is fully accomplished if the name applied has the same sound as the true name; a slight variation in spelling is immaterial if both modes of spelling have the same sound. Names are said to be *idem sonans* if the attentive ear finds difficulty in distinguishing them when pronounced or common and long-continued usage has, by corruption or abbreviation, made them identical or very similar in pronunciation.

Thus silent letters may be omitted. The conversion of letters like *d* and *t* and *c* and *k* is generally permitted, and final *s* may usually be added or omitted without harmful effect. The question often depends on the manner in which the syllables are accented, but no set of rules will reconcile all of the decisions. Among the names which have been held to be *idem sonans* are the following: *Blunt* and *Blount, Conada* and *Kennedy, Critz* and *Kreitz, Dugald* and *Dougal, Edward* and *Edwin, Johnson* and *Johnston, July* and *Julia, Meyer* and *Maier, Pillsby* and *Pillsbury*, and *Wilkerson* and *Wilkinson*. The following have, on the other hand, been held not to be *idem sonans: Burke* and *Bauks, Dunton* and *Denton, Guilfuss* and *Geilfuss, Hesse* and *Hesser, Keesel* and *Keisel, Lane* and *Leane, Shea* and *O'Shea, Wood* and *Woods*. Generally the question is one of fact for the jury, and consequently is often subordinate to other facts which the men and women in the jury box may consider to be of controlling importance.

In earlier times when reading and writing was not so universal as it is at the present time, and spelling was more in the discretion of the speller, this doctrine of *idem sonans* was quite important. Today, however, the courts are not likely to be quite so lenient in the matter as they have been in the past, because of our modern advance in universal education.

Even down to very recent times the English lawmakers seldom attempted to prescribe what names a subject might or might not bear, nor have they attempted to control changes of name. There are a few cases where Parliament did interfere in order to quell disturbances in the more remote parts of the kingdom, but the instances were rare and are now obsolete.

The most famous is that in 1465 when a statute for Ireland provided (5 Edw. IV, c. 3):

Every Irishman that dwells betwixt or amongst Englishmen in the county of Dublin, Myeth, Vriell and Kildare, shall go like to one englishman in apparel . . . and shall take to him an English surname of one town, as Sutton, Chester, Trym, Skryne, Corke, Kinsale: or colour, as white, blacke, browne: or arte or science, as smith or carpenter: or office, as cooke, butler, and . . . he and his issue shall use this name, under pain of forfeyting of his good yeareley. . . .

An Act of 1569 attempted to prohibit the name of *O'Neyle* in the following wording:

And forasmuch as the name of O'Neyle, in the judgments of the uncivill people of this realm, doth carrie in it selfe so great a soveraintie, as they suppose that all the lords and people of Ulster should rather live in servitude to that name, than in subjection to the crown of England: . . . what person soever he bee that shall hereafter challeng, execute, or take upon him that name of O Neyle . . . the same shall be deemed, adjudged, and taken high treason against your Majestie. . . .

Similarly the Scotch, in 1600, subsequent to the Gowrie conspiracy, enacted:

Forsamekle as the surname of Ruthven has bene sa naturalie bent . . . To attempt maist heich and horribill treassonis aganis his majestie and his maist nobill progenitors . . . That the surname of Ruthven sall now and in all tyme cumming be extinguischit and aboleissit for evir.

In 1603 the Privy Council banned the name *MacGregor* or *Gregor* in Scotland. This prohibition was removed in 1661, but again enforced in 1693, and finally rescinded in 1784.

The reason why so little attention has been paid to personal names by our English system of law is that by the time surnames were being adopted and the practice firmly established, the common law had become set in its ways. It developed a tendency to protect only tangible things, that is, property which could be owned or possessed. The Church successfully asserted jurisdiction over Christian names. At first surnames were only descriptions and were little regarded as a valuable right. The courts consequently decided generally that there was no property right in a name which required protection and denied relief.

While names in themselves are not protected, if one can prove that a writer has used one's name in a novel or play in order to bring ridicule upon him, a suit for libel will stand.

Authors are sometimes hard put to find a good name for their imaginary characters. The name must sound real. It is not enough that the name selected is actually a real name. If the character is something less than charming, there are sure to be one or more with the same name around threatening a libel suit. If an extremely uncommon or invented name is used, someone in the country will be found bearing it and will be certain that the author used it with malicious intent. A real Ichabod Crane harassed Washington Irving for use of his name in the *Legend of Sleepy Hollow*.

The Marx brothers have encountered difficulty in choosing fictitious names for their comedies. After they used Bernard B. Brindlebug, they were amazed when Mr. Brindlebug appeared, a real person, to seek balm for his sufferings. They were successful with Otis B. Driftwood and Ulysses Ungdunger but they still don't feel safe. Groucho contends that there are no fictitious names. The big radio broadcasters make it a practice to use real names, but obtain the consent of the bearers first.

Sol Hess, who draws the comic strip, *The Nebbs*, which features the bombastic Rudy Nebb, was sued by a real Rudy Nebb, of Savannah, Georgia, but a Federal New York Court dismissed the action.

The Federal District Court in Minnesota granted a motion for summary judgment in the libel case of *Clare v. Farrell*. There one Bernard Clare, a newspaper writer, sued James T. Farrell and the Vanguard Press because Mr. Farrell, in 1946, wrote the book, *Bernard Clare*, about the thoughts, hopes, observations, frustrations and sordid experiences of an aspiring young writer of that name. Mr. Farrell had never heard of the real Bernard Clare, and the court held that he would not be required to make a search throughout the whole country to avoid the imputation of negligence and observed that if an author used a name which was possessed by no one, it would be pure accident.

There is a growing tendency in the law governing the right of privacy, a comparatively new concept in Anglo-American law, to restrain the unauthorized use of one's name in connection with advertising or other commercial purposes. A case decided by the Oregon Supreme Court in 1941 is in point. After the legislature of that state passed a bill which would prevent certain corporations from maintaining optical departments, a company which engaged in the business of fitting and selling optical glasses to the public, unauthorizedly signed the name of George Hinish to a telegram which it sent to the

Governor of the State urging him to veto the bill. Hinish was a Civil Service employee of the United States and the rules of the Civil Service Commission prevented him from engaging in political activities. The court, after carefully considering the case pro and con, decided that he could sue and recover damages for mental anguish, even though they were difficult of ascertainment, and could also recover punitive damages if there was actual malice.

The publisher of a newspaper, magazine or book may use the name of another where the subject of inquiry is a person who has achieved or has had thrust upon him or her the status of a "public figure." Items of legitimate news or of historical fact may be freely published and names named. One who, by his or her fame, mode of life or actions, becomes a public personage thereby relinquishes to some extent his or her right of privacy. This is not considered to be an advertising or business use of names even though it may stimulate the sale of the publication.

Some courts have held that the initials of the Christian names with the surname do not constitute the full or legal name of an individual, while others have regarded them as sufficient if the person is so known, or has signed documents in such a manner. Courts will generally take judicial notice of the nicknames and abbreviations of Christian names as *Jack* for John, *Eliza* for Elizabeth, *Thos.* for Thomas, *Jos.* for Joseph, and the like. However, the abbreviation must be one universally recognized; courts have, for instance, held that *Mike* is not equivalent to Michael or *May* to Mary. A mistake in or omission of the middle initial is of no moment in most states, although the law in Massachusetts and a few other jurisdictions is otherwise.

The prefixes *Mr.* or *Mrs.*, like the prefix *Sir*, are not a part of a person's name; neither are the suffixes, *Junior* or *Senior;* these latter are merely words of description which better identify the person. The words *esquire, gentleman* and *yeoman* are regarded, in English law, as names of worship, that is, as descriptive suffixes or additions to indicate social standing.

A married woman's name consists, by almost universal custom both in England and America, of her own Christian name and her husband's surname, and all legal documents should be so signed. The question of her correct middle name is unimportant where the law does not recognize a middle name or initial. The courts have, however, generally recognized the use of the middle name, or initial of her maiden name to be proper. Many women use their maiden surname as a middle name. While from a genealogical point of view this is good procedure, on principle the better practice is to use the middle name of the maiden name because marriage changes only the family name. The custom of using the husband's surname is so firmly ingrained that it is generally continued even after divorce in cases where there are no children. Exceptions to this practice exist chiefly when the marriage was only of short duration. Almost never does a woman revert to her former name when the dissolution of the marriage is by death.

A few ardent feminists, bent upon exhibitionism, have insisted upon keeping their father's surname after marriage to accentuate their independence or rather to convince their own doubting selves that they were the "equal of men." The best-known example was the nineteenth century American woman suffragist, Lucy Stone, who kept her maiden name after her marriage to Henry Brown Blackwell (with his consent) to prove that she had not lost her individuality.

Most such departures from custom have been professional women who have built up a reputation and who would find it a handicap to change their professional names. This is particularly true of actresses. Many use their maiden name in their business life but use their husband's name in their personal and social life. In their legal contracts careful professional women use both names in some such expression as, "Sarah Johnson, otherwise known as Alice Penny."

In countries other than England and the United States this eclipse of the wife's maiden name is not nearly so complete, although in many the tendency is toward complete elimination of the woman's surname. In some of the Continental countries, as Belgium, Portugal and Italy, the woman sometimes keeps her maiden name but adds her husband's surname, by hyphenation, to her surname, particularly for legal purposes; and sometimes the husband also uses the hyphenated surname. When two professionals marry, it would be entirely proper to retain the name of each, connecting them by a hyphen.

As a general rule, unless prohibited by statute, an individual or partnership may legally transact business under an assumed or fictitious name so long as fraud, infringement of trademarks or trade-names, or unfair competition are not involved. A New York court in 1844 had before it the case of a man who could write but who endorsed a bill with the figures, "1.2,8.," no name being written. It decided that a person may become bound by any mark or designation he thinks proper to adopt, provided it be used as a substitute for his name and he intend to bind himself. Suits against persons doing business under such assumed names are generally entitled, "John Doe, doing business as (or d/b/a) The Smith Company."

Most states have enacted statutes to regulate the doing of business under fictitious or assumed names, their purpose being principally to force the disclosure of the real name and thus protect those with whom business is done. Many of them require the registration of an assumed business name, together with the real name, but business done under an unregistered assumed name is not, for that reason, invalid.

A curious feature of our law is that despite the protection given the use of one's name and likeness in connection with the advertising and good-will of an established business, the courts have, in general, repudiated the theory that persons have such a common-law property right to their names as to enable them to assign exclusive rights to use their names in advertising in a business in which they are not otherwise interested. The law does not greatly favor those seeking its protection in the use of their names.

In the famous "Mark Twain Case," Samuel Clemens brought suit to collect damages and to enjoin another from publishing a book called "Sketches by Mark Twain." Mr. Clemens called attention to his use of the *nom de plume* of Mark Twain for over twenty years. These two words were the leadsman's call as he counted the knots on the sounding line heaved from the deck of a Mississippi River steamboat. It meant that the second mark was out—that two fathoms of water lay beneath the keel—welcome news. It was one of the best-known calls on the river and Samuel Clemens, while a Mississippi pilot, was familiar with the term.

The court considered the right to one's own name and the right to a *nom de plume* and decided that he had no more legal right to one than to another. If the holding of the court had been otherwise, it might well have been a decision that Samuel Langhorne Clemens had no right to use the pen name of Mark Twain, for it is well known that Captain Isaiah Sellers, a Mississippi River steamboat pilot, attached this pseudonym to his writings long before it was used by Clemens. Clemens knew Sellers, too, for as a joke one day he wrote a piece satirizing the captain's literary style.

Famous ball players cannot give another a valid and exclusive right to their names. A permission given to another by such a person to use his name, for a designated purpose for a limited time, operates only to prevent the contracting notable from objecting to the use of his name and likeness. New York has a statute prohibiting the use of one's name without written consent.

Al Jolson was sued on May 5, 1941, by his brother Harry, who alleged that Al had agreed to pay him $150 per week for the exclusive right to use the Jolson name in the theatrical world. The agreement was conceded and payments had been made for three years, but the suit was dismissed because the contract was not in writing.

In Brooklyn a man appeared before Judge Grant in a petition for change of name.

"What is your name?" the Judge inquired.

"O. Hell," replied the applicant.

"What's that?" asked the startled court.

"Otto Hell—H-E-L-L," came the qualifying answer, and he then explained that he was opening a confectionery business and wanted his name in big lights over the door. "It would never do to tell people to go to Hell for candy, so I think Otto Hill would be a better name."

The Judge quickly agreed.

Another Otto Hell, a German immigrant, changed his surname to Hall because, he alleged, his neighbors delighted in addressing him by the initial of his first name and his last name in full.

Under the English common law (which common law is part of the law of the United States) a man could change his name or adopt any other name whenever he wished, and there was nothing to stop him as long as the change was not made for fraudulent purposes. A few British writers in England have contended that it is unlawful to change a surname notwithstanding what the law courts have decided because, they argued, this is a matter of "honour." The rule stated above is still the law in England (except for certain wartime regulations) and in most of the states in this country (also except for certain wartime measures against enemy aliens and their allies).

In most states there are statutes providing for a change of name by decree of court. About three-quarters of the states, by statute, provide that one desiring to change his name "may" apply to a court for judicial permission. The courts have been quite uniform in holding that these statutes in respect of change of name merely affirm, and are in aid of, the common law and do not change it. They merely give the individual an additional method of changing his name, and do not insist that he use such procedure. In some jurisdictions, notably North Carolina, a name may be changed only once, as the law provides that after the change has become effective, the applicant may be known by the new name and no other.

In a few states, statutes provide that change of name may be accomplished only by court action. Pennsylvania, for example, provides: "It shall be unlawful for any person to assume a name different from the name by which such person is and has been known, unless such change in name is made pursuant to proceedings in the court and approved by the court." Notwithstanding this law, a lower court in 1938 held that a divorced woman might, even without statutory authority, resume her maiden name. There are no recorded decisions of the courts in Pennsylvania penalizing anyone for violation of this law.

Massachusetts' law provides that change of name shall be unlawful unless made by the court. Texas, Delaware and Louisiana provide that one desiring to change his name "shall" apply to the court. Virginia and West Virginia provide a fine for changing a name "unlawfully," but do not define what unlawful means. The laws of a few states merely say what court has jurisdiction of applications for change of names. In none of these states, however, are there important court decisions penalizing people for altering their names.

In former times it mattered little whether a man changed his name by Act of Parliament, license from the king, act of a legislature, petition in court, or by informal change, except in those rare instances where it became necessary to prove just when the new name was adopted. Nowadays, because of social security laws, military service, life insurance and automobile registrations, and the many paternal statutes in existence, it is important that one have ample, documentary proof of change of name. It may become necessary to prove that one is the same person named in the birth certificate filed a few days after birth.

The question arises, when one has determined to change his name, whether or not to do it by decree of court. While legal procedure involves court and advertising costs and attorney's fees, it has distinct advantages: it is quick, definite, and constitutes a matter of record which is easily proved even after the death of all witnesses.

Most of the American statutes leave the decision to the reasonable discretion of the court and often require a sufficient and reasonable cause for a change of name. An appellate court may overrule the judge of the lower court if, in its opinion, he has abused his discretion.

In California the stage and motion picture actor, Ian Keith, attempted, by decree of court, to change his name from Keith Macaulay

Ross to Ian Keith. Although no one appeared to object, the lower court denied the application when it was discovered that the petitioner had gone through bankruptcy in New York and had not subsequently paid the debts as discharged. On appeal, in 1937, the California Supreme Court reversed, holding that the judge abused his discretion because he had the legal right to become a bankrupt and he was not to be denied any other legal right because he had done so. The court further was of the opinion that he could assume the name he desired without leave of court.

A court may exercise some discretion in granting or denying an application to change a name. In New York, in 1923, a divorced mother asked leave to change the surname of her five-year-old son to that of her present husband. Her former husband opposed the petition and the court denied it, with some asperity, saying that it would not foster any unnatural barrier between father and son.

Some statutes require a showing that pecuniary benefit will result from the change. American judges often berate an applicant for change of name, and then allow it.

The District Court of Appeal in California, in *In re Useldinger*, said, "Until such time as the common-law right to change one's name may be abrogated by statute, the courts should encourage rather than discourage the filing of petitions for change of name to the end that such changes may be a matter of public record."

At least one New York judge refused to allow a change of name merely because the old name was a common one. In 1936 Morris Cohen, a student at the First Institute of Podiatry, in New York, sought legal sanction to assume the name of Louis Murray Kagan, asserting, in his petition, that Cohen was a very common name which occurred with great frequency in the telephone directory. Justice Ryan denied the petition after observing that the desired surname of Kagan was derived from the name, Keegan, a distinguished Brehon family of Ireland. With a flourish (and tongue in cheek?) the august court, paid to adminster justice impartially to all, declared that the name of Cohen was graced by many distinguished and successful Americans and constituted a badge of noble heritage. "Have honesty, character, and skill," asked the judge, "no place in the character of this embryonic artisan?"

In 1888 George Vere Hobart Philpott filed his petition for change of name, in Chautauqua County, New York, frankly setting out his troubles:

The Petition of George Vere Hobart Philpott respectfully represents unto this honorable court:

That at Port Hawkesbury, Cape Breton, Nova Scotia, on the 17th day of January, in the year one thousand eight hundred and sixty-five, your petitioner was born, and straightway, as soon thereafter as was consonant with the age and strength of your petitioner, in combination of the surname of his father and his fore-fathers and certain family likes and traditions, without the affirmative consent of your petitioner who occupied a purely negative position except, as your petitioner is informed and is willing to believe, your petitioner rebelled inasmuch as was compatible with concomitant circumstances, by no right save parental prerogative and the rite of the church, he had thrust upon him the cumbersome and mirth-provoking name by him, amidst the jeers and taunts of an unfeeling kind for near the fourth of a century, borne in seeming fortitude and he hopes with rectitude, and by which, now being of full age and a permanent resident of this State and of the said county of Chautauqua, there being no suits pending nor outstanding commercial paper, nor judgments against him, whatsoever, he now petitions for such relief in the premises as is agreeable to equity and good conscience, and within, following the just laws and statutes in such case made and provided, the province of this honorable court, and praise, upon and because of the grounds and for the reasons herein and hereinafter, as by law required, fully and at large set out, that he may be lawfully stripped of his surname, and, as George Vere Hobart, from then, thenceforth and forever be known, because and for that the first syllable of the surname of your petitioner, when pronounced as phonetically spelled and then associated with the last syllable thereof, suggests to that vast and humorously inclined and punning portion of the common public, many and annoying calembours upon utensils more or less intimately connected with the household and the kitchen, of many metals and divers wares, which by many quibbles, much play upon words, and certain presumed apt expressions, with exasperating laughter and self-satisfied smiles, with never ending and ever varying changes constantly rung upon degrees of emptiness and fullness, and pots and kettles of all manner of use and kind from the humble yet seductive Jack-pot unto those of tinkling brass, "up and down and all around they hammer away like a nailer" with much synthetic reasoning and synonyms galore until both puns and punsters unto your petitioner are moss grown and ivy covered in their antiquity. And again, innocently, persons who never dreamed a pun, nor would they know one if they saw it, having never heard the name, right common too in England, are at loss how to proceed therewith, contract the same by speech and pen into all manner of shapes and forms and combinations of sounds, vowels, consonants and combinations of the alphabet, and the name the forefathers of your petitioner bore in honor, resignation, England and Nova Scotia where the good people are more staid and less humorously inclined, straightway is a by-word in the land and in the mouth of the unrefined, and is, in many renderings, lost in identity and your petitioner, by ignorant metamorphosis, is Mr. Philip Pott, Filpot, or worse than all Full Pot in which pseudonyme those same humorously inclined and many friends with a keen sense of the ridiculous find much themselves and admiring auditors to please, and many suggestions of the symposium, and, the more vulgar ones, by tentative and that same synthetic reasoning and apt association of ideas and things, are led to common-place expressions relative the "growler", whatever that same may be, and, by quick transition, unto the chasing thereof. Wherefore, with no disposition to lessen the sum of human happiness, having passed thro' the stages of "mewling infancy; of school-boy days", now proudly treading the busy stage of manhood; having stood the "taunts and jeers of outrageous fortune" through all those years of puns and punishment for no wrong by him committed; desiring a name that in this cosmopolitical country will add dignity to rather than detract from a promise to pay, through the conscience of this honorable court, he seeks an equalization of amusement and protection in the years to come as he glides down or struggles up the pathway of life, as the Fates decree, toward a setting sun, feeling that this honorable court will presume for the reasons aforesaid, and believe with him that all the "foul deeds" which may by him have been committed, or by those who came before him, lived like him afflicted, and died without an epitaph,—for what will rhyme with pot,—even unto the third and fourth generation, are outlawed or have in the crucible of puns been "burnt and purged away", your petitioner entreats the granting of his request and your petitioner will ever pray.

With such a candid disclosure of his afflictions the least the court could do was to grant the petition and it did.

There are other instances in which courts may countenance a change of name. In divorce actions the statutes may provide that the wife may resume her maiden name. The old divorce by the English Parliament restored a woman at once to her maiden name. In adoption cases the baby is given the surname of the new parents, together with a given name chosen by them. The naturalization laws of the United States provide that if an alien prays for a change of name in his petition for naturalization, the court may make a decree changing the name of the petitioner, and the certificate of naturalization shall be issued in accordance therewith.

Some states have restricted professional men from using assumed names or from changing them. A dentist became known as Painless Parker and practiced under that name. Other dentists objected and succeeded in obtaining the passage of a law preventing doctors and dentists from being known except by their "legal" names. Dr. Parker then went to court and, after some difficulty, had his given name changed from Edgar to Painless.

In sharp contrast with the common law is the old Roman law under which a change of name had to be made in a solemn way in the *curiate* (assembly). Although the method was liberalized later, it never could be done without the consent of the state. The free and easy change of name so familiar in England and America is not found in most other European countries.

Until recently names could be changed in Sweden without formality, providing the name of a nobleman was not adopted and no bearer of the name objected; now informal change is forbidden. France, in 1803, provided that the applicant for change of name must wait a year to give objectors a chance to oppose the assumption of their names by strangers. Denmark, in 1828, attempted to prevent the shifting of patronymics, but, starting in 1899, because of the many common names, the Danish Government encouraged the selection of names no longer in use by compiling a list and reducing the fee for change of name.

Because of the ease with which gypsies could alter their names and identities when accused of misdeeds, the Hungarian Government, in 1934, decreed that all gypsies born in the Farczali district of Hungary were to be branded with tattoo marks showing their name and the date and place of birth.

In 1938 the Nazis were deciding how many names a parent could bestow on a child. If more than one was given, the parent must designate which name would be used. If the child later wished to use another of his names, official sanction must be obtained.

Many of the regulations concerning change of name arose through the desire to nationalize foreigners. In 1654 Philip IV of Spain forced the Moors who lived in his kingdom to adopt Spanish names. The Hungarian Government decided in 1848 that every German surname must be turned, as far as possible, into an equivalent Hungarian name. Early Pennsylvania law required all Germans who received a grant of public lands to Anglicize their names.

In England a change of name may be accomplished by an Act of Parliament, by license from the king, by recording a deed poll or by an informal change.

Acts of Parliament, royal licenses and deeds poll do not in themselves change a name. The first two methods, generally, are merely permission to change a name and a deed poll simply gives publicity. In

England, as in America, a change of name is accomplished only by a change in reputation: that is, only after one has become known by the new name. As a name is acquired by reputation, so it is changed by a change of reputation. And when that has been done, an Act of Parliament, royal license or deed poll adds nothing more. Emily Post suggests that social and business associates should be notified of a change of name by a formal announcement card.

Changes of name by Act of Parliament were frequent during the eighteenth and early nineteenth centuries, with a few before the eighteenth century. In most of these cases the object of the change was to comply with the terms of a will wherein a testator imposed a condition that his name should be taken. By the middle of the nineteenth century recourse to Parliament had become rare, because of the expense and the realization by testators that the desired results could be attained by far less cumbersome methods.

In a recent case in England (*In re Fry: Reynolds v. Denne*, 200 Law Times 24) a man had died leaving a will in which he had given a life interest in the residue of his estate to a woman with remainder over to her eldest daughter under certain conditions. The testator provided that it should be a condition appurtenant to taking the residue, "that the person so taking shall take and continue to bear my surname." The daughter had married and thus changed her surname. She sued to avoid the name clause, and still get the property, as her husband did not want to change his name, although he was prepared to do so if it was absolutely necessary. The English court held that to require the lady to bear the testator's surname throughout her spinsterhood and also while married was contrary to public policy and void because, the judge reasoned, if the husband refused to change, the use of different surnames by husband and wife would be productive of many embarrassments and inconveniences to themselves and their children and friends and to society generally. The court also observed that many husbands would not agree to a change of surname.

Alfred Tennyson's father changed his surname to Tennyson in compliance with the will of his mother's brother who left money to the poet's father on condition that he take his mother's surname. Florence Nightingale's father changed his name from Smith to Nightingale when his mother's brother left him an estate on condition that he make the change. Change of name, by direction of a will, or upon inheriting an estate, has not been an uncommon occurrence in England.

When a younger son acquired an estate, he often assumed the name of his estate in place of his former surname.

Sometimes when the king granted land or did a favor for a subject, it was accompanied with the expression of a wish or command that a different name be taken. Under the circumstances the desire of the sovereign could not be ignored. This naturally led to a custom of applications for the royal license to change names because such acts of the king added prestige to the change and tended to make the act notorious. In the past the royal license for a change of name was easily procurable, but George V practically limited the grant of his warrant to those cases where the change was necessary because of the terms of a will or settlement requiring that the name and arms of the testator or settlor be taken. This method, too, has now become expensive and cumbersome.

Next, and in these times, the most common means employed by an Englishman to change his name is by enrolling a deed poll in the Central Office of the Supreme Court. This procedure was not used before the latter half of the nineteenth century. While not the first to change "by deed enrolled in Chancery," William Jones, of Clythia, by his advertisement in the London *Times* of February 21, 1862, taking the name of William Herbert, stirred up a veritable hornet's nest, the sound of which reverberated through debate in the House of Commons and provoked various pamphlets on the subject as well as numerous "letters to the editor." In the end William Jones-Herbert was fully accepted as William Herbert despite efforts of bureaucratic government officials to withhold recognition.

A touch of humor entered into the picture when one who claimed to be Joshua Bug, by advertisement in the London *Times* of June 26, 1862, solemnly became Norfolk Howard. Since no Joshua Bug could be found in the directories (and bug, in England, is equivalent to bedbug in America), it is generally assumed that this was just a hoax to caricature the ambition of Jones. However that one could be surnamed *Bedbug* is evidenced by the application of A. Bedbug for change of surname, who assigned as a reason for his requested change that he was known as A. Bedbug and he expected to marry a girl named Olivia who objected to becoming O. Bedbug and to any children they might have being called "Little Bedbugs."

Also a probable English fabrication was the advertisement in the *Times* of July 1, 1863, wherein Vere Jones, "the infant son of Thomas J. Jones of Cintra, Upper Norwood," took the name of Vere to be called Vere Jones Vere. If this was a serious case, the child was first given a baptismal name in preparation for the additional surname.

The Central Office now imposes definite restrictions on its acceptance of deeds poll. Stringent regulations were introduced in 1914 which required the production of a British birth certificate or a certificate of naturalization and advertisement in the London *Gazette*. The advantages to be obtained by use of a deed poll are that the change is formal, public and provides a permanent record—the same advantages obtained by a decree in an American court.

Among the English there is an automatic change of appellation when a title of nobility is conferred. The title takes the place of the surname for the time being and is used in lieu of the surname. Peers sue and are sued by their Christian names and their title, as "The Right Honorable Charles Earl of Suffolk." The same is also true of archbishops and bishops, but when they retire the surname again becomes part of their full names. Except in the case of knights, English law does not recognize foreign titles as part of one's name, but only as a description.

Many changes of names in America are by young people who find their names a burden and have not lived long enough to feel sentimental about them. Children, returning from school to their families, demand a change. At times the suggested change is strongly abetted by their teachers. This was true in the case of Mr. Pappatheodoro-komoundoronicolucopoulos, a Greek of Pontiac, Michigan, who stubbornly refused to consent to a shortening of his patronymic. If the parents refuse, the children often leave home and then change their names, occasionally keeping it a secret from their families.

One, Antoni Przybysz, applied to a Detroit, Michigan, court for legal permission to change his name. He appeared before Judge Joseph Murphy who remarked sympathetically, "Yes, I suppose a name like that probably causes a lot of confusion."

"It certainly does," replied Przybysz. "Some people call me Anthony, some Tony and some Anton. I want to change my name to Clinton Przybysz."

Some families have been adventurous in changing their names. The German family of Rahmsauer in this country, over a period of two hundred years, finally ended as Lamb, having successively become *Ramsauer, Ramsaur, Ramsour, Ramseur, Ramser, Ramsir, Sirram, Ram, Sheep* and then *Lamb*. They started slowly, but they picked up speed and with it that old spirit of "devil may care."

When a name comes to represent an unsavory character those bearing the name rush to change it. The papers recorded in 1942 that Albert John Capone, younger brother of Al Capone, the famous gangster, changed his surname to Rayola, and his wife and son did likewise. After William Heirens was convicted in Chicago as the sadistic killer of a child and two women, his parents and brother changed their name, but were careful to keep their new cognomen out of the papers. The children of Joseph Ignace Guillotin, after whom the guillotine was called, obtained permission to change their name after their father's death in 1814.

When Hitler came to power, there were two *Hitlers* and eleven *Hittlers* in the New York telephone directory; before the war ended there were none. During the First World War it was the *Kaisers* who altered their surnames. *Trotsky* was a common name in Russia. After he became a "traitor" many of those with that name hurried to change it. No one wanted to be identified with a national villain. After the purge trials in Russia, persons with the names of *Zinoviev* and *Kamenev* adopted new ones in place of them.

In 1939, before the war started, artist Hilaire Hiler sued the publishers of a San Francisco guidebook for $100,000 when they inserted his name as Hilaire Hitler.

Artists and writers have changed their names without incurring that opprobrium which seems to plague the ordinary citizen. In past times when freedom of the press was not even a phrase, a writer's personal safety might depend on his forethought in leaving his work anonymous or attaching a name made for the purpose.

Often manufactured names seem to smack of artificiality, although it cannot be denied that a list of real names could be easily compiled that would appear to be highly artificial. Pseudonyms or *noms de plume* often have a strangely unreal appearance, as, for example, *Cholly Knickerbocker, Oliver Optic* and *S. S. Van Dine*.

Because criminals have freely adopted "professional" names to help them cover up their activities, the use of an alias has been in disrepute. Although condemned, an alias is not always wrongful. Camden tells us that when Judge Cataline took exception to the alias of a man appearing before him, saying that no honest man had a double name, he was asked what exception could be taken to Jesus Christ, alias Jesus of Nazareth.

In late years musicians, artists and especially teachers of music and art have adopted queer and foreign-sounding names. Just enter a building devoted to such activities and look at the names on the doors. In Chicago's Fine Arts Building the author walked around and noticed the names, *Vitaly Schnee, Margit Varro, Anna Dazé, Ettore Titta Ruffo, Delphine, Gino S. Monaco* and *Maestro Silvio Insana,* among many others. Are these names assumed for professional reasons? An outstanding woman conductor of symphony orchestras is known as *Ethel Leginska,* although she was born Liggins in Hull, England.

Joseph Benton was born in Oklahoma. To sing before the Italian public in Italy, he became *Giuseppi Bentonelli.* Returning from Milan, he was so billed with the Chicago Civic Opera Company. While the Italians would not tolerate a foreign singer, American opera audiences actually crave foreign names. But American radio billed him as Joe Benton. Opera singers generally flourish under names with a definite Italian flavor. Ballet performers and some musicians prefer Russian or Polish-sounding names.

The biggest artificial name factory in the world is Hollywood. The movie moguls are forever looking for appropriate names carrying eye, ear, memory or sex appeal for new actors. Some studios even keep a file of names handy for new discoveries. Every year a fresh supply of material is released to the public under assumed names.

The system of changing names of movie stars was probably launched back in 1914 when the William Fox Company decided to build a great myth around an unknown personality, a Cincinnati girl named Theodosia Goodman, who was transformed into the vampire, *Theda Bara.* She was exploited as the daughter of a French artist and an Arabian mistress. *Bara* was Arab spelled backward, a mere cypher. *Theda* was a rearrangement of the letters of *Death.*

Not all changes of name in the entertainment world are sudden and unpremeditated. There is Chris-Pin Martin, the Mexican comedian, who started life south of the border as *Ysabel Ponciano Chris-Pin Paiz.* When he first came to Hollywood, he dropped the *Paiz* because it was pronounced "Pies," and they called him "Pie Face." He took the name Martin, because he was once a messenger boy for a drug store of that name. Because *Ysabel* carried a feminine connotation in English, he dropped it. As he was afraid of being nicknamed "Punchy," he eliminated *Ponciano.* "In Mexico," he explained, "Chris-Pin is the carpenter saint and my father was a carpenter. It was his favorite name."

In most cases it is the studio, or a producer or director that is responsible for rechristening actors. They may try out several names before one clicks. Gig Young was born Byron Barr but the studio changed it to Bryant Fleming. When he played the character "Gig Young" and received so much fan mail so addressed, his studio quickly made the new name permanent. The actress Dona Drake was born *Rita Novella* in Mexico City. At thirteen she changed her name to *Una Vilon*. Three years later she became *Rita Rio*, then *Rita Shaw*, and finally *Dona Drake*.

Requirements of space on theater marquees tends to limit the length and number of the names adopted by entertainers. From time to time film notables become so enamored with their professional names that they go to court to drop their original names and use the name by which they are so well known in all their business. For example, Spangler Arlington Brugh, in 1943, became officially Robert Taylor.

A few film folk who are known by names other than those they had at birth are:

Known as	*Original Name*
Don Ameche	Dominic Felix Amici
Jack Benny	John Kubelsky
Bruce Cabot	Jacques de Bujac
Ricardo Cortez	Jack Kranz
Joan Crawford	Lucille Le Sueur
Dennis Day	Eugene Patrick McNulty
Judy Garland	Frances Gumm
Cary Grant	Archibald Leach
Hedda Hopper	Elda Furry
Al Jolson	Asa Yoleson
Bert Lahr	Isidore Lahrheim
Carole Landis	Frances Lillian Ridste
Mary Livingstone	Sadye Marks
Paul Muni	Muni Weisenfreund
Mary Pickford	Gladys Smith
Ginger Rogers	Virginia Katherine McMath
Gilbert Roland	Luis Antonio Demoso De Alonzo
Barbara Stanwyck	Ruby Stevens

Two actresses, Maxime Sheppard and Nancy Clark, planned to engage in the theater as a partnership. Since publicity and personal fame was the central core of their work, and as they wished to operate on an absolute equality, they conceived the idea of each using the same name. They petitioned the New York court to allow each of them to assume the one name of Nancy Clark-Sheppard, thinking thus "to circumvent the possibility of having the spotlight of publicity trained more upon one of us than the other." They averred, "We wish to share and share alike in publicity, the life blood of a performer." But the court, in December, 1948, denied their applications, Mr. Justice Aurelio observing, "To approve these requests would create a situation which may veritably lead to a 'Comedy of Errors.'"

Sometimes one's original name is valuable in the entertainment world. When Alexis Smith was signed to a term contract by Warner Brothers, the picture officials suggested that she adopt a more romantic appellation. But Alexis insisted on keeping her name, and the studio reluctantly consented. When she rose to stardom, she found that it paid. Many fan letters came from the more than a million Smiths in the country. And not only did the Smiths take a personal interest in her, but the Browns, Joneses, Millers, and other Americans with common names did too.

Upon being elected Pope in 844, a priest by the name of *Boca de Porco* (translation would be Pig's mouth) changed his name to *Sergius II*. Since then most of his successors have changed their names on being advanced to the pontificate. A superstition arose that Popes who did not change their names would die within a year. So Adrian of Utrecht (Adrian VI) died; Marcello Cervini, in 1555, despite the protests and prayers of the entire College of Cardinals, called himself Marcellus II, and died in twenty-two days.

All elective Popes have avoided the name of Peter, due to modesty. Sergius III, John XXI, Paul II, Paul IV, and Alexander V were all named Peter originally but changed their names upon their elevation to the papal throne. Some ascribe the change of name in Popes to Christ who changed Simon into Peter.

John was a favorite with the Popes, being the official name of at least twenty-one of them, but John XXIII, considered by some to be an anti-Pope, was so profane that since 1415 the name has not been used in the Vatican. Pope Pius XII, the present Pope, was Eugene Mary Joseph John Pacelli before his election. The custom is now thoroughly established for a Cardinal, upon being elected Pope, to choose the name of one of his predecessors.

Nuns from early times have been quite careful to assume new names when they are professed, and this practice continues to the present day. Some of them receive the names of male saints. Prior to the Reformation it was the custom for a cleric on ordination to receive the name of the town in which he was born in place of his father's surname.

Changing of names in early times has not been without its dangers.

Platina, the historian at Rome, who, in a solemn ceremonial, took the name of *Callimachus* in place of Phillip, was imprisoned and most cruelly tortured by command of Pope Paul II to make him confess. This Pope, who had himself changed his name on his elevation to the Roman See, was suspicious and thought a man would not change his name unless he had an evil design in mind. Similarly, one of the charges against the learned Paleario, who was burned at the stake in 1570 for heresy, was that he had changed his first name from *Antonio* to *Aonio.*

Men of learning in Denmark, Germany, Holland, Sweden and Switzerland Latinized their surnames. Many added *-ius* or *-us* to their names. There are the Americans Edward R. Stettinius, father and son, whose early forebears probably came from Stettin, Germany. The Swedish botanist Linnaeus is best known by the Latinized form of his surname. Nicolaus Kaufmann, German mathematician, translated his surname to the Latin, *Mercator.* Also Flemish Gerhard Kremer Latinized his name to become the *Mercator* of map-making fame. *Melanchton*, the German scholar and religious reformer, Grecized his surname of Schwarzert. *Xylander*, the German classical philologist, was born Holtzmann.

Before July 17, 1917, the Royal House in England had no surname. On that date, by a Royal Proclamation, it was declared that thereafter it was to be styled and known as the House and Family of Windsor (after the royal castle of that name) and as such it is now known. King Edward VIII, when he left the throne and received a title of nobility, chose to be known as the Duke of Windsor. The only ones who sign by their Christian name alone are the king, nobles and certain high ecclesiastics.

Many and varied are the reasons given for change of name. Most of them boil down to a desire to avoid ridicule and that sense of strangeness which comes from being a foreigner, not "one of the group." In times of war or other national emergency the rate of change is stepped up greatly. Our entry into both world wars stimulated many name changes, particularly by persons with German-sounding names. With some it is "business reasons." With others the reasons are political; American communists have secret names. After Dickens wrote *Pickwick Papers* some people of that name changed their name.

In 1882 the widow of Henry Carter, the well-known publisher, had her name legally changed to Frank Leslie, which was the pseudonym under which her late husband had managed his book and magazine publishing enterprises (he legally adopted the name in 1857). As Frank Leslie, the lady ably conducted the business, bankrupt three years before her husband's death, so as to amass a very large fortune.

Now and then when a member of a foreign group changes his name and meets disapproval among his compatriots, he reappears in court to change back again. A Chicago dealer in meats, christened Elias *Harlampopoulas*, changed his name to Louis *Harris*. Soon he was back in court asking for the return of Harlampopoulas, and explaining that most of his customers were Greek and could not pronounce Harris. During the First World War when the top sergeant could not pronounce the surname of George *Stanislauskas*, he called him *Sprague* and changed his records to read accordingly. Twenty-odd years later Sprague appeared in a Chicago court and said that he was tired of Sprague and wanted his real name back. He left the court as Stanislauskas.

The list of famous men who have altered or changed their names is endless. Just to name a few without tiring the reader: Jeremiah Jones Colbath became Henry Wilson in 1834 and Vice-President of the United States in 1873. Ulysses Hiram Grant became Ulysses Simpson Grant when he entered West Point and learned that his congressman had so registered his name. Although he never officially changed his name, he served two terms as President of the United States under his adopted name. Stephen Grover Cleveland, Thomas Woodrow Wilson, and John Calvin Coolidge all dropped their first names before being elected President; Herbert Clark Hoover eliminated his middle name long before becoming President.

The Italian poet *Dante* was formerly *Durante*. The French actor and playwright, Jean Baptiste *Poquelin*, was always known as *Molière*, and the French writer, François Marie *Arouet*, assumed the name of *Voltaire*. Desiderius *Erasmus*, the Dutch religious scholar, was originally Herasmus *Gerardus*. The famous African explorer, Sir Henry M. Stanley, started life as John Rowlands. Painters have in many cases altered their names or are known in art by a fragment of their full appellations. We all know the Dutch Rembrandt. His full name was Rembrandt Harmensz van Rijn.

One determined lady changed her name as part of an act of revenge. Mrs. Irene Margaret Campbell Sneyd thought that she was ill-treated in the Old Bailey in London by Barrister Derck *Curtiss-Bennett*. To strike back she changed her name, by publication, to Irene *Kurttis-benet*, adopting the pronunciation but not the spelling. About a week later she caused her picture to appear in a London newspaper together with a letter saying that she had altered her name because she had so fallen in love with Mr. Curtiss-Bennett's "roguish devastating profile" that day in court that she wished to hug to her breast the relationship, even though it arose only phonetically, through her new name. She closed her letter by stating that she was grateful that Mr. Curtiss-Bennett was not called Winterbotham, as "that is a cold name to take for an airing." Mr. Curtiss-Bennett only laughed.

In the early years of the New Deal, John Ehmig of Akron, Ohio, named a son, Franklin Delano Ehmig, and a daughter Eleanor Elizabeth Ehmig. Later when he appeared in court to change their names to Lincoln Franklin and Jessie Elizabeth, he explained that he reached the decision to make the change when his WPA check arrived too late for Christmas. In 1928 a man in Tennessee named his son Herbert Hoover Holden. Four years later he was in court petitioning for permission to change to Franklin Roosevelt Holden.

Some change their names to give them good luck. The most startling example of this was in April, 1947, when *Miswald Cenda Wrandvakist*, a numerologist, petitioned the court in Oakland, California, to change his name—to *Linkolis Dislgrowels Wrangvaufgilmotkets*. Perhaps his name, before changing this time, was a manufactured one, but it certainly looks unlucky. However, the man must be an optimist to expect luck with his new name. One can hardly accuse him of not following his own system of numerology.

Patrick Francis Butler, a printer of Colorado Springs, Colorado, applied to the court to change his name to Patrick Francis Rameses. He explained to the court that he was a spiritualist and through spirit communication had been adopted into the family of the Egyptian King, Rameses II, and that he wanted to complete the spiritual adoption by taking the name of the old king. The court granted the petition!

A writer in the *Liverpool Echo*, in 1931, enquired why names should not be changed to reflect the personalities of their owners, and observed that many a Miss Williams would be more accurately recalled as Miss Dimple. To remedy the situation he suggested a periodical renaming festival for those desiring it. Wouldn't that create a lot of fancy confusion?

CHAPTER XI

Curious Names

*Few men have grown into greatness
whose names are allied to ridicule.*
—M. F. TUPPER, *Proverbial Philosophy,* I, 1838

B UT what is the long and short of it? We shall first consider the
longest single names, and then the greatest aggregation of names
given to one person.

There are many long surnames, such as Mr. *Ahrenhoersterbaeumer*
of St. Louis, and Mr. *Aledasnabaladiedoescheda* of Detroit. Mr. James
J. *Pappatheodorokoummountourgeotopoulos* was a confectioner in Chicago and his elongated business card contained his complete name. A
long Dutch surname is *Inkeervankodsdorspanckinpadrachdern.* The
church at Llangollen in Wales is said to be dedicated to St. Collen-ap
Gwyunawg-ap Clyndawg-ap Cowrda-ap Caradoc Freichfras-ap Llynn-
Merim-ap Einion-Yrth ap Cunedha-Wledig. A female child born into
the Bowen family in Providence, R. I., in June, 1906, was named *Alda-
berontophoscophornia.* That she came by her name properly is shown
by the entry in Boston official records that *Aldiborontiphoscophornio*
Bowen married Andrew Fearing on April 29, 1829. With a name like
that, one cannot insist on too much accuracy in spelling. A man in
New Orleans carries the full name of *Maillillikageyeaaegyaye Ede-
youeayearayilo Anlillyilayio.* He must have acquired it from a Swiss
yodeler.

The New York *Times* of August 21, 1936, relates the name Mr. and
Mrs. Raymond Murray Judd of Honolulu, Hawaii, bestowed on their
son: *Kananinoheaokuuhomeopuukaimanaalohilohinokeaweaweulama-
kaokalani.* To save you counting, it has sixty-three letters and, translated

from the Hawaiian, means "the-beautiful-aroma-of-my-home-at-spar-kling-diamond-hill-is-carried-to-the-eyes-of-heaven."

Arthur Chiles, son of the Reverend R. W. Chiles of Cleveland, was drowned, and then his full name was mentioned. It was *Arthur Hugh Thomas T. DeWitt Talmage Hardin Eddy Lane Arland Linnie Marion Branch Sam Joness Pigg Reuben Walker Chiles*—all names of ministers the parents admired.

One of the kings of Burma, according to *The Glass Palace Chronicle of the Kings of Burma*, translated by Pe Maung Tin and G. H. Luce, had, among other long names, that of *Siritaribhavanadityapavar-apanditasudhammarajamahadhipatinarapatisithu*, which, it is recited, was given by Sakra at the foot of the rose-apple tree. Perhaps it was too long to be bestowed indoors. Sometimes he was referred to by parts of this long name, but other times the full name was used.

The late Empress Dowager of China, concubine of the Emperor, Hsien Fêng, had, at the end of her long life as a virtual dictator in China, the complete official designation of *Tzŭ-Hsi-Tuan-yu-K'ang-yi-Chao-yu-Chuang-ch'eng-Shou-kung-Ch'in-hsien-Ch'ung-hsi-Huang-Tai-hou*, which would be translated as "the Empress Dowager, mo-therly, auspicious, orthodox, heaven-blessed, prosperous, all-nourishing, brightly manifest, calm, sedate, perfect, long-lived, respectful, reverend, worshipful, illustrious and exalted." Sixteen Chinese characters were needed to record her full name and six more were added on the occasion of her death in 1908. During her lifetime she was popularly known to the world as "the Empress Dowager" or "the Old Buddha."

A man in India was named *Joy Joy Sree Sree Amia Nemai Kishore Chandra Gour Bishoumvara Soondara Sachinondona Hari Mahamaha Sharaisharjya Madhurjyamaya Paramparipooruahtamottoma Vagaban*, according to the *Japan Advertiser* of June 28, 1925.

Because most of these long foreign names originate in a language that does not use the Roman alphabet, and because the exact number of Roman letters depends on the system of transliteration used, it is difficult to choose the *longest* name. The wit says it is our English *Smiley* because there is a mile between the first letter and the last.

Deciding what is the shortest name is not nearly so difficult. There are many surnames with only two letters as Mr. *Py* of Fairmont, Minn., Mr. *Au* of Clinton, Ia., Mr. *Oi* of Chicago, Mr. *Ax* of Indianapolis, Mr. *Ur* of Torrington, Conn., and Mr. *Ek* and Mr. *Sy* of Duluth. But these gentlemen are not even in the running for the shortest name in the world.

A few years ago Mr. Earl F. Gerske of Chicago caused his name to be legally changed to *Aaron A*, in order to obtain the shortest surname, and cause his name to lead all others in the telephone directory. After changing his name, he made a deal with a laundry company to use it for advertising purposes. A woman from Burma, in this country, had the surname of *E*.

Is there a surname shorter than *A* or *E*? There is! Graduating from medical school in 1925, in this country, was a Chinese student whose last name consisted of only the letter "I." Upon only a brief inspection everyone will agree that *I* is shorter than *A* or *E*, it being a much slimmer letter.

When something is done in an alphabetical manner, most people begin to covet those whose names begin with A. The name of a person listed first in many directories is *Aaberg*, but *Aab* leads in the Queens telephone book. However, in most telephone books there are a group of corporations which have the first part of the name composed only of letters which come first. Thus Boston, Minneapolis, New Orleans and Washington telephone directories list *AAA*, without otherwise identifying it. In Los Angeles the *AAAAAAAAAAAA Alteration and Repair Co.* manages to be first.

The very last name in directories is usually a surname, and a search will uncover some dandies. Perhaps the lowest down in any list will be the *Zzzpt* of the Detroit telephone directory whose first name is *Zeke*. Incidentally, the New York Telephone Company in 1934 routed from its Manhattan directory the *Zzyn's* and even *Zzzyzyvara's* when they discovered all the double and triple Z's to be invented names adopted by subscribers who wanted to be listed last in the book, yet Manhattan's parting hiss is *Zzyzz, Inc.* In the First World War, Private Edwin B. *Aaae* led the list of fighting men while Corporal Alfred A. *Zzeppenfeldt* brought up the rear.

Now that I have gone this far and have given the longest and shortest and the first and the last names, I might as well go on and discourse on other fancy, odd or esoteric names. The staid scholar who insists on taking himself and his work seriously will frown on the levity with which some unusual names are handled, and will find in this chapter proof of the lack of the so-called true scientific approach to the study of personal names, but it is from the unusual or exceptional that aid can be obtained in formulating rules.

Many odd names, both surnames and Christian names, have been fashioned from the names given foundlings. As late as 1934 the

Spanish Ministry of Justice decreed that thereafter foundlings might receive names common in the locality of their birth instead of the surname, *Exposita* (Exposed) which had heretofore branded them for life. When a child was to be baptized and named before it was born, because of the precarious health of the mother, a name often given in the early English Church was *Creature*. If the baby lived, the name might be changed upon birth, but there are instances where this word was borne throughout life.

Many curious and eccentric names have appeared in other chapters but as everyone is interested in the queer names persons have actually borne, many of the most striking will be noted here. Newspapers and magazines are full of references to these appellations and the peculiar situations to which they sometimes give rise.

A name which has repeatedly been mentioned in the newspapers is that of *Llieusszuieisszei Willitrimnitzzisstdizziiu Hurrizzissteizil,* who is said to be known to his acquaintances as Leo Hurst. He is a Siamese, though not a twin, although his name is enough for more than one. The names are said to translate into "Great Mountain, Wonderful Strength, Bear of the Lake." Newspapers referring to this name year after year do not, of course, spell it the same each time. Perhaps the owner can't even do that. Certainly printers can't. Some newspaper reporters contend that he calls himself Leo Ward for everyday purposes.

Men with odd names have sometimes attained such fame that the queerness of their names has been forgotten. In this country alone there were *Preserved Fish*, the New York merchant, *Cotton* and *Increase Mather*, the New England divines, and *Henry Wadsworth Longfellow* and *Jones Very*, poets.

The people who have received first names intended to be complementary to their surnames are legion. After his name was especially verified, *Katz Meow*, of Hoquiam, Washington, received a warrant from the State Auditor in payment of a gasoline tax refund. Mr. *Ache Payne* of Allerton, Illinois, contended that his only illness had resulted from eating too many green apples. *R. V. Arvey*, a duplicated name, is so listed in the Chicago telephone directory.

A railway mail clerk of Meridan, Wisconsin, is *Darling Dear*. A high school music teacher of Little Falls, New York, is named *Love Sweetheart Walachek*. Does she have trouble with the male students? *Fish Hook* lives in Pike County in the Sucker state (Illinois). The *Apple* family of Chicago had a son they named *Orange*. In 1935 a daughter arrived in September but they named her *June*. *Orange Vanilla Lemon* resides in Boise, Idaho.

Really unusual names are found to be not uncommon when one begins to look for them. Some tickle the fancy more than others. In this classification would certainly come Mrs. Molly *Ticklepitcher* of Turnip Top Ridge, Tenn. The English official *Dingle Foot* received a lot of good-humored publicity while he was in the United States during the last war. The name of *Singular Onions Gallyhawks* became a matter of record when he appeared in court some years ago to change it.

A resident of Hood River, Oregon, was named *Asad Experience Wilson*. He was killed in an auto smashup in 1946 and his full name, Asad Experience Wilson, was chiseled on his grave marker. Two of the sailors on post office duty in the navy were *Billy B. Good* and *Billy B. Quick*. Rev. *O. B. Quick* is a negro pastor in Boston. Jeanette Miss is married and is therefore *Mrs. Miss*. In Chicago there is *Mr. Mister* and his wife, *Mrs. Mister*. In the last century in England, Mr. *Doubleday* and Miss *Halfknight* lived in the same house; and Philadelphia had both a *Halfman* and a *Doubleman*.

Sam Damm resided at Dickens, Iowa. *Dr. Donat Yelle* (do not yell) is a dentist at Dayton, Ohio, while *Dr. Toothache* practices the same profession at Burlington, Iowa. *I Will Sing* is a Chinese laundryman in Thomasville, Georgia. In 1948 the papers recorded that *Please Wright* was a candidate for postmaster at Oceana, West Virginia.

Every year when the holidays come around, the papers mention *Mary Christmas*. There are several people with this name in the United States. One lives in Racine, Wisconsin. When doing her Christmas shopping, she found it a bit difficult to satisfy busy store clerks. Some children think that she is Santa Claus' wife, and she is swamped with telephone calls and thousands of cards every year asking for toys or just her signature. Others of this name live in New Orleans, Chicago, and in practically every large city. After Christmas, when the head of the family is painfully surprised by the size of the bills coming in, it is no consolation to tell him that Chicago can boast of a man named *Christmas Hurts*.

Mr. and Mrs. James A. *Buck* of Clear Lake, Iowa, named their new daughter, *Helen May*. A newspaper item opined that she may when she finds out her name. Mr. and Mrs. John Rogers of Shenandoah, Iowa, allowed their doctor to christen one son *Herbert Hoover Depression* Rogers and a later son *Franklin Delano Roosevelt Recession*

Rogers. You know when they were born. When John and Mary *States* had a son in 1923, they could not resist naming him *United*.

A surname may be only a number expressed in Roman numerals. The New York *Times* of July 25, 1944, printed an item to the effect that Pvt. Louis *XVI*, son of Mr. and Mrs. Francis XVI, returned to Ottawa, Canada. Mr. XVI said his name was pronounced "Vee." Mr. and Mrs. Jack First, of South Bend, Indiana, expected their baby to be born April 1, 1948, and even though their baby daughter arrived a few days early they named her *April First*. April has an aunt named *June First* who was born in January. An English family was named *And*, and it had for arms the character *&*.

For identification some have adopted startling middle names. Because there was another William Harris in the same neighborhood, William Harris of 43 Whitcomb Street, London, in 1927, adopted the middle name of *No. 1*, and is listed in Kelly's London Postoffice Directory for 1927 as William No. 1 Harris. A negro in Homerville, Georgia, was named Willie 5/8 Smith.

Then there was one, J. John *B. B. B.* Brown, living only in a cartoon, who explained his appellation by saying that he was christened by a minister who stuttered. Likewise existing only in a squib, was the boy named *Banana* after his father, Ben, and his mother, Anna.

Mr. and Mrs. Arlos Rogers of Wallace, West Virginia, called their eight children *Winter, Snow, Icy, Frost, Hale, Raine, June* and *Day*. Homer Frost of Roswell, New Mexico, named his six children *Winter Night, Jack White, Snow, Dew, Hail* and *Cold Frost*. *Summers Autumn Winters* lives in Sunbury, Pennsylvania.

In Nebraska Mr. and Mrs. Ira W. *Ready* named their son *Ira Maynard* and he used his initials only. He had two uncles, one named *B. Ready* and the other *R. U. Ready*. *Odd Albert* was a faculty lecturer at New York University, while *Oa Lloyd* served as an instructor at Brigham Young University. At the same university *Newburn I. Butt* was a library assistant in 1936.

But just for names—you attach your own meaning—there is an *Otto Flug* of Chicago, *St. Elmo Bug* of Beverly Hills, California and *J. Flipper Derricotte* of Washington, D. C. *My Ubl* was Chicago district traffic manager of Northwest Airlines before the war. *Mr. George Leopold Augustus Octavius Wilhelm Scheuchenpflug* of Highland Park, Illinois, is widely known as "Mr. X" and receives mail so addressed. His daughter in school signs her reports and papers as "Doris X."

Then there are just some odd surnames. Mr. *Kusswurm* is a Chicago lawyer. John *Knowlittle* was an English author in 1820. Nettie Neff *Smart* was Dean of Women at Brigham Young University. Professor *Rainwater* taught history at the University of Mississippi. Pierre *Forget* was a Paris writer in 1646. Mr. *Whynaught* lives in Cambridge, Mass. In the latter part of the eighteenth century, in Maidstone, England, William *Scaredevil* was a whitesmith. William *Brotherhead* published a book in 1861. Mr. and Mrs. *Kitchenmaster* live in Green Bay, Wisconsin. A correspondent in *Notes and Queries* found the surname *Naughtiboy* in the English registers. Some other surnames mentioned in that interesting English periodical are *Argument, Brasskettle, Eightshilling, Laughter* and *Yessir*.

Families named *Outhouse* and *Backhouse* can be found in the directories of almost any large city. People born in a city may not recognize these buildings so essential to every farm home, but followers of Chic Sale will surely see what is meant. A John *Smalbehynd* lived in nineteenth century England. In 1783 when Edward Miller *Mundy* became a member of the English parliament, he succeeded a representative of the name of *Noon* and became known as "Mundy afterNoon."

While the newspapers are full of odd names, some of them must be taken *cum grano salis*. When the author noted that many newspapers printed the fact that "Mrs. Twice gave birth to twins," he investigated, and W. G. Whitby of Royal Oak, Vancouver Island, verified the story, saying that Mrs. Twice had twice given birth to twins, but did not read or write, and sent a picture of Mrs. Twice to prove her existence. The photograph clearly proved that Mrs. Twice was a cat, but no newspaper item referred to this salient fact. The author also found that many other odd names narrated in the press could not be verified by reference to city or telephone directories or by letter and consequently had to leave them out of this chapter.

A Chicago policeman found a man asleep near the Chicago Avenue Police Station. "Who are you?" he enquired, arousing the man.

"What? I'm Drunk," was the reply.

"I didn't ask you what you were. I asked who you were," the officer insisted.

"Drunk, I told you," the erstwhile sleeper irritably shouted.

Much to his surprise the policeman finally understood that he was talking with Carter *Drunk*, 238 West Division Street, Chicago, Illinois.

This misunderstanding was not tragic, however, like the name of the seventeenth century French general, Count *Valavoir*. While his forces were lying encamped before the enemy, the Count attempted to pass a sentinel after sunset. To the sentinel's challenge the Count answered, *"Va-la-voir,"* which literally signified, "go and see." The soldier taking the name in this sense indignantly repeated the challenge. When he was again answered in the same manner, he fired and the unfortunate Count fell dead—a victim to the whimsicality of his surname.

Luther *Wright* and Hermann *Rongg* appeared before Judge Leon R. Yankwich of the Federal Court in Los Angeles in 1937, in a controversy over a patent. Can't you just hear the court say, "One of you must be wrong"?

"That's right," declared Wright. "He's Rongg."

Rongg interrupted, "I'm right, although I'm Rongg."

"No, I am Wright and he's wrong," said you know who.

"Well," came from the judge, "you can't both be right; one must be right and the other wrong, just as sure as one of you is Wright and the other Rongg."

And the judge ruled, "Wright is wrong and Rongg is right."

In 1932 a student at the University of Texas applied to the librarian for certain books, and she asked his name.

"Guess," he replied.

She asked again and received the same answer. She then suggested that if he would come around when they were not quite so busy she would be glad to play guessing and other childhood games with him. Only then did he inform her that his full name was William *Guess*.

The lady registering ship-workers for pay-as-you-go income tax deduction had had a busy day and was perhaps a little curt in her questions toward the end of the afternoon.

"Give me your last name first," she said.

"First," he answered.

"Yes," she said, "give me your last name first."

"First," he repeated. "My last name is First."

"What's your first name?" she asked.

"Last," he replied.

The clerk was in no mood for play—she was more tired than ever. "Here, fill the form out yourself, if you don't want to cooperate."

"Last Gale First, 1106 Louisiana Avenue, Tampa, Florida," he wrote.

"And that's really my name," he explained.

In Cleveland, in 1934, Harry *First* managed a drug store with Leo

Last as his clerk. When they were held up by thieves, Last told police, "It was our first holdup together," while First chimed in, "Let's hope it's the last."

Mr. Jones, the dominating head of a publicity agency, liked to have his wife work with him in the business. The story goes that Garfinkel, one of his clients, was manufacturing an article which had no disagreeable odor, as competing brands had, and needed a good "selling name" for it. Mr. Jones made all the family decisions but Mr. Garfinkel's request came just as Mrs. Jones was presenting her husband with a son and heir. Having to do everything, Mr. Jones was very busy and someone made a deplorable error in mixing up his brief memoranda. Mr. Garfinkel was disappointed at the suggestion that his product be called *Johanjane*. Mrs. Jones read the next morning that her son had been named *Garfinko Nostinko Jones*.

The Kelly-Arvey political machine was quite powerful in Chicago before and during the Second World War. In the 1946 election, when the Republicans made important gains in Cook County, and Kelly appeared to be on his way out as mayor, the question was posed: "Will Arvey run the county now?" And the answer was "Like Kelly will."

This is similar to the old nineteenth century tribute to the memory of a certain American writer. The man said he was going to *Helen Hunt Jackson's* grave. Many names may be found to be distinctive because they produce a startling connotation when used in certain sentences.

One of the most quoted of all limericks is that created by that irrepressible funster, Oliver Wendell Holmes:

> The Reverend Henry Ward Beecher
> Called a hen a most elegant creature.
> The hen, pleased with that,
> Laid an egg in his hat—
> And thus did the hen reward Beecher.

In 1936 the punning game of Knock-Knock, originated by the song, "Knock Knock Who's There?," swept the country, everyone being at liberty to produce his own ditty, the more atrocious the pun the better. The full conversation went:

> Knock, Knock.
> Who's there?
> Marshall.

Marshall who?
Marshall come in like a lion.

Or,

Who's there?
Ophelia.
Ophelia who?
Ophelia pulse.

The full possibilities of this awful epidemic of punning may be
realized by these deteriorated examples,

Paula who?
Paula, bedroom and bawth.

Toots and Theresa who?
Toots company, Theresa crowd.

This form of insanity is not much worse than the ancient diversion
of anagrams, that is, making a sentence or motto from the letters of
one's name.

Acrostics were a great source of indoor amusement in the last
century. The Boston Public Library, a dignified, cultural institution,
was designed by the architectural firm of McKim, Mead and White.
On three sides of the building, cut in solid blocks of granite, are
immortal names, culled after great deliberation from the pages of
universal history. An observant newspaper reporter, soon after the
building was finished, noticed that certain of the names were grouped
as follows:

Moses	Mozart	Wren
Cicero	Euclid	Herrick
Kalidasa	Aeschylus	Irving
Isocrates	Dante	Titian
Milton		Erasmus

and wrote a story pointing out that the initials of each name spelled
out the firm's name, McKim, Mead and White. When New York
laughed, Boston and the library's board of trustees became indignant
and quickly had the names chiseled off, and substituted a new plaque
which would not provide a clever advertisement for the architects.

When Doris Doe, the contralto singer, first went to New York, her
funds were low and she received a money order from her father, John
Doe. Hurrying to the post office to cash it she was surrounded by

alert guards and suspicious postal clerks. Finally she convinced them that the signature was good—her father's name really was *John Doe*.

St. Louis Estes, the health lecturer, and Esther Estes, his wife, have named all their sons (six) *St. Louis*. The girls (five in number) have received no names at all, but respond to *Dimple* and *Chickadee*. Mrs. Estes explained, "Names are really inconsequential so we have not taken the time to name them." Mrs. Estes is really quite busy; she lectures and talks over the radio on child rearing.

Sometimes the name chosen for the baby betrays only too clearly that it was not wanted. The English General Registrar Office for the years, 1861, 1870 and 1886 disclose the following unChristian names: *Not-Wanted-James, One-Too-Many* and *That's-It-Who'd-Have-Thought-It*. A woman once named her baby *Alpha Omega* with the explanation that it was her first and she fervently hoped that it would be her last.

The story is told of the bookish family that had too many children. Another child was born and, supposing it to be the last, it was called *Finis*. Later a daughter came along to be called *Addenda*, and then two boys were christened *Appendix* and *Supplement*. Another version of the story says that the five children in one family were *Imprimus, Finis, Appendix, Addenda* (the first daughter) and *Errata* (the second daughter and last child).

One who lived his entire life without a Christian name was the late Dr. Gatewood of Chicago. Dr. Gatewood often explained that his parents decided to let him choose his own name and he never got around to it. When he attained fame as a doctor and spoke at medical meetings, the programs read "Dr. Blank Gatewood" or "Dr. Gatewood Gatewood" when formality required something for a first name.

Another American who has struggled through life without a given name is *Tifft* of Tifft Road, Dover, N. H., a former New York businessman. His parents had the same reasons for not bestowing a name as Mr. and Mrs. Gatewood. Mr. Tifft, now in business for himself, finds that people who hear of his name never forget it, and the lack of a given name is thus of some advertising value. He contends that the only inconvenience he suffers in not having a first name is the more or less continuous explanation he has to make, and he points out that even the explanations have about petered out since his name has become so well known in his community.

Now and then the jointure of two odd names in marriage is mentioned in the public press. In Los Angeles in 1938 the records show that

Rosalin Oh married *Henry You. Him* and *Shee* obtained a marriage license in San Francisco the same year, that is, Tom Him and Wong Shee—now you know their nationality. When Gladys *Mann* married Bernard Herman *Groome* in Matoaca, Virginia, in 1942, the husband observed that his wife was a woman, a Mann, a bride and a Groome the same day. In Palmer, Texas, Martha Ellen Combs married Mr. Daly to become *Martha Ellen Combs Daly*; but whether she does or not, one cannot really say.

Marriage has produced some startling combinations. When Mary *Broker*, who lived in Nebraska in 1927, married the man of her choice, who happened to be surnamed *Mothershead*, she found it inconvenient to use her maiden surname as a middle name as she wished. Most of these odd combinations arise from the queer combination of given name and new surname. Miss *Ima Wunder* is said to have married Mr. *Goodwin* and became *Ima Goodwin*.

A woman in England, Alice Mann, wrote to a newspaper that she was born *A. Mann*, married a Mr. *Husband* and so became *A. Husband*. After his death she married Mr. *Maiden*. Thus a woman who was a *Mann* became a *Husband* and then died a *Maiden*. In Galveston, Texas, Miss *Tubbs* recently wed Mr. *Barrell*. Before the judge in Chicago, in 1934, came Seymour *Ex* to divorce Kay S. *Ex,* his wife, and thus make her the *ex-Mrs. Ex.*

The Reverend Mr. Pomp in 1827, at Easton, Pennsylvania, married Abraham *Kind* to Susan *Queer* and the following verse commemorating the odd names appeared:

> Is it strange that a female, when wed to her mind,
> Should cease to be Queer, and become truly Kind?
> Since Queer-ness is not the best trait in a wife,
> While Kind-ness subdues half the evils of life.

This is only matched by the following epigram which appeared in England, in the latter part of the nineteenth century, when Mr. *Day,* an Eton Master, married a lady surnamed *Week*:

> A Day the more—a Week the less—
> But Time shall not complain;
> There'll soon be little Days enough
> To make a Week again.

Elizabeth *Bird* was born near Paris, Kentucky. Not being satisfied with being just a winged creature, she married Mr. *Martin*. After his death she married Edward *Crow*. When she next changed nests it was after marriage with a widower, David *Buzzard,* certainly about as low as she could get in the bird family. To the Buzzard nest she brought one little Martin and two little Crows, to find one little Buzzard already there.

The first wife of the Rev. Dr. *Nott* composed the following verse in reply when he proposed to her:

> Why urge, dear sir, a bashful maid
> To change her single lot,
> When well you know I've often said,
> In truth I love you, *Nott.*
> For all your pain I do not care,
> And trust me on my life,
> Though you had thousands—I declare
> I would, *Nott,* be your wife.

If she recited the verse to him, he might have had a little trouble in seeing just where the commas were meant to be placed.

In an English cemetery on the grave of a man who was named *Knott* is the following inscription:

> Here lies a man who was Knott born
> He did Knott live
> He did Knott die
> And is Knott buried here.

Almost everyone has heard of the old New York law firm known as *Ketcham and Cheatham,* said to have been a partnership between I. Ketcham and U. Cheatham in the latter part of the nineteenth century. Miami, Florida, has its law partnership called *Ruff and Ready.* Yes, *Dilly, Dally, Doolittle and Stahl* (maybe speed was not necessary) really practiced law in Akron, Ohio. *Wind & Wind* appeared in the courts of the Windy City of Chicago. Sligo, Ireland, has a firm of solicitors known as *Argue & Phibbs.* Worthy of note here, outside of law partnerships, is a firm of funeral directors in Jacksonville, Florida—*Geter and Baker.* This is—one supposes—just the modern turning toward cremation.

A Clinton, Iowa, attorney, Ernest *Otto Work,* has a son he named George *Will Work.* In Mt. Vernon, Illinois, a laborer, Clarence *Will Work,* had a wife, Hattie *May Work.* In an Illinois court, Tillie *May Fail* sued John *Will Fail* for separate maintenance. The N. M. Fails of Oklahoma City, Oklahoma, named their two sons, *Will Fail* and *Never Fail*—both have been successful.

In England the names of three Cambridge physicians gave occasion to the following punning conundrum:

What's *Doctor*, and *Dr.* and D^{octor} writ so?
Doctor *Long*, Doctor *Short*, and Doctor *Askew*.

William James Judge appeared before Judge William James to take the oath of allegiance in federal court in Los Angeles, California. The certificate for William James Judge was then signed William James, Judge.

After a bad check was returned in Falls City, Nebraska, the proprietors of the Silver Grill Cafe noticed that it was signed *U. R. Stung*. The authorities in California arrested a Japanese for passing worthless checks which he signed *I. Nogota*. A confidence man can possess a sense of humor.

During the war the draft uncovered many odd names and the newspapers and magazines carried many such items as fillers. For instance, there was General *Twaddle* in the Army, in full—Brig. Gen. Harry L. Twaddle. His sketch in *Who's Who* proves that he does not hide behind any off-pronunciation, but boldly pronounces his surname as it is spelled.

Since surnames like *Sergeant, Major* and *Ensign* exist, it is not too surprising to find a *Sergeant Sergeant* and a *Major Major* in the Army and, in the Navy, *Ensign Ensign*. When *Captain Major* was promoted, the newspapers, true to form, picked up the item, and wrote about Major Major.

In 1943 at the Topeka (Kansas) army air base a voice told the clerk who answered: "This is the sergeant major calling Major Sergeant."

"How's that?" asked the clerk.

The caller repeated his statement several times but still the clerk didn't get it. Finally the caller broke it down, "I'm Master Sergeant Southiller, the sergeant major," he said. "I want to speak to your major, Major Sergeant. His name is Sergeant."

The clerk finally caught on, but, after making the connection, continued to mutter to himself, "Sergeant Major, Major, Major Sergeant, Brrr."

These military and naval titles have also been given as Christian names and, during the war, the flying school at Mather Field had enrolled Pvt. Lieutenant Carnes, Pvt. General Rudolph Merriweather as well as Sergt. Admiral C. Allen. Private Colonel Underwood found it convenient to drop the title when requesting hotel reservations while on leave. He would say, "This is Colonel Underwood speaking." It usually worked.

Just after the war some people were startled when they telephoned the chaplain's office, at Buckley Field in Colorado, to hear a voice answer, "Chaplain's office—St. Peter speaking." A few callers complained of this seeming levity but Army authorities explained that Private *Saint Peter*, of Omak, Washington, had been assigned to answer the telephone.

During the war, at the USO center in Highwood, Illinois, attendants were amazed to find that *Alexander Dumas, Julius Caesar* and *Henry Ford* registered in one evening. An American soldier, named Julius W. Caesar, was stationed in Italy after the invasion, and he told interviewers that he had never heard of any other person with a name like his—except his uncle, Julius D. Caesar.

In the first World War, Phil Graves of Neosha, Mo., was an officer in the United States Marine Corps. When he first joined the company they thought his full name was the ominous *Phillip R. Graves,* but he soon assured them that the middle initial was *H* and not *R*. Those facing death were relieved. What a difference an innocent middle initial can make!

People with names having an obvious significance pay little attention to them. A few years ago, on a radio quiz program, a woman was asked to name six countries beginning with the letter *I*. By the time she had slowly and hesitantly remembered Iran, Iraq, India and Italy her time was up. Then, when the announcer inquired as to her name, she answered, "Mrs. Iceland."

The Chinese in America sometimes have their names transformed into jokes. The new immigration official inquired for the name.

"Sneeze," the Chinese replied proudly.

The official looked at him warily. "Is that your real Chinese name?"

"No, English name."

"Well, let's have your native name."

"Ah Choo."

After Lindbergh's successful flight, the wits spoke of the little Chinese boy named after the event—*Wun Long Hop.*

People with the same name, but not related, have formed associations. The one which has received the widest publicity is the Benevolent and Protective and Completely Universal Order of Fred Smiths of America, founded in 1936. They first met in a hotel and had page boys call out, "Fred Smith," until they all got together. The group has held dinners in New York, Chicago and elsewhere. Only those called *Fred Smith* are allowed to attend. At the New York dinner, however, they did permit Smith Frederick to back into the banquet hall and eat out of his lap with his back to the table. To eliminate confusion the society uses a parenthetical nickname, as Fred (Headmaster) Smith and Fred (Lily Cup) Smith.

Other groups have done something similar. At a luncheon meeting of the Executives Club in Chicago those christened *Benjamin Franklin* sat at the speakers' table, and there were eighteen of them. Benjamin Franklin Affleck was president of the club and introduced Professor Benjamin Franklin Shambaugh to speak on Benjamin Franklin. The Murphys in Massachusetts have had several very large meetings. The Thompsons formed a club in Chicago. As a group the Smiths founded TNSDUNSPHI—The National Society to Discourage Use of the Name Smith for Purposes of Hypothetical Illustration. When a member hears anyone refer to an imaginary character as Smith, it is his duty to present his membership card. The only qualification for membership is a pledge to produce his membership card to those who say, "Take the average man, we'll call him John Q. Smith."

One of the best known "associations" is the SPCSCPG, that is the Society for the Prevention of Calling Sleeping Car Porters George. It was started as a joke by George W. Dulany, Jr., at Clinton, Iowa, in 1916. He discovered that less than two per cent were so named. Only a "George" may belong. George Washington and Admiral George Dewey are patron saints of the organization. A membership of more than thirty thousand is claimed. *George,* for a sleeping car porter, is said to have started when a salesman, finding none in sight called out "George" because that was the first name of the founder of the Pullman Company.

Elder Brewster of the Plymouth Colony had sons named *Love* and *Wrestling,* and daughters named *Fear* and *Patience.*

Santiago Iglesias, former resident commissioner of Puerto Rico, named his six daughters *Peace, Light, Justice, Liberty, Equality* and *Fraternity.* In a traffic court in Los Angeles, a violator had a hard time convincing the judge that his name was really *Safety First.*

Many families have used only names beginning with one letter of the alphabet. The thirteen children of the W. O. Prince family of Peoria, Illinois, are *Darrell, Delmar, Donald, Dallas, David, Dale, Delbert, Doris, Darline, Dorothy, Duwayne, Dora* and *Dena*. The William Flynn family of Boswell, Indiana, have ten boys named *Oakley, Oral, Odie, Othie, Ovie, Orval, Otis, Oscar, Oliver* and *Omer*. The idea came from Mrs. Flynn's first name which is *Ollie*. The Mayards of Abbeville, Louisiana, also put their children in the "O" line. Their children are *Odile, Odelia, Odalia, Olive, Oliver, Olivia, Ophelia, Odelin, Octave, Octavia, Ovide, Onesia, Olite, Otta, Omea* and *Opta*. The children of Mrs. James R. Hickok line up as *Zelum, Zatha, Zella, Zarnell, Zelmond, Zorna, Zorin, Zelpha, Zerril, Zale, Zelbert, Zoland* and *Zane*. The four daughters are the ones whose names terminate in *-a*. There is another large family with *Z* names, the Cox children of North Carolina: *Zadie, Zadoc, Zeber, Zylphia, Zenobia, Zeronial, Zeslie, Zeola, Zero, Zula* and *Zelbert*. It is curious to note that of the Hickok and Cox children only *Zelbert* is found in both families.

Two brothers in Fairview, Oklahoma, were named *Younger Stringer* and *Older Stringer*. But the oldest is named Younger and the youngest is Older. Doremus French of Calagua, Maine, named each of his four sons, *Doremus, Jr.* They are known as *Junior One, Junior Two, Junior Three* and *Junior Four*, and they sign checks that way.

The twin sons of Mr. and Mrs. Pistel of Baltimore were christened *Bing* and *Bang*. Mr. and Mrs. Buren E. Hamm of Dallas, Texas, had five sets of twins and tried to give them appropriate names. The last pair they called *Hilda* and *Wilda*. The others were *Era* and *Vera, Tom* and *Jerry, Troy* and *Roy* and *Sylvia* and *Sylvester*. The Council Bluffs, Iowa, twins named *Oscar Oliver Over* and *Oliver Oscar Over* make the news columns every once in a while. Their father was named Oliver Oscar Over and the paternal grandfather, Oscar Oliver Over.

The old joke of naming twin boys *Pete* and *Repeat* or *Max* and *Climax*, and girls *Kate* and *Duplicate* really was re-enacted in England. In 1946 the newspapers reported that a London clergyman flatly refused to perform a christening ceremony when a mother wanted her twins named Kate and Duplicate. The angry mother appealed to the Chancellor of the Diocese who ruled that the minister acted properly. The British press took sides on the issue, one group claiming that a parent has the right to give children any name desired. Disregarding the raging storm, the London mother calmly registered one daughter as Duplicate on the birth certificate and induced another minister to perform the ceremony.

In 1944, the newspapers called attention to the twins named *Charlie* and *Extra Charlie*. Charlie was picked up by the F.B.I. for not carrying his Selective Service card. Mr. and Mrs. Hawkins of Chicago solved the problem of twins' names by calling them both *Richard Hawkins*. In Derbyshire, England, twin children were named *Jeru* and *Salem* so that the word Jerusalem would do for both.

Compared with quadruplets, twins are commonplace. What do surprised parents do when babies come in fours and have to be identified? Well, the Badgett family christened them *Jeraldine, Joan, Jean* and *Janet*. The Browns said *Connie, Claire, Cleo* and *Clayton*. Mr. and Mrs. Kasper solved the problem with *Frances, Frank, Felix* and *Ferdinand*. The Morloks were contented with *Helen, Wilma, Sarah* and *Edna*. The Perricones called them *A, B, C* and *D*, or more exactly *Anthony, Bernard, Carl* and *Donald*. And when it happened to Mrs. Schense, the new arrivals became *Joan, Jean, Jay* and *James*.

Palindromes are those sentences, words or names, which spell the same forward and backward. Common ones are *Anna* and *Otto*. M. *Laval* of France is one of the most famous. *Otto Rentner* and *Anna Renner* of Chicago and *Otto Laval* of Evansville, Indiana, have names where both the first name and the surname are reversible. A triple one is *Hannah Anna Tippit* of McAlester, Oklahoma. *Edna Lalande*, together is a palindrome. Illinois produced a *Revilo Oliver*, and Chicago has a *Ronnoc Connor*, both of which are not exactly palindromes. Indeed, the practice of giving the surname spelled backward as a Christian name is observed every now and then, as *Norabel Le Baron*. In the last century, *Asa* Reynolds married *Hannah* Wells. They had twelve children, all of whom were given palindromic Christian names: *Hannah, Asa, Emme, Iri, Aziza, Anna, Zerez, Axa, Atta, Alila, Numun* and *Harrah*.

When a serious dispute arose between the Venetian houses, *Ponti* and *Canali*, the quarrel spontaneously turned to their names and the former alleged that they, the Bridges, were over the Canals. The Senate was obliged to remind the rival houses that its authority included both the pulling down of Bridges as well as the stopping of Canals, when they became public nuisances.

The comedian Mathews bought his groceries from a dealer named *Berry*, who once sent his bill before it was due, whereupon the actor is said to have exclaimed, "You have sent in your *bill*, Berry, before it is *due*, Berry; your father, the *elder*, Berry, would not have been such a *goose*, Berry; but you need not look so *Black*, Berry, for I don't care a *straw*, Berry, and shan't pay your bill till *Christmas*, Berry."

In line with Dibdin's punning reference to Shakespeare's Anne Hathaway are the following lines found written by a guest, not wholly satisfied, on a pane of glass at an inn in South Wales, in the early part of the nineteenth century, where the proprietor's name was *Long-fellow*:

> Tom Longfellow's name is most justly h˙s due,
> Long his neck, long his bill, which is very long too;
> Long the time ere your horse to the stable is led,
> Long before he's rubb'd down, and much longer till fed;
> Long, indeed, may you sit in a comfortless room,
> 'Till from kitchen long dirty, your dinner shall come;
> Long the often-told-tale that your host will relate,
> Long his face whilst complaining, how long people eat;
> Long may Longfellow long ere he see me again,
> Long 'twill be ere I long for Tom Longfellow's inn.

Some year ago a duel took place between Mr. *Schott* and Mr. *Willing*. A wag then composed the following:

> Schott and Willing did engage
> In duel fierce and hot:
> Schott shot Willing willingly, and
> Willing he shot Schott.
> The shot Schott shot, made Willing
> Quite a spectacle to see,
> Since Willing's willing shot went right
> Through Schott's anatomy.

Whenever a new issue of the telephone book comes out in a big city, some newspaper reporter, in order to fill a little space, makes a search for names under a certain classification. One examined for fishing terms and found *Lakes, Streams, Rivers, Ponds, Seas* and many others, as well as *Reels, Hooks, Rodds, Lines*, etc. Then looking for various kinds of fish, besides Fish, he found *Dolphins, Shadd, Salmon, Sturgeon, Codd, Trout* and a host of others. But he failed to find a single *Bite*.

A reader sought for numerical names in the Chicago directory and found *Wann, Tew, Tree, Fore, Fife, Six, Severn, Ayotte, Nyhun, Tann* and even *Leven*, and then ended up with *Twety, Forty, Honert, Thowsen* and *Million*. Another went into the same directory and came up with *Aye, Bee, See, Dee, Hee, Effa, Gee, Haisch, Hie, Jay, Kay*,

El, Emm, Engh, Hoe, Peek, Kew, Ahr, Esse, Tei, You, Vee, Dubia, Ex, Wye and *Zee.* Any directory is a fertile field for opposites like *Long* and *Short, Light* and *Dark, Thinn* and *Fatt* and *Love* and *Loveless.*

Initials can provoke consternation. For confirmation consult the lawyer, *Daniel Ashton Martin,* who hired *Irene Thompson* to do his stenographic work. In the lower left hand corner of the letters he dictated she dutifully wrote, "Dict. DAM/IT."

An odd name can often be a distinct asset. A salesman, for example, wants to attract attention and favorable comments. C. C. C. Tatum, a California realtor, discovered that his name attracted so much attention that he considered it a major factor in his success. On the other hand, an accountant in Chicago, named *Clark Gable,* had his applications for jobs rejected because of his name. The argument was that to add a Clark Gable to the staff, where many girls were employed, would interfere with office routine. At Quincy, Mass., the judge asked a man appearing before him why he was not working. The unfortunate contended: "I can't get a job because no one remembers my name." His name was *Urho E. Waimionpaa.*

Absurdity is inherent in all personal names. After the meaning has been lost or pushed into the background, this ridiculous quality is not so apparent. When we contemplate names like those borne by the early Puritans or by the American Indian, their grotesque nature is brought home to us. If our English names are translated into English phrases, they are quite as comical as the most primitive name. If the *Johns,* the *Williams,* the *Benjamins,* the *Ursulas* were set out as *Gracious-Gift-of-God, Helmet-of-Resolution, Son-of-My-Right-Hand,* or *Little-She-Bear,* and if every *Miller, Fairfax* and *Cramer* were called *Man-Who-Grinds-Wheat, Light-Haired* and *One-Who-Sells-Things,* our names would no more than equal *Fight-the-Good-Fight-of-Faith* or the Indians' *White Eagle, Sitting Bull,* or *Yellow Hair,* or some of the odd "foreign" names. Their names are quite as honorable as our own. Really the only way we can enjoy a hearty laugh over the odd names of others is to keep ourselves in complete ignorance over our "common and ordinary" appellations.

The names mentioned in this chapter are, to put it mildly, eccentricities. But, as Bardsley pointed out in his *Curiosities of Puritan Nomenclature,* eccentricities follow a well-beaten path and have their use in outlining the name customs of a people. Odd or queer names are only exaggerations of the prevailing customs.

CHAPTER XII

The Psychology of Names

Names and natures do often agree.
—JOHN CLARKE, *Paroemiologia Anglo-Latina, 1639*

WHAT is the origin of the urge that causes people to write their names on walls or carve them on the wooden sides of depots and station stops for the general public to gaze upon? Is it mere vanity, or is it an awkward attempt to acquire fame by flaunting one's name before the community? The more cultured and educated look with anticipation for their names in the public prints. This is the basis of the society pages and gossip columns in our newspapers. Others like to write their name in the album of a friend, or insert it in the visitor's lists kept at some hotels and show places. Seeing one's name frequently is a gratification of one's self-esteem. A most subtile form of flattery is to remember a man's name correctly and to use it often in dealings with him.

Therefore an examination of our mental attitude toward the various aspects of names will be profitable. The significance of personal names arises more from our mental reactions than from the original meanings, which are generally obscured by the mists of antiquity. People do not often consider the psychological side of personal names, yet few are entirely indifferent to the influence of the names conferred on others.

Psychologists have given little attention to the attitude of people toward their names. The extreme importance attached to names by all primitive peoples is an intimation that the subject merits more consideration among civilized peoples.

People may alter their names to commemorate a significant event in their lives. George Waggner, the producer, explained that he inserted the extra *g* in his name to express his pride when he unexpectedly received two "G's" for a story early in his career.

In general we like or dislike certain Christian names because of the personality of the bearers of such names we have known in early life and since then. If a childhood friend you particularly admired bore a certain name, you like that name; it is a "pretty" name. On the contrary, a name borne by one who tormented you during your early life is distasteful. Of course those appellations which we have never known before are often strongly liked or disliked. Here the reason is that their spelling or sound more or less faintly suggests a name or word which is pleasant or unpleasant. Names which are familiar are more likely to be preferred than others.

A few years ago Professor William E. Walton, of the University of Nebraska, did some experimental work to learn what Christian names were most liked or disliked. He believed that this could be ascertained by his tests and claimed to find that there was little correlation between the pleasantness of the name and the pleasantness of the letters making up the name. From his report of his experiments it is apparent that they were inconclusive. When one considers it carefully, it is clear that the most popular names given to babies are the best-liked ones. Naturally they will vary among different groups of people. Any test that fails to show, for example, that John or Robert is the best-liked name for a boy and Mary or Elizabeth for a girl, is either inconclusive or has not included a sufficiently wide cross section of the population.

In the same manner several members of the Department of Psychology of the Central State Teachers College, in Michigan, made tests on some students and came to the same conclusions one would expect from an examination of lists of the most common Christian names for men and women, that is, that in general people prefer those names which are most popular at the moment. Else how could such names become the most popular?

They also found that men possess and prefer the common names more than women do. This conclusion is easily verified from the fact that there are quite a few more popular women's names than men's names. These investigators also discovered that some names are preferred because of their nicknames—not a startling bit of information. Perhaps the most notable fact they uncovered was, that among the students questioned, about forty per cent of the men and forty-six per cent of the women were dissatisfied with their given names. Of the men who were dissatisfied with their own names, the majority had the more uncommon names and seemed to prefer the more popular ones. Among women satisfaction or dissatisfaction with their names did not appear to be definitely related to frequency of occurrence.

Also at the Central State Teachers College some research has been made into the liking people have for their surnames. The researchers found that familiar surnames were preferred over the very uncommon names; but the most common family names were not in favor, on the theory, perhaps, that familiarity breeds contempt. In the United States English-sounding surnames are regarded as more desirable than others.

Persons like or dislike their own names in accordance with the sound and meaning of the words with which they have associated the name. This, indeed, is the secret of the powerful effect of names in Dickens' novels, which is discussed later in this chapter.

People have a kindly feeling for others with the same Christian name or surname. If both the Christian name and surname are alike, the bearers are likely to feel that they must be particularly friendly. A strong bond of brotherhood cements them together. When Jennifer Jones, the actress, won the Academy award in 1944, it was noticed that about 1,500 of her weekly fan mail of 8,000 letters came from people named *Jones*. Actually her real name was Phyllis Isley. Naming a baby after another is generally considered by the older person to be a great compliment. Fortunes have been bequeathed to namesakes.

Some of the mix-ups most far-reaching in their effects are caused by the coincidental meeting of two with the same name. If the name is unusual, the effect is heightened, due to the fact that no one expects another so named.

The story is told of two men bearing the same name, one a clergyman and the other a businessman, both living in the same small city. The clergyman died, and about the same time the other had to go on a business trip to Southern California. When the businessman arrived there, he telegraphed his wife to relieve her anxiety, but, unfortunately, his wire was delivered to the widow of the late minister. The horrified woman read, "Arrived safely—heat terrific."

Personal names are more apt to be forgotten than any other item retained in our memory. Professor Sigmund Freud, the Austrian founder of psychoanalysis, points out that there is not only forgetfulness, but false recollection. We forget a name, and, in striving to remember it, bring to our mind many other names which we immediately reject as false. Some of them cling to our recollection with great tenacity. We may fail to remember the name of Mr. Johnson, whom we know well. In attempting to force it from our mind such names as Hansen, Jones, Honley, Honland and others come up; we discard them as false, but they seem to crowd the name we seek further from our memory. When we finally remember the name, or someone else mentions it, we immediately recognize it. A curious point is that this forgetfulness tends to be reproduced in those with whom we converse so that they are often unable to supply the missing name.

Of course Freud maintains that this forgetting of a name is motivated by repression, usually sex repression, but many modern psychologists do not agree with him.

The memory experts assert that names may be retained by us and brought to mind at will by associating them with something else, particularly something odd or ridiculous. The difficulty is that we sometimes unconsciously use some other name by thought transference to a synonym. Take, for example, the clergyman who proposed to remember Mrs. *Sumach* by associating her name with "stomach." The next time he saw her he confidently called her Mrs. *Kelly*! The old system of learning a name that has slipped one's memory by inquiring if it is spelled with an *e* or an *i* worked, until the earnest young man asked the question of Miss Hill.

Freud reasons that we are much more apt to forget names of persons whom we consciously or unconsciously dislike, or resent their intimate association with something very close to us. Names are forgotten when they can be associated in some manner with some thing or event we fear. As an example, Freud points to the tendency of some wealthy and aristocratic people to distort the names of the physicians they consult, from which he concludes that while they greet the doctors with especial courtesy, inwardly they slight them. Critics of Freud believe that the tenuous associations he seizes upon may lead in any direction and so either of two opposite conclusions may be reached depending on the associations selected.

Few people can avoid a feeling of resentment when they find that their names have been forgotten, or are spelled incorrectly, or pronounced wrong, when they hoped or expected them to be remembered and used correctly. They instinctively realize that if they had made a greater impression on the person's mind, he would remember them. On the other hand, few things are more flattering to a person than to find himself addressed correctly by a celebrity when he had little reason to expect to be remembered.

This faculty of remembering and using correct personal names is an attribute often found among the truly great and leads many to support them who would not otherwise do so. In Rome, during the Republican periods and under the early emperors, a candidate for public office commonly took a slave with him, called the nomenclator, whose business it was to know everyone by name, and whose sole duty it was to whisper the name of the voter into the candidate's ear so that he could greet the citizen by name as if he knew him.

Conversely, one can affront another easily by pretending to forget his name; the insinuation is that the person whose name is forgotten is so unimportant that we cannot bother to remember it. Falsification of a name has the same signification as forgetting it. The arrogant, newmade knight in Shakespeare's *King John* knew this when he exclaimed, "And if his name be George, I'll call him Peter." Percy Hammond, the late drama critic, frequently used the device of an incorrect name when he wished to annoy someone. He would ring the misspelled name and write "stet" on the margin of his copy to prevent the linotype operator and proofreader from making the correction.

That people are very sensitive as to the spelling of their names is illustrated by the annoyed subscriber who complained to the Cleveland, Ohio, *Press*, in 1939, that it had spelled his name wrong when printing notice of his application for a marriage license. The *Press* had called him *Mieczipylaws Dzesidosz*, whereas the correct name was, he wrote sternly, *Mieczyslaws Dziadosz*, and added, "My friends are asking me whether I have changed my name."

It was said that anyone wishing to see a jurist in a fury had only to omit the extra *t* in the spelling of Chief Justice David Kellog Cartter of the Supreme Court of the District of Columbia, appointed by Lincoln in 1863.

People are irritated when utter strangers use their first names only. If a peddler obtains one's name and then uses it in a familiar manner in conversation, exasperation surges to the surface. If the president of a large corporation calls us by our first name, we are flattered; if the office boy so addresses us, we are affronted. The explanation is that in the first instance our ego is pleasantly inflated; in the second it is abruptly deflated.

A name at once sets a person on the step of dignity he should occupy. The *Salem Gazette* relates a sentence passed by a Massachusetts court in 1630. After finding one, Josias Plastoree, guilty of the theft of four baskets of corn from the Indians, the court ordered him to return eight baskets, be fined five pounds and thereafter to be called by the name of Josias, "not Mister as formerly he used to be." It has been observed that Charlie Chaplin has been raised *per saltum* to the high dignity of "Mr. Charles Chaplin." At any rate where he used to be billed as Charlie Chaplin he is now sedately set out on theatre marquees as Charles Chaplin.

First names of others than servants are reserved for one's friends. Not only is the person addressed irritated, but third parties dislike it because they think the tactless user of the intimate form of address is attempting to parade a friendship which he does not have. The common use of given names between casual acquaintances has become more usual in this generation. People resent the use of their surnames alone, without any title appended, as something less than respectful. To be crudely addressed as *Jones*, instead of *Mr. Jones*, by bare acquaintances, just does not set well with us.

The present-day practice of calling everyone by his first name, or by a diminutive or pet name, is bitterly assailed by the fastidious among the older generation. Rotary was about the first club to make it a rule that members must know each other by their first names and use them. Much fun was made of the practice, but it stuck, and many other men's clubs followed suit. Business men found that it was a most democratizing and humanizing influence, and the practice is still growing.

Perhaps sports writers were among the first to use baptismal names freely. On the golf course businessmen adopted this simple and intimate style of address. A desire to push ahead in business induced some to pretend to influence by casually referring to important persons by their intimate names.

This free and easy mode of address was not always the custom. In the last years of the nineteenth century or the beginning of the twentieth century *Molly Brown* was different from *Mrs. Brown*; a clean-cut social distinction was involved. The maid might be called *Nora* by her mistress, but the lady of the house was careful to refer to most other servants as *Jones* or *Flanagan*. All the tradesmen were *Mr. Hanson* or *Mr. Graves*. In England even the house servants were called by their surnames alone. The hired man would be mentioned only by his cognomen. The laundress or seamstress who came to the house was *Miss Weaver* or *Mrs. Thomason*.

The only ones who then used first names in conversation were children. Indeed, for an older person to refer to another by his or her given name was almost equal to a declaration that they had attended grammar school together. In college, a generation ago, everyone was *Harrison* or *Bennett* or *Johnson*.

Acquaintances and friends, in the last century, had a rigid last-name status. Even close friends of the family were *Mr. Schmidt* or *Mrs. Seagraves.* If a social friend of your mother's asked to be called by her first name it was a declaration of the most intimate kind of friendship. Scarcely anyone knew that Mrs. Astor had a Christian name. She certainly didn't need it at all. The society reporter who related that a debutante was "known among her friends as Sandy" was being a bit daring. Presidents Cleveland and McKinley were never known as *Grover* or *William.*

In business the formal use of the last name was the invariable rule. Even young men in one's office were granted the courtesy of reference only to their family name.

Nowadays, all one's friends are called by their first name or by an affectionate nickname, and the stilted use of a last name bespeaks utter strangeness. The breezy life insurance salesman is quick to call the prospect by his given name. It is related how the salesman stepped on the elevator with his prospect on the third floor and started the conversation, "Now Mr. Williams, about this. . . ," and at the second floor he was saying, "As I said, Williams, this is the best. . . ," and before the operator could open the gate at the first floor, he heard the prospect being told, "Yes, Al, the best I can do is. . . ."

Today when an announcer interviews someone on the radio, he uses the familiar style of address, although he may never have heard of the celebrity ten minutes before. One celebrity on the radio always calls another by an intimate nickname although they may be mortal enemies. If Hope wishes to show his contempt for Crosby on the radio, he calls him *Harry,* the name by which he was baptized. Crosby badgers Hope by calling him *Robert* and refusing to say *Bob.* Everyone in radio, with little regard for age, has a first name which is more important than a family name.

No politician of our era would think of referring to a man he had known longer than five minutes by other than his first name. To do so would be tantamount to a confession that he could not expect the man to do a "favor" for him. It is a cheap way of showing friendliness. From the top down, this familiar style of address is used. Roosevelt writes to "Dear Alben," and Barkley becomes majority leader of the United States Senate.

Now people in business flaunt their first names. As you drive along the highway you have your choice of eating places and taverns, all run by *Bill* or *Dan* or *Jack*. Perhaps both the man and his wife sell gasoline and the sign reads, MARY AND JOE'S or if the place is operated by a woman alone, it is just JANE'S EATERY. The signboard may inform you that the owner is *Bobbie* and you don't know whether the proprietor is a man or a woman.

The use of pet forms, like *Mollie, Tommy* and *Sal,* in the privacy of one's home, may sound well. But the practice carried into formal clubs, formal parties and churches often sounds flat and vapid. That the problem is not new is shown by the observation made by Horace in his *Satires,* before the Christian era, when he wrote, "Sensitive ears delight in being called by the first name."

In mentioning great writers the use of surnames is almost universal. We speak "of Burns," "of Dickens," "of Thackeray" and others by their surnames only, but we say "of Miss Austen." We speak "of Milton," "of Kierkegaard," but we say "of Henry James."

A man learns his name in infancy; during his childhood he laboriously writes it out. It is the symbol of his personality, the best evidence of himself. To his ears it is the sweetest sound in the language. If he gets into trouble or runs into debt, it is by his name. To its sound he greets an acquaintance, walks into a room, or rises nervously to make a speech. At the sudden sound of his name he will start. When he sees it in a newspaper or magazine, he will exhibit pleasure or mortification. Even though he knows it is there, he will pore over long lists to find it. And, tracing it out with a shaking hand on his will may be one of the last acts of his life.

A name can emphasize a thought. In conversation its pronunciation, in places where its use is not imperative, is felt to be an act of homage. It cements the attention of the listener to hear his name in the mouth of one conversing with him. Lovers fairly revel in the sound of their names from their beloved.

Men are more interested in their own name than in all others put together. If a man remembers our full name correctly, we are flattered to find that we are so important in his eyes, and we consequently feel that he is a great man, if for nothing else than for recognizing our worth and merit. In Papua it is bad manners to ask a native his name —everyone is supposed to know it instantly. James A. Farley has claimed that he could call 50,000 men by their first names and this ability was no small factor in his success.

In order to keep his name fresh in the minds of his fellow Ephesians, Herostratus set fire to the Temple of Diana (Artemis) at Ephesus on the same night that Alexander the Great was born (B.C. 356). The outraged Ephesians decreed the condemnation of his name to oblivion, but, as might be expected, this action just made certain that his name would be remembered and his goal attained.

Andrew Carnegie is said to have learned the importance of names when he was only ten years old. He had some rabbits but had nothing to feed them. He told the boys in the neighborhood that if they would gather enough clover to feed the bunnies, he would name his pets in their honor. The plan worked like magic and Carnegie never forgot it. Years later, when he wanted the business of the Pennsylvania Railroad, he built a huge steel mill in Pittsburgh and called it the J. Edgar Thompson Steel Works after J. Edgar Thompson, the president of the Pennsylvania Railroad. When the railroad needed steel rails, in what mill do you think the order was placed?

Back in 1924 the Controller General of the United States, J. R. McCarl, ruled that married women employees of the Federal Government must be carried on the payroll by their husband's surname and not by their maiden name. What a hornet's nest he brought down on his ears! The feminists denounced him. To the attack came the Lucy Stone League and sailed in with the utmost indignation, loudly declaring that the law allowed married women to use their maiden names. It was pointed out, however, that for a long time the State Department had insisted that passports be drawn in the husband's surname.

The National Woman's Party, in 1925, decided to bring a test case attacking the regulation specifically stating that passports could only be given to married women in their husbands' surnames. Ruby Black was the wife of Herbert A. Little and both were eminent journalists. There would have been some confusion if Ruby Black had used her husband's surname on her passport. After a prolonged hearing, attended by the legal staffs of the Departments of State, War and Navy at Washington, the Secretary of State ruled that the petitioner might have, as an emergency and particular measure of relief, a passport in her maiden surname. All the Government departments were so hostile in the matter that only a heavy preponderance of English common law and legal precedent prevented an adverse decision. The general question was thought to be of such importance that it was sent to the President for a final ruling.

Another woman, Doris E. Fleischman, the wife of Edward L.

Bernays, the public relations counsel, insisted on a passport in her maiden name and, in 1925, received it. Despite the embarrassment she continued to be known as Miss Fleischman even after the birth of her two daughters, although they protested when they were old enough to understand. Registrations in hotels and visits in hospitals proved to be productive of fierce altercations. Complications of her domestic and social life under the two-name system finally caused her to give up, and, twenty-six years after her marriage, she announced her abandonment of the hopeless fight to "maintain her individuality" in an indifferent world wedded to a firm adherence to tradition, with the observation that it was "like swimming upstream through molasses."

In all ages man has had an innate feeling for the fitness of personal names. Not only children, but adults, are quick to perceive an agreement between a name and the person who bears it. If Mr. *Short* is short of stature, the fact is immediately noted. There are many instances of this in the Bible, although, owing to the difficulty of reproducing them in English, they are not so apparent. Abigail, in commenting on her husband, says, "As his name is, so is he; Nabal [fool] is his name, and folly is with him." (*I Samuel*, xxv, 25.) In another instance a widow says, "Call me not Naomi [pleasantness], call me Mara [bitterness]: for the Almighty hath dealt very bitterly with me." (*Ruth* i, 20.)

Particularly when one is engaged in a quarrel or controversy his adversary will lay hold of his name and seek to show a contradiction between the name, if it imports something good, and the actions of the bearer of the name, thus making it appear that one is presenting himself under false colors, affecting a merit which he does not really possess. Examples abound in ancient writings. In the early church there was one, *Vigilantius*, whose name might be interpreted "the Watchful," who got into dispute with St. Jerome over certain vigils which he thought perilous to Christian morality, while Jerome was an eager promoter of them. The latter quickly seized upon the name and proclaimed that he, the enemy of these watches, the partisan of slumber and sloth, should not have been named Vigilantius, but rather *Dormitantius*, or "the Sleeper." In the eighth century *Felix*, Bishop of Urgel, a champion of the Adoptionist heresy, was constantly referred to as *Infelix* in the writings of his adversary, Alcuin, just as our modern writers would do. At the time of the Peninsular War, the Spanish people would not hear of *Bonaparte*, but insisted on calling him *Malaparte*.

During the war, people, in order to puncture a lot of the pomposity built around the man's personality, derisively referred to *Hitler* as *Schicklgruber* and called on others to do the same. Many alleged that he had changed his name to Hitler. Even the *Reader's Digest* loudly summoned people to "Help defeat Hitler by calling him by his right name, Schicklgruber." The true facts are that Hitler's father was the illegitimate son of Maria Anna Schicklgruber, who married Johann Hiedler, generally believed to have been her seducer. Hitler *père* bore the name of his mother until he was forty, when he legally adopted the name of his maternal grandmother. Adolf Hitler was born twelve years after the change of name.

Reichsmarshal Hermann Goering confidently advised the people of Berlin that, if one single Allied bomb ever fell on Berlin, his name would be Meyer. When the Berliners were tense with fear of the violent bombs raining on the city, they remembered their gangster leader, even if somewhat less than fondly, and from one end of the city to the other he was known as *Herr Meyer*.

If the name has a bad import and does not need to be reversed, the adversary is even quicker to take it up and triumphantly point out the agreement as if it were a public confession of the worthlessness or wrong thinking of the bearer. Indeed, the antagonist often then regards his task at an end, his argument fully proved. Examples are numerous in early writings and continue right down to our own day. Every reader will remember back to his childhood when he has attacked a youthful opponent by seizing upon his name.

Mr. Allen Steven, writing a letter to the *Chicago Daily News* during the late war, observed that the German leaders could not but be cruel with the names they bore, as would be seen when associated with English words: *Hitler* made him think of hitting, *von Ribbentrop* of ripping. *Goering* reminded him of a bull goring its victims, *Goebbels* of a hog gobbling up everything; *Mussolini* was the unwelcome character who muscled in. *Hirohito* made him think of hot, *Laval*, of molten lava that destroys all life. *Vichy* reminded him of vicious, while *Rommel* brought up the picture of a drunk. On the other hand Mr. Steven pointed out that *Winston Churchill's* name brought before him the prospect of winning while *Roosevelt* reminded him of rosy. Perhaps the same uncomplimentary idea could be worked out by the Nazi writer, and it probably was printed in the German press. The point is that people's names do remind us both consciously and unconsciously of good or bad words.

On the other hand, when we desire to honor a man, if his name in any way bears an honorable significance or is capable of a good interpretation, the fact is always brought out. John Careless, in writing to Philpot, exclaims, "Oh good master Philpot, which art a principal pot indeed, filled with much precious liquor,—oh pot most happy! of the High Potter ordained to honour."

The often secret regard a man has for his name is sometimes revealed in his will. Many testators have given money to persons upon the express condition that the beneficiary adopt the testator's name and the English Home Office has expressly recognized this as the most logical reason for a change of name. John Nicholson, by his will, dated April 28, 1717, gave the residue of his estate toward the support and maintenance of such poor persons in England as should appear to be of the name of Nicholson, being Protestants. William Stanislaus Murphy, a bachelor, left his entire estate to Harvard University, in 1916, to be used as a scholarship fund "for the collegiate education of any young man or men named Murphy." In 1882 Elias W. Leavenworth established a scholarship at Yale University, "for any student of good character and promise and good standing in the academical department of the college, of the surname of Leavenworth." The Spaniard, Alonso Días de Montalvo, who died in 1499, by his will, disposed of his surname, as well as his property, among his sons.

An eccentric Frenchman left his estate to six nephews and six nieces on the condition that everyone of the nephews marry a woman named *Antonie* and that everyone of the nieces marry a man named *Anton*. They were further required to give the Christian name *Antonie* or *Anton* to every first-born child according to the sex. The marriage of each nephew was to be celebrated on one of the *St. Anthony's* days, either January 17, May 10, or June 13, and if, in any instance, this last provision was not complied with before July, 1896, one-half of the legacy was to be forfeited.

A man named Furstone, of Alton, Hampshire, England, by his will, left £7,000 to any man, legitimately bearing the name of Furstone, who should discover and marry a woman named Furstone. If the marriage should result in children, the sum was to descend to the male offspring, if any, or to any child or children of the opposite sex who should, after marriage, retain the name. P. T. Barnum, the great circus promoter, made careful provision for the perpetuation of his surname, since he had no sons. In his will he left an additional $25,000 to his grandson, C. H. Seeley, if he would change his name to C. Barnum Seeley, "so that the name of Barnum shall always be known as his name."

Paul Revere, father of the famous revolutionary patriot, in his will, cut off his grandson, Frank, "who now signs his name Francis," with one dollar. However Paul Revere, Sr., was not always opposed to the alteration of names as disclosed by his changing from Apollos Rivoire shortly before he was married, "merely on account that the bumpkins pronounce it easier."

Surnames can be changed quite easily compared with first names, that is, it is easier to persuade people to use the new name. The man who dares to change his given name faces an almost hopeless task in forcing his acquaintances to forget the old name. Alfred, formerly Algernon, will continually meet acquaintances who will insist on displaying their old intimacy with him by familiarly calling him Algy.

No one has published a comprehensive analysis of the influence of personal names in political campaigns, yet the fact that personal names have a very real influence and significance in politics is recognized by all practical politicians. A young man may be chosen to run for office because the party bosses think that he has a name that will attract votes. Newspaper items disclose the power of names when, as in the Roosevelt-Dewey race in 1944, they show how inhabitants of towns named *Roosevelt* have tended to vote for him while natives of towns named *Dewey* seemed to prefer the Republican candidate. This is true even though the Roosevelt towns were named after Theodore Roosevelt and the Dewey towns after Admiral Dewey.

Voters may have real reasons for voting for or against the head of the ticket, because of their policies and abilities about which they have heard for months before election day, but when they begin to examine their ballot alone in the voting booth, many discover, for the first time, that they are also going to make a choice for representatives, lieutenant-governors, auditors, legislators, judges, court clerks, university trustees, and others far too numerous for the average man to be familiar with their qualifications, particularly in large cities. Some will select their party nominees but this solution is not always available in the primary elections. When one comes right down to it, many will be picked because of their name as that will be the only criterion the voter can muster at the last minute. If the voter is American, and there is one out-and-out American name in a group of foreign-looking names, he quickly selects the American for whom to cast his vote. But the candidate with the American name may have only recently changed his name and really be more foreign than the rest. For the same reason a Polish or German or other name may be a great asset when the candidate is running before a Polish or German or other constituency.

A favorite trick of unscrupulous politicians is to persuade some one with the same or a similar name as an opponent to enter the race and thus divide the opposition vote. Voters, only partially informed, are befuddled. Through coincidence, two candidates for the same office, with the same or similar surnames, will spend a great deal of their campaign just in identifying themselves.

If the name of a candidate can be used as a slogan, well and good. When Governor Dunn of Illinois and President Wilson were running for reelection, the Democratic buttons read, "Well Done—Wilson and Dunn." In 1940 the campaign cry for Dewey was "Do we want Dewey? We do." This name recalls the verse by Eugene Ware, in 1898, about another Dewey:

> Oh dewey was the morning
> Upon the first of May.
> And Dewey was the Admiral
> Down in Manila Bay
> And Dewey were the Regent's eyes
> Them orbs of royal blue
> And dew we feel discouraged?
> I do not think we dew.

A man may be so startled and alarmed by the sudden sound of his name that he may retire in confusion without thinking. Hazlitt speaks of a student who had lately come to London and, in a playhouse, seeing one of his college tutors in a box near him, called out, "Dr. Topping!" in a low voice. There being no answer he called the name a little louder and then louder and louder. The Doctor took no notice. Other persons started to call "Dr. Topping," and soon the whole audience rose and roared out, "Dr. Topping," with loud and repeated cries. The Doctor was so confused and frightened at the sound of his own name that he was impelled to leave.

We are all familiar with the Fourth of July orator who appeals, in quivering accents, to the name of Abraham Lincoln, letting his voice dwell caressingly on the name so his hearers can interrupt to applaud properly. Everyone has heard the preacher, telling of the three saved from the fiery furnace, who enunciates, in a sonorous, majestic voice, with rising accents, *"Shadrach, Meshach* and *Abednego."* The rhythmic sound of these names has produced a popular song about them.

It is said that Alexander the Great, before going on a war, ordered the Jews to erect a monument to him for his inspection upon his return from the expedition years later. When he came back he could find no stone commemorating him. Angrily, he summoned the High Priest, who came with hosts of children in his suite, and was asked if he had forgotten his duty. "Sire," the High Priest replied, "it is contrary to our religion to make any graven image. But look!" And he asked each boy in his train his name. Each replied, "Alexander." "Sire," the High Priest continued, "you see we have fulfilled your command by naming each boy, born in your absence, Alexander, and as your name will go down from generation to generation, a living monument will be better than a cold stone one."

Names can die quickly. George W. Goethals, the American engineer, was on every man's tongue when the Panama canal was finished. Pancho Villa, the Mexican bandit, drew the United States into a practice war in 1916. And do many remember Emile Coué, the French exponent of autosuggestion, who, on his trip to the United States, induced many people to affirm, hopefully, to themselves, "Every day, in every way, I grow better and better"?

During the war the Dutch needled their conquerors by naming their sons *Winston* and *Franklin* until the Germans forbade it. The Nazis sentenced a Belgian father, during the war, to nine months imprisonment for christening his son, *Winston.* The Germans also became suspicious of all given names beginning with *V,* fearing that it referred to victory.

The mystic aura cast over one by the professional use of a foreign name is well known. London-born *Charles Edward Pratt,* in order to make as much of a menace of himself as possible, changed his name to *Boris Karloff* when he began to act in horror stories. This was a catering to the idea, prevalent in America, as well as elsewhere, that "foreigners are evil."

The story is told of how the Spanish Ambassador to the English court, *Don Pedro de la Silva,* proud of his haughty and resounding name, rode through the streets of London, aware of the whispers and subdued hum of admiration of the people, who murmured his awe-inspiring name to each other. When a comedian pointed out that it meant only *Peter Wood,* the admiration of the populace turned to derision. Their taunts and the indignities heaped upon the common name caused him to return to Spain, his mission unaccomplished.

Musicians and artists are convinced that they cannot be successful before the English and American people unless they can display an exotic name. If *Ignace Paderewski* had translated his surname to its English equivalent, *Patterson*, before his concert tours, would his success have been so outstanding? The pianist, *Lucy Hickenlooper*, from San Antonio, Texas, of English stock in this country long before the Revolution, must adopt the name, *Olga Samaroff*, to assure the success of her musical career. This is no modern innovation. Dr. Allan A. MacRae discovered that the scribes of the ancient Assyrian city of Nuzi, as long ago as 1500 B.C., adopted Akkadian names as a subtle method of professional advertising.

A name can, in itself, achieve immortality for a man or push him into obscurity. Almost unknown is William Dawes, the American patriot, who rode with Paul Revere on that fateful ride, that "eighteenth of April, in Seventy-five" toward Lexington, warning the people of the coming of the British. Ten years younger than Paul Revere, he got through and attained his goal, while Paul Revere was captured by the British soldiers and failed to reach Lexington that night. Longfellow immortalized Revere in his celebrated poem, *The Midnight Ride of Paul Revere*, in which slight attention was paid to historical fact. Thus every child knows of Paul Revere and his ride while almost none know of the more successful ride of the man Longfellow so shamefully ignored, and our history books and encyclopedias barely mention his name. The basic reason? *Paul Revere* has a more musical rhythm to it than *William Dawes,* and is more susceptible to rhyming.

Amerigo Vespucci, the explorer, merits our attention simply because the New World was named after him, although it is doubtful whether he ever set foot on the American continent. Again he owes his fame in this naming episode to an obscure map maker, Martin Waldseemüller, who suggested the name, *America*, and first so labeled a shadowy portion of the Western Hemisphere. Even the name of Martin Waldseemüller lives today in our histories and reference books solely because he was instrumental in fixing the name of two continents.

Among the Chinese, the middle man, who has the task of choosing a wife for his client, takes care to inquire first as to the lady's name. Mr. *Cash* and Miss *Waste* would not make a good marriage. If the man's family name were *Ox* and the girl's *Red*, the parents of the young lady might object to such a match on the grounds that after the marriage Mr. Ox might see Red. On the other hand, *Water* and *Well* or *Happy* and *Sing* or *Time* and *Sand* might make a happy marriage.

Two ambassadors, in the year 1200, were sent from France to Spain to choose one of the daughters of King Alfonso IX for marriage to the French King, Louis VIII. The beautiful one was called *Urraca* and everyone assumed that the choice would fall upon her, but *Blanche* was selected, as history records, because, the envoys said, her name would be better received in France. Camden, quoting Herodotus, tells us that in the time of Galienus, one *Regilianus* was chosen emperor merely from the royal sound of his name.

Often names, through the operation of fate, exert a most disastrous influence on our lives or even are the means of terminating them. During the French Revolution there were two persons named *Biron*, of which one was known to be guilty. As there was little time for proper investigation, Fouquier ordered both of them sent to the scaffold. When Bossa Ahadi, the King of Dahomey, ascended the throne, he had everyone beheaded who bore the name of *Bossa*. What price name?

Another historical instance of death, solely by reason of one's name, is that supplied by the cruelty of Valens, Roman Emperor of the East from 364 to 378 A.D. When Hilarius, an oracle, about 371 A.D., prophesied, by means of the principle of involuntary movement (which we know as "Ouija"), that Valens would be succeeded by one whose name began *Theod-*, the despotic monarch decreed the death of *Theodorus*, *Theodulus*, *Theodoretus*, *Theodosius* and others so styled. The prophecy came true when *Theodosius*, the Great, became emperor as his successor.

Names thus do affect the bearers, sometimes seriously. After the late Sir Arthur Pinero titled one of his plays, *The Notorious Mrs. Ebbsmith*, a weak-minded lady of that name, of whom he had never heard, committed suicide, under the delusion that her lurid past had been discovered. Mrs. Marian Ocala Stegowski, with her twelve-year-old son, impulsively jumped into icy Lake Michigan, in 1936, to end it all. Even after she was pulled out and thought her son had been rescued, she said she didn't want to live with the name *Stegowski*. Six years before, she had attempted suicide by slashing her wrists; and worry over her name prompted that attempt also. This is an extreme case, but nevertheless true.

The dictator of Paraguay from 1813 to 1840, Dr. José Caspar Rodriguez de Francia, decreed that anyone who addressed him other than as "El Supremo" would be shot. He meant it, too, and did it, keeping the people of that nation in unhappy subjection to his odious terrorism for twenty-six years. It was the ignorant and uneducated natives who enabled this cruel despot to control the country, and perhaps they were the reason why he was so determined that his stern edict be strictly obeyed. In the language of the Paraguayans' ancient paganism, the Most High was referred to as *El Supremo* and many of them believed that this man had by law made himself omnipotent.

The name of the Japanese Mikado is so hallowed that it is seldom mentioned and a great proportion of the public does not know it. Some years ago the mayor of a small town unwittingly gave his son the emperor's name. When he discovered his horrible mistake, he resigned and dutifully committed hara-kiri.

The inscription "Kilroy was here," found in so many places during the second World War, was both a lift and a drag to many of the good people named *Kilroy*. Some found that it helped their business with the ex-GI's. Others would have enjoyed shooting the "original Kilroy," particularly after they had answered the telephone too many times to the inquiry about Kilroy's whereabouts. John Kilroy, shortly after the war, was arrested for drunken driving in Chicago. Instead of being booked, released on bond, fined and forgotten by the police, as any ordinary man would have been, he had to listen to a lot of monotonous jokes, and his stay in jail cost him his job. When the judge began to feel sorry for him and offered to request his employers to give him his job back, the harassed Kilroy exclaimed, "No thanks, I was kidded too much on that job."

Carry Amelia Moore, the American temperance agitator and hatchet woman, married Mr. Nation to become Carry A. Nation (not spelled Carrie). Her suggestive name then helped convince her that she had been providentially selected to Carry A Nation to prohibition, and with great self-sacrifice she carried on.

That names have an effect on character and behavior, from their association or meaning, cannot be doubted. This is the reason why the Catholic church insists that babies be given the names of saints of the church. That Christ was alive to the influence of names on character was evident when he said, "Thou art Peter, and upon this rock I will build my church." (*Matthew* xvi, 18.)

Christian names are often suggestive of the person because they are bestowed by the parents and reflect the characteristics of the parents, which are inherited, in a sense, by the children bearing them. Weak, indecisive parents are likely to bestow weak, indecisive names and their children inherit the weak, indecisive character of their parents.

To many persons the name of an unknown calls forth, in imagery, a portrait of the person. They are disappointed when the person later fails to fit the picture conjured in their minds and they are apt to remark about it. The sound of a name, from its association with others with the same or a similar name, or from word association, brings to mind a person thought to fit the name. Other things being equal, names containing heavy or repeated syllables produce a representation of stout, heavy-set, stodgy individuals; short, easy-sounding appellations suggest slender, vivacious, attractive personalities. In the mind's eye Miss *Blablatiford* represents a person with entirely different characteristics from Miss *Tan*. While names often suggest distinct images to various persons, those images are not the same for all people due to their heterogeneous background and experience.

Further proof that a certain, unidentifiable importance exists in names is seen in the copious allusions to them by poets and novelists. James Russell Lowell remarked, in an essay on Keats, that Fame loves best high-sounding names, names from which sonorous epithets can be formed, such as *Spencerian, Shakespearean* and *Wordsworthian.* Keats is a good instance of the falsity of the dictum of Robert Louis Stevenson that men of high destiny always have magnificent names.

Keats knew the value of a name. In a letter to his sister-in-law, in America, dated January 13, 1820, Keats wrote, "If you should have a boy, do not christen him John, and persuade George not to let his partiality for me come across. 'Tis a bad name and goes against a man. If my name had been Edmund, I should have been more fortunate." Certainly an awkward name for a poet is Percy Bysshe Shelley.

Emile Zola said, in his Introduction to *Dr. Pascal,*

I am quite a fatalist in the matter of names, believing firmly that a mysterious correlation exists between the man and the name he bears. Thus I always judge a young author by the names which he bestows upon his characters. If the names seem to be weak or to be unsuitable to the people who bear them, I put the author down as a man of little talent, and am no further interested in his book.

Scott and Dickens have been particularly noted for the apt names they have chosen for their characters. Balzac successfully spent hours and days in searching for appropriate names. Bunyan's allusive names are familiar to all. Thackeray has been called a great master of illustrative nomenclature. Edgar Rice Burroughs, the originator of the Tarzan stories, admits that the sound of the name *Tarzan* is the secret of his phenomenal, world-wide success with the Tarzan books.

Dickens' names are so appropriate because they contain a subtle, half-suggestion of words in our language which are associated with the traits embodied in the characters so named. *Squeers* suggests "squints" and "queer"; *Moddle* was weak, bringing to mind "mollycoddle"; *Phunky* signifies both "flunky and "funk." Others, like *Blathers* and *Bumble*, are fairly obvious. Many other names used by Dickens seem to be peculiarly appropriate, and essentially subconscious and intangible, though they may not suggest the same words to all persons. We all know Mr. *Micawber, Barkis* and *Uriah Heep.* There is a limitation on the suggestiveness of names. What one sees, another doesn't.

Names which may readily be made the subject of a pun are distasteful to some sensitive souls. *Shenstone*, the poet, thanked God that his name was not liable to a pun. *John Huss*, the early Czech religious reformer, is said to have punned on his name when he was burned at the stake, in 1415, by exclaiming, "They burn a goose [German, *huss*], but in a hundred years a swan [German, *luther*] will rise from the ashes," thus predicting the rise of Martin Luther.

Because of the small amount of careful research which has been done in connection with the psychological aspect of names, it is extremely difficult to make accurate generalizations. Some writers have written on the influence of the name on the selection of an occupation and have referred to many examples of correlation of meaning of name and occupation. Undoubtedly the meaning of the name is often considered when choosing an occupation but it is doubtful, in many cases, whether the meaning of the name was a weighty reason for adopting or failing to adopt a certain occupation.

For example, a boyhood friend of the author contended that he would like to become a doctor, but that his ambition was impossible of fulfillment because his surname was *Kilham*, pronounced "Killem." Some psychologists, with an instance of this kind before them, would search no further, but would point to it as an incontrovertible example of the influence of the name in the mind of the bearer. The probability is, in this case, as in so many others, that the Kilham boy had little desire to enter the medical profession, but thought the sound of his name, as a reason for not becoming a doctor, made a good conversational piece. If he had had a strong inclination to become a doctor, he could have done so in spite of his name, or could have resolved the difficulty by changing his name.

Thus even a talk with the person as to the influence of his name upon occupation is likely to fail to bring out the real psychological effect of the name upon the occupation. Psychologists will point to the instances of persons with surnames of *Doctor* or *Lawyer* who became doctors or lawyers, but few of them have made any effort to show that more than the average number of persons named Doctor or Lawyer have become doctors or lawyers than persons with other surnames. Yet it cannot be doubted that the surname does have some effect, however slight, upon the choice of occupation. Naturally it sways those contented with shallow thinking more than the determined person. Many persons with apt names are so used to them that the aptness of the name never occurs to them.

Albert Fancher tells of a man who applied to the head of an international organization for a job, and sent his name in by the secretary. The tycoon was not thinking of hiring anyone, but was intrigued when the name was announced to him as Mr. *Welcome*. He interviewed the visitor, saw that he was in earnest and serious, and offered to try him out on one condition. The applicant was told, "Live up to that name of yours. When you call on a man, go in with a real smile on your face. Be glad, really glad, to see him. Show him that, make him feel it. Make yourself a Welcome visitor." The young man had not given much thought to his name, but decided to capitalize upon it and became an important salesman for his firm.

The study of the effect of the name on choice of love object is no more advanced than its effect on choice of profession, and of course the same number of examples can be given. Here, again, little effort has been made to separate the examples which result from coincidence from those where the name had some real effect. Those emanating from coincidence give rise to observations on the subject and after they have been made, it is hard to say how much is really coincidence. It has been suggested that girls with foreign names in America are sometimes influenced to marry men of their own nationality who have Americanized their surnames as a simple means of easing their own names.

Byron had many attachments for women bearing the name of Mary, or one of its derivatives, and was thus undoubtedly justified when he wrote, in *Don Juan*:

I have a passion for the name of Mary,
For once it was a magic sound to me:
And still it half calls up the realms of fairy,
Where I beheld what never was to be:
All feelings change, but this was last to vary
A spell from which even yet I am not free.

When one sees a celebrity with an odd or eye-arresting appellation, the thought presents itself: just how much of an asset or a liability has the name been? A great many report that their name has been neither an asset nor a liability. If the appellation has been merely odd or unusual, not ridiculous, the general agreement is that it has been more of an asset than a liability. People, in general, are proud of their names whether they are queer to others or not. Many aver that they have been useful as a topic of conversation. Names that are subject to puns are sometimes embarrassing, and many of these persons are wont to affirm that they have not heard a new variation since they were six years of age.

The eminent Federal judge, *Learned Hand*, of New York, wrote the author that people with punning natures have used his first name as a source of innocent merriment to his mild distress. The judge was originally christened Billings Learned Hand—three surnames, but when he was about twenty-five they seemed to be too much baggage to carry and he dropped *Billings* and has never used it since.

When he visited England, in 1933, he traveled on board the *Olympic*, at that time one of the large ships. The London newspapers always used to send down reporters to the big liners to pick up any gossip they could. While Judge Hand was on the train bound for London a rather unpleasant young reporter, going through the different cars, stopped and asked whether he was Judge Learned Hand. Upon receiving the affable judge's reply the young man said, "Your name on the passenger list raised considerable interest among the reporters in London, and they asked me to find how you came by it." The jurist answered, "It was my mother's surname." This plainly was a disappointment and the newspaper man made it clear that he had hoped to find that this was an American judge, who, thinking to enhance his dignity, had taken on the name Learned. The interviewer even argued that England had no such surname when the Judge declared that his mother's family came from England. Still trying to get something sensational he asked, "Has it ever caused you any embarrassment?"

Upon receiving an answer in the negative his parting, ill-natured shot was, "I fancy it may in this country."

Mr. Jay F. Christ, of the University of Chicago, has had some interesting experiences with his byname. He writes, in a letter to the author:

Once when I was on the way from Kansas City to Omaha, back in 1908, I had just fifteen cents when I went to sleep at night. I thought that I could borrow a couple dollars from an operator in Omaha, to get me back to Sioux City, where I was employed at the time. As I sat in the smoking compartment, wishing I had some breakfast, a stranger sat down beside me and began to talk about names. Odd names, he mentioned. Before long he wanted to bet me that he had a harder name to live up to than I had. So, with my fifteen cents, I bet him a breakfast. He handed me a card which said, "W. E. Drinkwater"; but my card which I used when I was young and foolish, said merely, "J. Christ." I got a good breakfast in spite of the fact that I told him how I had been betting on a sure thing; but he had bet on what he thought was a sure thing, too.

This same Mr. Christ likes to relate how, years ago, when he was handling correspondence for a home-study school, an inquiry came from a Filipino who signed his name, "B. Jesus." Mr. Christ replied and, without thought, signed his name, "J. Christ." The student took offense, thinking that fun was being made of his name. Mr. Christ reported that it took several letters to convince the man that J. Christ was really his name.

The psychological influence of personal names may be best illustrated by a study of one or two specific names. For an ordinary person the most common is *John Smith*; a most unusual one is *William Shakespeare.* Fortunately we have articles on these two names writen by two dissatisfied bearers, one John Smith writing bitterly in *The Galaxy* of April, 1876, and one William Shakespeare, with a sense of humor, taking a more tolerant view of the matter in the *Rotarian* of July, 1936, this latter article being condensed in the *Reader's Digest* of August, 1936.

Although these names might be thought to be opposites, strangely enough we find both of these writers complaining of people thinking that they were giving wrong names when they identified themselves correctly. John Smith, lacking a sense of humor, said that his college career had been ruined by his name.

John Smith related how a kinsman had invited him for a visit in New York and had then invited all the Smiths of his acquaintance to meet him at an evening party. Everybody, knowing nothing of the trick, were all smiles and affability at first, then became flushed and embarrassed. As each party approached the host the "Mr. Smith, Mr. Smith, Mr. Smith, Mr. Smith" caused the whole room to hiss with aspirates like a serpent's den. Smith glared at Smith, each believing himself to be the victim of a practical joke, but suppressing his rage out of deference to the occasion.

The writer, John Smith, complained that premiums were put on the heads of catamounts and wolves, but that we let the Smiths go free. He would not put a price on their scalps, but would give them the largest possible liberty to get rid of themselves. He told how easy it was to change names, but neglected to say why he had never pursued that remedy when his name gave him such concern.

The modern William Shakespeare also explained how his name had made his school life miserable. His greatest complaint was that for the past twenty years he had not heard an original comment on his name. He asked the reader, however, to imagine that someone brought a man up at a party and introduced him, "May I present my friend, William Shakespeare?" The reader would have to say something on the spur of the moment, but what? Mr. Shakespeare told of almost being discharged from a job when a patron, thinking he was making fun of her, complained when he answered her question as to his name.

The climax of this article came when William Shakespeare told of visiting the psychopathic ward of a hospital at a time when General Hines was inspecting it. When the General stated who he was, a burly patient told the General that he would get over it in a couple of weeks. The General, seeing that Mr. Shakespeare had observed the incident, struck up a conversation with him about it, and eventually asked him his name. All the modern William Shakespeare could do was say, "Oh, what the hell," and walk away.

William Shakespeare stressed the disadvantages of his appellation when he told of being arrested in the evening for a traffic violation and of being held all night by the enraged police when he gave his right name. When he contributed an article to a magazine he was advised not to use the *nom de plume* of William Shakespeare. He ended his narration by wishing with all his heart that his parents had called him *Oswald*.

Concluding, it should be emphasized that names have influenced people, their property, their pursuit of happiness and their very lives, throughout all history. To assume otherwise is simply to ignore the facts. For civilized man names are almost as important as they were thought to be by primitive man, although in different ways. And the difference is more subtle than is apparent on the surface.

CHAPTER XIII

Names of the Famous

It is a heavy burden to bear a name that is too famous.
—Voltaire, *La Henriade* III, 1723

ABLE sons of famous fathers have complained of the blighting influence of a famous name, but succeed nevertheless. Justice Oliver Wendell Holmes, named after his father, Dr. Oliver Wendell Holmes, succeeded admirably, in fact outstripped the Autocrat for immortal honors. Alexandre Dumas, the French playwright and novelist, was the famous son of Alexandre Dumas, famous playwright and novelist, son of Alexandre Dumas, the famous soldier. William Pitt, the Younger, was a greater statesman than his father, William Pitt, the Great Commoner. Naming these who outstripped their famous ancestors merely serves, however, to point to the numerous able sons who went down because of the famous name which they did not measure up to. A desire to bear the exact name of a famous sire came to light on June 20, 1947, when a Massachusetts court granted permission to Second Lieutenant George Patton to assume the name of the colorful General, his father, George Smith Patton.

Probably the most famous men with the same name, not father and son, are the American and English Winston Churchills. Both writers, they were born within three years of each other. Others are the American industrialists: Charles E. Wilson became president of General Electric Company in 1940, while another Charles E. Wilson succeeded to the presidency of General Motors Corporation in 1941.

Before laying this book down, let us examine some of the names of outstanding men. For a start we may as well look at the surnames of those who have been elected to the Hall of Fame for Great Americans established at New York University in 1900, now numbering seventy-seven men.

Heading the list are the two names known by every school child, Washington and Lincoln, both place-names. As they are the great national heroes of the United States, it is meet that something be known of the origin of their names.

Anyone with the forename of *George*, because of the meaning "farmer," may find himself called "Farmer George," and the Father of our country was no exception. His ancestry has been traced back to the twelfth century, where "Willus de Herteburn habet Wessyngton" is mentioned in the *Bolden Book* (1183). A Norman with the name of William exchanged his manor of Hertburn for that of Wessyngton, both in the county of Durham, England, and, as was to be expected, thereafter dropped the name *Hertburn* and became known as *de Wessyngton*.

The Saxon village name was much older than the Conquest and was mentioned in a charter in 973 as *Wassengtone*. In 1264 we find William Weshington of Weshington mentioned. The tun or manor was probably founded by the Wessyng family, that is the sons or descendants of Wess. The seignorial *de* gradually disappeared from the family name and the surname went through various forms until it was finally spelled *Washington* and thus it remains. This final spelling has caused some shallow writers to aver that the great name merely signifies "the washing place," a manifest absurdity.

While the relationship of the American ancestors of Abraham Lincoln to the English Lincolns is a bit obscure, it may be conceded that the sixteenth president of the United States was descended from English Lincolns who acquired their surname from the circumstance that they had removed from the city of Lincoln or from Lincolnshire, of which Lincoln is the principal city. Like other surnames from place-names, the name of Lincoln is found to be rare in the city of Lincoln, but rather common in the nearby counties of Suffolk and Norfolk, especially the latter.

The early English Lincolns usually, but not uniformly, spelled the name *Lincolne*. The crude spellings of *Linker*, *Linkern*, and *Linkhorn* are chiefly from the American backwoods, and are not nearly so common as many of the Lincoln authors, intent on a story, would have one believe. The Germans have seized on some of these spellings with the argument that they represented the original form of the name in order to prove that the Great Commoner was of German descent. No substantial foundation for this claim has ever been shown. The Kentucky misspellings merely prove that names are often incorrectly spelled by people with little formal education.

Lincoln was first the name of a place, and so the earliest personal form was *de Lincoln,* and as such it is listed in *Domesday Book* in 1086. As a very early Roman settlement it was *Lindon,* later *Lindum-colonia* or, translated, "Lake colony." As a place-name Lincoln arises through the faint mists of English antiquity. The Venerable Bede referred to it as *Lindcylene.* One has little difficulty in understanding how it could be telescoped easily to Lincoln.

Names of persons elected to the Hall of Fame like Adams, Bryant, Clemens (Clement), Eads, Edwards, Emerson, Henry, Hopkins, Jackson, Jefferson, Jones, Madison, Mitchell (palatal form of Michael), Morse (Maurice), Willard and Williams are usual and common patronymic surnames and require no further explanations. Likewise, the occupational and official names of Channing (palatal form of Canning, the ecclesiastical Canon), Cooper, Cushman (from *cuish-man,* maker of cuish or thigh armor), Foster (forrester), Franklin, Marshall (farrier), Parkman, Sherman (the shearman or cutter of wool or cloth), Stuart (steward), Webster, and Whittier (the white tawer or white-leather dresser), are familiar. Names derived from places can excite little wonder from readers such as Bancroft (bean field), Beecher, Booth (hut or stall), Brooks, Cleveland, Fulton, Hamilton, Hawthorne, Holmes, Howe (hill), Irving, Kent, Lee, Monroe (red morass), Morton (if not little Mortimer), Penn (Welsh, head or height), Stowe (place), and Whitney (Hwita's island). Some of the personally descriptive family names are obvious such as Gray, Reed (red) and Whitman (white man).

Other personal descriptive names are more interesting. Simon Newcomb, the astronomer, owes his family name to the fact that an early ancestor was a stranger, or "newcomer," in the vicinity. Thomas Paine's surname is not what it sounds like; it is from Old French *payen,* the pagan of the early struggle between Christianity and Mahomet, as displayed in medieval pageantry.

James Abbott McNeill Whistler descended from a "whistler" or "piper." Henry Wadsworth Longfellow derives his patronymic from one who was distinguished for the distance his head was separated from his feet (although it might be from the French *Longueville* or "great town"). Ulysses Simpson Grant's remote ancestor was "grand," i.e., large. Joseph Storey has an odd name which has developed through the years; it is composed of *store*, meaning "big" or "powerful," and the diminutive suffix -*y* meaning little, although the -*ey* may be from Old English *ea*, "a stream."

Henry Clay came from an original dweller by the clay bank. Daniel Boone's masculine forebears were either "good" or "ready"; probably the latter best fits the great scout. Horace Mann's surname is the early word for a vassal or servant. Augustus Saint-Gaudens takes his name from *Gaudentius*, the name of five different saints revered by the Catholic Church.

Edgar Allan Poe's family name undoubtedly came from an inn sign representing the peacock. This bird was formerly known as the *pokoc* or *poecock*, the earliest form being without the -*cock* termination. George Peabody's name also refers to the peacock and may be a nickname for the brightly-dressed individual. Mary Lyon's surname also probably came from an inn sign, the lion. This name was also applied as a nickname for lion-like qualities. James Russell Lowell's name, likewise, is of the same type, referring to the "little wolf."

John Lothrop Motley, if his surname is not a place-name, probably derives from a nickname, Middle English *mottelye*, "a dress of many colors." The surname of Rufus Choate has puzzled many. However, it undoubtedly is derived from a Kentish provincial word *Choaty* meaning "chubby" or "fat," and thus described the stout appearance of the first bearer of the name.

John Paul Jones was born John Paul in Scotland. After settling in Fredericksburg, Virginia, about 1793, he added the "Jones," for reasons still undetermined. The common surname did add some slight length and made it easier for school children to remember. The New York *Times*, of July 4, 1947, reported that there were thirteen John Paul Joneses in the Navy, only one of whom was an officer.

Alice Freeman Palmer, the educator, brings to our mind the palm-bearing pilgrim newly returned from Rome or the Holy Land. Since Palmer is a rather popular surname and it was conferred out of respect and reverence only on the small number of persons who had visited Jerusalem, it seems probable that many boasted of their travels who had not been anywhere.

The two naturalists in the Hall of Fame, John James Audubon and Louis Agassiz, both had French surnames. Audubon, the natural son of an adventurous, French father, Captain Jean Audubon, has a name which is quite rare. Literally translated it is "of the good," possibly a shortened form of some name including a noun modified by the adjective "good," although *bon* is also a noun in French. David Glasgow Farragut had a family name which also included the adjective *good*. It may be translated, from the German, as "the good traveller." The name Agassiz probably means "magpie." Another French surname Matthew Fontaine Maury, the naval officer, probably refers to a Moor, a native of North Africa, or to one of dark complexion.

The origin of the surname of Sidney Lanier, the Southern poet, is not clear. It probably has three distinct origins. First, it may be the dweller by the lane or narrow rural road. Second, it is the wool comber, from French *lainier*. Third, it is an animal nickname from the falcon, Middle English *laner* and Old French *lanier*.

Since Booker T. Washington was once a slave, his name was acquired in this country. In his *Up From Slavery* he tells how, when he went to school and first heard the roll call, he was surprised to learn that most of his fellow students had two names and some of them had three names. Booker was the only name he could remember. When the time came to give his name, he calmly stood up and said, "Booker Washington." Later he learned that his mother had named him Booker Taliaferro, so he became Booker Taliaferro Washington. He wrote, "I think there are not many men in our country who have had the privilege of naming themselves in the way that I have."

Turning from the galaxy of names in the American Hall of Fame, we find other famous men whose names command our attention. Consider the Roosevelts who became presidents.

Roosevelt is a Dutch farm name meaning "the rose farm" or "field." It originated in Holland in the sixteenth century. At this time the rose was a novelty in the Low Countries, and the farm may have been so named because the owner had in his yard one or more rosebushes which attracted attention. An ancestor of our presidents bought this farm in 1649, and then probably moved to the New World the next year. Thus, residence on a farm for a year created a surname which has attracted the respect of the world. The usual pronunciation in both branches of the family is *rō'zě-vělt*, although it formerly was often pronounced *rōō'zě-vělt*, and still is sometimes so enunciated. The earliest emigrant was Claes Martenssen Van Roosevelt.

Succeeding Franklin D. Roosevelt as thirty-third president was Harry S. Truman. His name is unusual in two particulars. He was baptized with a pet form, Harry for Henry. However, Harry is so common that many people never recognize it as a nickname form. The *S* in Truman's name is a letter only, not an initial. It seems that one of his grandfathers bore the name of Shippe and the other the name of Solomon, and, as his parents did not want to please one and antagonize the other, they used only the "S."

The surname is a pleasant one to consider, and certainly denoted a trustworthy quality in the first ancestor so designated. Truman means the "true man," that is, "the faithful or loyal servant." Bardsley suggests that it was probably the sobriquet of some herald or messenger. Truman, spelled *Treweman* and *Treueman*, is found as an English name as early as the *Hundred Rolls* (1273).

During the war the outstanding English and American generals were Sir Bernard Law Montgomery, Douglas MacArthur and Dwight David Eisenhower. Montgomery is a Norman place name meaning the "hill of Gomeric." As a surname it is very old, coming to England with the Conqueror in 1066. MacArthur is, of course, "the son of Arthur." Eisenhower is German for "the iron miner."

National leaders during the Second World War, outside of the English speaking countries, were men who had changed their names. The real name of Marshal Tito of Yugoslavia was Josip Broz, but he adopted the pseudonym before the war in connection with his Communist Party work. Joseph Stalin couldn't stand his original name of Iosif Vissarionovich Dzhugashvili, and you can scarcely blame him. Even the Russian people would feel their burdens more if they had to worship Iosif Vissarionovich Dzhugashvili. Compare this with the original family name of Napoleon Bonaparte, which was Kalomeris, when the family was a resident of Southern Greece.

The Russian Communist leaders were not satisfied with their original names. Lenin was originally Vladimir Ilich Ulyanov. He adopted the name N Lenin. The N did not stand for any name, but many assumed that it stood for *Nikolai* and he was so known. Leon Trotsky was originally Leib Davydovich Bronstein, but discarded that mouthful because it marked him as a Jew. Zinoviev started life as Hirsch Apfelbaum. Litvinoff was born Finkelstein. Molotov was originally Skryabin. One reason for change by these Russian officials was to enable them to keep a step ahead of the old Tzarist police.

To Americans, Chiang Kai-shek, the former Chinese generalissimo and statesman, is probably as well known as any living Chinese, although newspapers are apt to refer to him as "Mr. Kai-shek." His family name, however, is Chiang. As a boy he was called *Jui-tai*. When he reached adolescence, he kept his family name but selected the name *Kai-shek*, also transliterated *Chieh-shih*, which means "boundary stone." His "official" name is Chiang Chung-cheng, which means "central righteousness." It is said that the approximately correct pronunciation of the general's name is "Jiahng Gai-shek."

Controversy over the origin and derivation of the name Shakespeare has been waged more bitterly than over any other surname. In addition, men have quarreled volubly over the spelling of the name, particularly whether the first *e* and the second *a* should be included. The orthography of many other names in years past has been regarded as a trivial matter, but not the name of the great bard. Reputable scholars have taken their stand with a do-or-die attitude. *Shakspeare* and *Shakespear* had their champions, but the real fight, from about 1840 to 1910, was between *Shakspere* and *Shakespeare*, ending in victory for the latter.

Until about forty years ago, when John Louis Haney published his *The Name of William Shakespeare: A Study in Orthography*, Shakespearean scholars each had his individual opinion. Even after the publication of this excellent monograph the critics continued to cling to their opinions but appeared more reticent about airing them in print. The early nineteenth-century writers on the subject displayed little knowledge of surnames, but did that deter them? No! The libraries of the world are cluttered with works by men who were ignorant of the fact that they did not know much about the subject on which they endeavored to write.

Those who argued for *Shakspere* based their opinion on the six genuine signatures and also on the Florio Montaigne autograph, now generally regarded as spurious. While most of these autograph spellings are illegible, they are not uniform except in the probability that none of them can be clearly transliterated as *Shakespeare*. Followers of *Shakspere* contended that a man could spell his name as he pleased and that his autograph was necessarily correct. This argument blandly ignores the difficulty which arises from the fact that the authentic signatures are not uniform in spelling.

The generally accepted form, *Shakespeare*, is supported by the spelling in the text of most of the legal documents relating to the poet's property, including the royal license granted to him in the capacity of a player in 1603, the inscriptions on the graves of his wife, his daughter Susanna and her husband, the spelling on the title pages of the *Sonnets* and twenty-two out of the twenty-four contemporary quarto editions of his plays, and the printed signatures, affixed by his authority on the original editions of his two narrative poems published in his early career as a dramatist.

For many it is difficult to see sufficient reason for the heated argument. Some say it is embarrassing and a reproach to the English-speaking world, that they cannot agree on the spelling of the family name of the greatest English author. It may be more embarrassing for them to fail to agree on whether Shakespeare wrote Shakespeare. More than eighty different ways of spelling the name may be found in print or in official records. George Wise listed four thousand ways of spelling *Shakespeare*, and then did not exhaust all the ways found.

The controversy over the spelling is equaled only by the disagreement over the etymology of the name. More than fourteen different meanings have been seriously suggested, some with considerable asperity. Those who disapproved the spear-shaking theory suggested that it came from *Sigisbert*; from the French *Jacques-pierre* (James-peter), the initial *J* being pronounced *sh*; a corruption of *Shachsburh* (otherwise Isaacbury); the Celtic *Shacspeir* meaning "dry shanks"; the Saxon *Seaxberht*; the Norman-French *Saquespée*; from the place names, *Saxby*, and the French *Saquespée*; and from *Schalkesboer* (the knave's farm). Other forms have also been found in Ireland and in France. The more absurd the suggestion, the more likely that ridicule would tend to make a researcher stubbornly insist that he was right, whereas he had at first only timidly suggested the possibility. Some have suggested that the name is derived from several distinct sources and this may be quite right, particularly in view of the fact that it is found in many parts of England.

The two most likely origins are: (1) that it is *Schalkesboer* (the knave's farm), and (2) a nickname for a soldier, a shake-spear, one who wielded a spear, a spearman or pikeman. Old English phrase nicknames of this type are found as early as *Domesday Book* (1086). And in modern times a nickname composed of a verb and an object is not rare. The writer remembers a character in his boyhood who was familiarly known as *Chew-Tobacco*. *Shakespeare* as a nickname meaning "shake spear" probably refers to a blusterer who liked to act like a brave warrior who brandished his spear. It may also have been the nickname of an overzealous and overbearing officer of the law.

To express an opinion on this name of *Shakespeare* is to thrust out one's neck for the blow of one who cannot give a convincing reason for his own pet theory. The name has been said to be interchangeable with *Breakspear* and *Shakestaff*. It may also be related to *Levelance* and *Drawsword*.

Ewen suggests that the name *Shakespeare* was formed, by the doctrine of synonymous change, probably from *Brekespere*, which he conjectures to have been a place-name, or from *Saxby*, also a place-name. He thinks it may also be from *Shakelok*, which he deduces to be an old English personal name. In support of his theory of origin by synonymous change he points to undeniable instances of persons who have been known by several interchangeable surnames which have the same meaning.

The earliest occurrence of the name was found by that great Shakespearean biographer, Sidney Lee, a William *Sakespere* (of Clopton, seven miles from Stratford-on-Avon) who was convicted of robbery and hanged in 1248. Here is an example of a man who became notorious (at least among Shakespearean critics) centuries after his death by virtue of his crime and his name. Curious is the case of Hugo Shakspere who, about 1487, changed his family name to Sawndare because Shakspere *"vile reputatum est."*

By virtue of his wartime occupation of the office of Prime Minister of England, Winston Leonard Spencer Churchill, known as Winston Churchill, was a national hero and, as such, had a great influence on boys' names. His surname is an old honored English appellation referring to "the dweller near the church hill."

An important "famous man" with reference to his name is the youthful Prince of Edinburgh, born in late 1948 in direct line to the English throne, the first such birth since the present Duke of Windsor was born fifty-four years before. For a month after he was born there was much speculation on what his names would be. When it was announced, the day before his christening, that the decision was *Charles Philip Arthur George*, the newspapers promptly displayed the news on their front pages. In a poll the English people had favored *Philip*, with *George* a close second. The present ruler, King George VI, was named Albert Frederick Arthur George. Compared to his great uncle, the present Duke of Windsor, the infant has received only a few names. To please both the royal family and the Empire, the Duke received the names Edward Albert Christian George Andrew Patrick David.

The Scotch were elated to find that *Charles* was to be the name used, and happily exclaimed that, "England now has another Bonnie Prince Charlie." The royal family, it was said, scored a triumph in Anglo-Scottish relations at a time when Ireland was leaving the Empire and

the Scotch were watching, again calling attention to the subtle importance of a name.

The four names *Charles Philip Arthur George* are a euphonious and
harmonious series. *Charles* comes from the young prince's royal ancestor of the Stuart line; *Philip* from his father; *Arthur* from the legendary
king, hero of the Round Table; and *George* from his ancestors of the
house of Hanover, also the name of his great-grandfather, King George
I of Greece. If and when the boy succeeds to the English throne, he
will have an excellent choice of names to use for crown-bearing purposes.

He could become George VII, which would make the King Georges
rival the King Henrys and King Edwards. If he picked Arthur, it
would have to be as Arthur I, because there is no proof that the earlier
King Arthur actually reigned over all England. As King Philip I he
would bring a new name to the list of reigning monarchs of England.
Philip is popular: France has had six Philips, Spain five and Macedonia
five. King Philip II of Spain was husband of Mary I, Queen of England in the sixteenth century.

But, barring future adverse circumstances, he will probably find that
Charles III will be the most popular name under which to rule over
the British Empire of his time. Indeed, the wise choice of the proper
name, when the time comes, will be of vast importance in his success.
Charles will connote kingly dignity while *Charlie* will mark the affection of his subjects.

Is an odd name a help or a hindrance in attaining fame? If it is not
so unusual as to provoke ridicule, it may be a distinct aid. The most
famous names in this country are Washington, Lincoln and Roosevelt,
certainly not common names, yet they are not "unique." Perhaps the
most famous name England has produced is *Shakespeare.* Then in a
second group there are common names, well known—*Cooper, Jackson,
Jones, Reed* and *Williams.* Of the men in the American Hall of Fame
six have the above names, which are also listed in the fifty most
common surnames in the United States; while six others (*Adams* (2),
Bennett, Foster, Lee and *Stuart*) have surnames which were among
the fifty most common names in America in 1790, but which are not
in the present-day list.

Those listed in the American Hall of Fame have names more unusual than the ordinary run of names. What is the underlying cause
for this? Perhaps heredity is a factor. The unusual names are often
those derived from place-names. Even in early times the more able

men were those whose families had, by their ability and activity, acquired titles and lands, and these adopted the names of their lands as their family names. Common names are not so easily remembered.

On the other hand, there are more Smiths in *Who's Who in America* than is warranted by their numbers in the general population. There are fewer Johnsons and Joneses in that book than might be expected. Perhaps this, too, is a matter of heredity. The Smiths were respected; the sons of John carried no other mark on which a byname could be based.

One might argue that since those with common names are the English, Irish, Welsh and Scotch, who came to this country early, they had an advantage in the race to gain eminence over those of other nationalities. A study of the correlation of names and ability, compared with nationality, remains to be done by some one preparing his doctoral thesis.

CHAPTER XIV

If You Wish to Read Further

The beginning of all instruction is the study of names.
—ANTISTHENES, C. 400 B.C.

THE first work on personal names in the English language was a rather comprehensive vocabulary of Bible names with explanations in both Latin and English, entitled *The Calender of Scripture*, written by William Patton and published in London in 1575. Little is known of the author. His book is compiled, for the most part, from the Polyglot edition of the Bible by Cardinal Francisco Ximenez de Cisneros, printed in 1514, and the *Dictionarium Theologicum* of John Arquerius, published in 1567.

Since Queen Elizabeth was then on the English throne, the author, as was not unusual among sixteenth- and seventeenth-century writers, devoted thirty-seven pages, in Latin, to the entry *Elizabeth*, including an extravagant, eulogistic poem about the Queen. No other entry in the book occupied more than a few lines.

Next, in 1581, William Warren, "Gent.," an unknown poet, published, in London, *A pleasant new Fancie of a fondlings deuice: Intitled and cald THE NVRCERIE of names. Wherein is presented (to the order of our Alphabet) the brandishing brightness of our English Gentlewomen. Contriued and written, in this last time of vacation: and now first published and committed to printing, this present month of mery May.* They reveled in titles in those days. *The Nurcerie of Names* consisted of a few poems in fourteen syllable verse on women's names. Although the poems are extravagant and fanciful, the versification is unusually true. Apart from this work nothing else is known of the author. Only two copies of the work are known to exist, one of which is in the Henry E. Huntington Library in San Marino, California.

The first really important writing on surnames and Christian names in English is that by William Camden in his *Remaines of a Greater Worke Concerning Britaine, the inhabitants thereof, their Languages, Names, Surnames, Empreses, Wise Speeches, Poesies, and Epitaphes,* published in London in 1605, although the Dedication is dated June 12, 1603. Camden does not attach his name to his book but does sign his final letters, *M.N.*

As the title indicates, it is merely the material he had left over after publishing his illustrious *Britannia*, in elegant Latin, in 1586. Camden himself calls the *Remaines* a "silly, pittiful, and poore Treatise . . . being only the rude rubble and out-cast rubbish of a greater and more serious worke." Yet today the *Britannia*, which brought Camden fame, is all but forgotten and the *Remaines* is the prized masterpiece. It went through seven editions before the seventeenth century came to an end, and the last edition was twice reprinted in the nineteenth century.

In this work Camden set out his reflections on English Christian names and surnames in some detail. When one considers that he could not rely on other scholars, but had to depend entirely on his own observations, the result is truly remarkable. Of course, some of his statements are open to question in the light of centuries of later research. Nevertheless, one reading his comprehensive essays on names cannot but be impressed by the careful, meticulous work he has done.

William Camden, born in 1551, was the son of a London house painter who died when William was very young. He started out to make his living as a schoolmaster. His writings brought him into contact with the learned men of his time and he counted as friends many illustrious and influential persons both in England and on the Continent. In 1597, he was made Clarencieux King-at-Arms, which gave him more time for pursuit of his antiquarian subjects.

Looked upon as a common oracle in the latter years of his life, he was a jovial, friendly, sincere, easy-going old bachelor, a most interesting conversationalist. Known outside of the British Isles, as well as at home, travelers from the Continent thought it a very grave omission to visit England and return without seeing Camden. Upon his death he was immortalized by being buried in Westminster Abbey near the remains of Chaucer. Innate modesty had caused him to refuse the honor of Knighthood.

Like Camden, Richard Rowlands, who wrote under the alias of Richard Verstegan, also included chapters on Christian names and on surnames in a work of his published in 1605, the same year as the

Remaines. Although in English, it was first issued at Antwerp, Belgium. Verstegan's work is greatly inferior to Camden's. The title he chose is curious: *A Restitution of Decayed Intelligence: In antiquities. Concerning the most noble and renowned English nation.*

John Penkethman, an accountant, dabbled in the translation of Old Latin manuscripts. In 1626 he published his *Onomatophylacium* or *The Christian Names of Men and Women, now used within this Realme of GREAT BRITAINE, alphabetically expressed, aswell in Latine as in English, with the true interpretations thereof,* and listed it as by "I. P. Publike Writer." It is a curious little work, now exceedingly rare.

Then, in 1655, there was published *The true Interpretation and Etymologie of Christian Names,* a small work by Edward Lyford on the significations of Christian names. Like most of the modern works, it is divided into two parts, one for men's names and the other concerning names of women. Lyford was a non-conformist divine who held Calvinistic views. Educated at Magdalen College, Oxford, he received the degree of B.A. in 1618. He published two books before his death, in 1653, and the above work and two others were issued posthumously.

Next, we might notice an anonymous English dictionary, entitled *Gazophylacium Anglicanum,* one of our earliest English lexicons, published in 1689, which contained a section on "Proper Names of Men and Women." Two years later another edition was brought out under that most popular title for dictionaries, *A New English Dictionary.*

The eighteenth century produced little of note on the subject of names of people. The nineteenth century burst forth with a host of works on names, most of them of little real value, as scholarship and accuracy did not appear to be considered important objectives.

Now, for those who have read the story of our names and, having become interested in this most fascinating subject, wish to pursue it further, the following are the best books on personal names published in the English language:

CHRISTIAN NAMES:

Ames, Winthrop and Doody, Florence A., *What Shall We Name the Baby?* New York, 1935. Pp. 187.
Attwater, Donald, *Names and Name-Days.* London, 1939. Pp. xv, 124. (Catholic)
Bardsley, Charles Wareing, *Curiosities of Puritan Nomenclature.* New Edition, London, 1897. Pp. xii, 252.

Kolatch, Alfred J., *These Are The Names*. New York, 1948. Pp. 288. (Jewish)

Loughead, Flora Haines, *Dictionary of Given Names*. Glendale, 1934. Pp. 384.

Moody, Sophy, *What Is Your Name?* London, 1863. Pp. x, 314.

Musser, Benjamin Francis, *What Is Your Name? The Catholic Church and Nomenclature*. Manchester (N. H.), 1937. Pp. xv, 199.

Partridge, Eric, *Name This Child*. Second Edition, New York, 1942. Pp. ix, 233.

Smith, Edward Francis, *Baptismal and Confirmation Names*. New York, 1935. Pp. viii, 280. (Catholic)

Smith, Elsdon C., *Naming Your Baby*. New York, 1943. Pp. 96. Also London, 1946. Pp. 95.

Swan, Helena, *Girls' Christian Names*. London, 1900. Pp. xv, 516.

Weekley, Ernest, *Jack and Jill, A Study in Our Christian Names*. London, 1939. Pp. xii, 193.

Weidenhan, Joseph Louis, *Baptismal Names*. Fourth Edition, Baltimore, 1931. Pp. 347. (Catholic)

Wells, Evelyn, *A Treasury of Names*. New York, 1946. Pp. viii, 326.

Withycombe, Elizabeth Gidley, *The Oxford Dictionary of English Christian Names*. Oxford, 1945. Pp. xxxvi, 136.

Yonge, Charlotte Mary, *History of Christian Names*. New Edition, London, 1884. Pp. cxliii, 476.

SURNAMES:

Barber, Henry, *British Family Names, Their Origin and Meaning*. Second Edition, London, 1902. Pp. xii, 286.

Bardsley, Charles Wareing, *A Dictionary of English and Welsh Surnames with Special American Instances*. London, 1901. Pp. xvi, 837.

Bardsley, Charles Wareing, *English Surnames, Their Sources and Significations*. Ninth Impression, London, 1915. Pp. xxviii, 612.

Baring-Gould, Sabine, *Family Names and Their Story*. London, 1913. Pp. 43.

Black, George Fraser, *The Surnames of Scotland*. New York, 1946. Pp. lxxii, 838.

Bowditch, Nathaniel Ingersoll, *Suffolk Surnames*. Third Edition, New York, 1861. Pp. xxv, 757.

Bowman, William Dodgson, *The Story of Surnames*. New York, 1931. Pp. vii, 280.

Bowman, William Dodgson, *What Is Your Surname?* London, 1932. Pp. 317.

Dellquest, Augustus Wilfrid, *These Names of Ours*. New York, 1938. Pp. xxiii, 296.

Ewen, Cecil L'Estrange, *A Guide to the Origin of British Surnames.* London, 1938. Pp. 206.

Ewen, Cecil L'Estrange, *A History of Surnames of the British Isles.* London, 1931. Pp. xx, 508.

Fransson, Gustav, *Middle English Surnames of Occupation, 1100-1350.* Lund, 1935. Pp. 217.

Guppy, Henry Brougham, *Homes of Family Names in Great Britain.* London, 1890. Pp. lxvi, 601.

Harrison, Henry, *Surnames of the United Kingdom.* London, 1912-1918. 2 vol.; Pp. iv, 290; viii, xvi, 332.

Löfvenberg, Mattias Teodor, *Studies on Middle English Local Surnames.* Lund, 1942. Pp. XLVIII, 255.

Lower, Mark Antony, *English Surnames.* Fourth Edition, London, 1875. 2 vol.; Pp. xxvii, 276; vi, 271.

Moore, Arthur William, *Manx Names.* Second Edition, London, 1903. Pp. xvi, 261.

Tengvik, Gösta, *Old English Bynames.* Uppsala, 1938. Pp. xxii, 407.

Weekley, Ernest, *The Romance of Names.* Fourth Edition, London, 1928. Pp. xiii, 250.

Weekley, Ernest, *Surnames.* Third Edition, New York, 1937. Pp. xxii, 360.

NICKNAMES:

Frey, Albert Romer, *Sobriquets and Nicknames.* Boston, 1887. Pp. iii, 482.

Latham, Edward, *A Dictionary of Names, Nicknames and Surnames.* London, 1904. Pp. vii, 334.

Shankle, George Earlie, *American Nicknames.* New York, 1937. Pp. vi, 599.

BIBLICAL NAMES:

Gray, George Buchanan, *Studies in Hebrew Proper Names.* London, 1896. Pp. xv, 338.

Jeffries, Letitia D., *Ancient Hebrew Names.* London, 1906. Pp. xiii, 186.

Potts, Cyrus Alvin, *Dictionary of Bible Proper Names.* Second Edition. [New York], 1923. Pp. 288.

Skinner, John, *The Divine Names in Genesis.* London, 1914. Pp. viii, 303.

Wilkinson, William Francis, *Personal Names in the Bible.* London, 1866. Pp. xii, 556.

Williams, Thomas David, *A Concordance of the Proper Names in the Holy Scriptures.* St. Louis, 1923. Pp. iv, 1056.

PRIMITIVE NAMES:

Clodd, Edward, *Magic in Names and in Other Things.* London, 1920. Pp. vii, 238.

CHANGE OF NAMES AND THE LAW CONCERNING NAMES:

Adamic, Louis, *What's Your Name?* New York, 1942. Pp. xv, 248.
Fox-Davies, Arthur Charles, and Carlyon-Britton, P.W.P., *A Treatise on the Law Concerning Names and Changes of Names.* London, 1906. Pp. 118.
Linell, Anthony, *The Law of Names Public Private & Corporate.* London, 1938. Pp. xxxvi, 236, 19.

GENERAL:

Ekwall, Eilert, *Early London Personal Names.* Lund, 1947. Pp. XIX, 208.
Forssner, Thorvald, *Continental-Germanic Personal Names in England in Old and Middle English Times.* Uppsala, 1916. Pp. lxiii, 289.
Greet, William Cabell, *World Words.* Second Edition, New York, 1948. Pp. liii, 608. (Pronunciation)
Kneen, John Joseph, *The Personal Names of the Isle of Man.* London, 1937. Pp. lx, 295.
Long, Harry Alfred, *Personal and Family Names.* London, 1883. Pp. 362.
Mawson, C. O. Sylvester, *International Book of Names.* New York, 1936. Pp. lxiv, 308.
Redin, Mats, *Studies on Uncompounded Personal Names in Old English.* Uppsala, 1919. Pp. XLV, 196.
Reinius, Josef, *On Transferred Appellations of Human Beings.* Göteborg, 1903, Pp. xv, 296; Supplement, Pp. 10.
von Feilitzen, Olof, *The Pre-Conquest Personal Names of Domesday Book.* Uppsala, 1937. Pp. XXXI, 429.
Woolf, Henry Bosley, *The Old Germanic Principles of Name-Giving.* Baltimore, 1939. Pp. xii, 299.
Woulfe, Patrick, *Sloinnte Gaedheal is Gall Irish Names and Surnames.* Dublin, 1923. Pp. XLVI, 696.

In addition to the list of nomenclatural books here given there are a great many excellent studies in periodicals and specialized works. For a more complete listing of books on personal names see the author's *Bibliography of Personal Names,* published by the New York Public Library in 1950.

This is a list of the best books on the subject of personal names but there are scores of other onomatological works that are waiting to be written. Some works have been published on Indian names, but there is no comprehensive book on the names of the Indian aboriginals of the Americas.

While some very good work has been done in short articles on Negro names by Professor Newbell Niles Puckett, Mr. Howard F. Barker and a few others, a careful, book-length study of the subject would be of outstanding value in the field of nomenclature.

Index

283